DEMOCRACY IN
AFRICA

SAIS African Studies Library

General Editor
I. William Zartman

DEMOCRACY IN
AFRICA

The Hard Road Ahead

edited by
Marina Ottaway

LYNNE
RIENNER
PUBLISHERS

BOULDER
LONDON

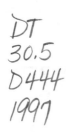

Published in the United States of America in 1997 by
Lynne Rienner Publishers, Inc.
1800 30th Street, Boulder, Colorado 80301

and in the United Kingdom by
Lynne Rienner Publishers, Inc.
3 Henrietta Street, Covent Garden, London WC2E 8LU

Library of Congress Cataloging-in-Publication Data
Democracy in Africa :   the hard road ahead / edited by Marina Ottaway.
     p.   cm.—(SAIS African studies library)
  Includes bibliographical references and index.
  ISBN 1-55587-312-X (cloth : alk. paper)
  1. Africa—Politics and government—1960– 2. Democracy—Africa.
I. Ottaway, Marina.   II. Series: SAIS African studies library
DT30.5.D444   1997
320.96—dc21   96-39895
                                                            CIP

British Cataloguing in Publication Data
A Cataloguing in Publication record for this book
is available from the British Library.

Printed and bound in the United States of America

     The paper used in this publication meets the requirements
∞ of the American National Standard for Permanence of
     Paper for Printed Library Materials Z39.48-1984.

  5   4   3   2   1

Contents

Acknowledgments

Democracy in Africa is the fourteenth in the series of books based on the SAIS African Studies Program's annual country day conferences. We are grateful for the participation of the contributors to the "Democracy in Africa" conference and for the comments from the audience.

We wish to thank the U.S. Army War College for the financial assistance it provided for the conference and Theresa Simmons for her efficiency in organizing the conference and coordinating the editing of this book. Our thanks also go to Kellie B. Anderson, who compiled the index, and to Lynne Rienner and her staff, who were particularly helpful in this effort.

1

From Political Opening to Democratization?

Marina Ottaway

The political change occurring in Africa since 1990 has been remarkable. In the space of a few years, the formal political systems of
African countries have become virtually unrecognizable. A continent characterized for twenty-five years by single- or no-party systems, military
regimes, and personal rule was suddenly ablaze with change. Everywhere
constitutions were revised to allow the formation of multiple political parties, and competitive presidential and parliamentary multiparty elections
were held in over thirty countries. Some leaders whose tenure went back to
the dawn of African independence, like Zambia's Kenneth Kaunda and
Malawi's Hastings Kamuzu Banda, were voted out of power. Once again,
the wind of change appeared to be blowing across Africa. This time, it was
the wind of democratization rather than decolonization.

But democratization is proving to be a complex and at times stormy
process, as is to be expected given the complexity of the transformation.
Political openings have indeed taken place in many countries, as shown by
constitutional reform, the organization of new political parties, the growth
of independent media, the strengthening of voluntary organizations, or the
holding of "national conferences" and elections. Nevertheless, it is far too
early to talk of democracy in Africa. At best, these changes will prove to be
the beginning of a long, rocky process eventually leading to democracy—a
process that entails not only the consolidation of institutions but also a
change in the political culture. At worst, they will turn out to be short-lived
experiments, mere interludes between different authoritarian regimes.
Indeed, the most difficult part of a democratic transformation—the move
from an initial opening to a sustained process of liberalization and of consolidation of institutions—is still ahead for most countries.

The chapters in this book examine the aftermath of the political openings that have taken place in the last five years in Africa. They should not
be looked at as studies of the consolidation of democracy, because it is not
clear that consolidation is occurring yet. Rather, the authors take a sober
look at some major issues that arise in countries that have experienced a

political opening. A process of political and often economic change as well has started in these countries, but its outcome is not predetermined, either in the short or in the long run. History is not a journey with democracy as its obligatory, although sometimes distant, destination.

There are many reasons why the prospects for democracy in Africa remain uncertain. While the ideological climate of the 1990s is undoubtedly favorable to democracy, the same is not always true for the political climate. Many leaders, old and new, still resist changes that put limitations on their authority. Western governments, on paper strong supporters of democracy, inevitably balance in the formulation of their policies the commitment to democracy with the desire for political stability and the pursuit of their national interest, as the chapter by David Gordon shows. As a result, they are often inclined to accept friendly governments with dubious democratic credentials rather than to risk the instability and unpredictability that accompanies far-reaching change. Kenya, under Daniel arap Moi's leadership, is not an admirable country, but it is at least predictable.

Most fundamentally, the outcome remains uncertain because a transition from authoritarianism to democracy requires a radical change of political, and probably of social and economic, relations, and radical change never occurs easily and smoothly. "The strategic problem of transition," Adam Przeworski writes, "is to get to democracy without being either killed by those who have arms or starved by those who control productive resources."[1] Few countries navigate such shoals smoothly.

It has become fashionable today to discuss democratic transformation as something that can be deliberately engineered by leaders of goodwill assisted by international experts working for Western governments and newly organized nongovernmental organizations (NGOs). Although policymakers inevitably have to think in terms of what can be done, thus in terms of engineering change, it is dangerous for analysts to forget that existing democracies emerged not from engineering, but from conflict, violence, bargaining and compromises, reverses, and new attempts at reform. Successful democratic transformation in most countries would require radical, almost revolutionary change. The outcome of any process of radical change is not easily predictable and even less easily controllable. Although democratization does not entail a project of radical social transformation such as the one foreseen by socialist revolutions, it does require a considerable shift in the balance of political power certain to be opposed by those who have much to lose. This does not mean that democratization necessarily entails violence, although violence has been part of the process through which many countries became democratic.[2] But democratization certainly involves conflict, and it is not inevitable that the good guys will win. The outcome of conflict can be the consolidation of a new repressive system as well as the emergence of a more democratic one.

All open-ended situations eventually must come to closure. There are at least three ways in which the process underway in African countries can close. The best-case scenario, from the point of view of democracy, is the gradual transition from the conflicts and tensions that made possible the initial opening to a deliberate, controlled process of liberalization and institutional development. Indeed, this is the engineering scenario. Such closure cannot take place in a short period of time, and it is likely that even the most successful countries will experience some reversals before reaching it. The worst-case scenario is a reversal of the opening, with a return to unabashed authoritarianism and repression. This has happened in Nigeria already—Peter M. Lewis explores the reasons in Chapter 7—and to a large extent in Zaire, where President Mobutu Sese Seko has reconsolidated his power after the challenge of the national conference, as Michael Schatzberg shows in Chapter 6. Finally, a less clear-cut but more likely outcome is the premature closure of the process of transformation through the establishment of formal procedures and institutions before a real change in the nature of power has taken place. Premature closure can be brought about through laws that impose difficult requirements on still disorganized parties or voluntary associations, through regulations that purportedly guarantee the responsible behavior of the independent media but in reality muzzle them while they are barely getting off the ground, or through elections that sideline the opposition before it gets organized. Couched in the trappings of democracy, such premature closures can be as detrimental to democratization as repression and much more insidious.[3]

■ Democratization, Politics, and Social Change

The uncertain process of democratization Africa is experiencing at the present time belongs to a special category that could be defined as "purely political" democratization. It is an attempt to bring about a profound change in the nature of African political systems, although no such profound change has taken place in the economic and social realm.

Scholars disagree on whether there are specific socioeconomic preconditions for democratization, and if so, on what they are—degree of development, the existence of a bourgeoisie, high levels of literacy, a rich "social capital," and a vibrant civil society are only some of the factors that have been singled out as preconditions for democracy.[4] The assumption made in this chapter is not that there are specific socioeconomic preconditions that have to be met before democracy becomes possible, but that there are conditions that facilitate a democratic transition. If those conditions do not exist—and they do not in Africa—then democracy has to be attained purely through politics: Political action by small democratic groups has to provide the leverage for change that has not been provided by social or economic transformation. Democratization, in other words, takes on a curious Leninist twist, becoming a process where political organizing must make up for the unfavorable underlying socioeconomic conditions.

As far as economy and society are concerned, the conditions for democracy in Africa are no more favorable in the 1990s than they were in any of the preceding periods. Indeed, in some respects they probably have deteriorated. The African bourgeoisie is still very small. Even if we enlarge the concept of a bourgeoisie to include not only the entrepreneurial class but more broadly a middle class or a petty bourgeoisie, the situation is poor. The brain drain from Africa, coupled with the reduction in the size and income of the civil service caused by economic crisis and structural adjustment, has left the African middle class diminished and disheartened. There simply is no buoyant middle class, confident of its future, secure in its prosperity, and ready to claim its rightful place in the political process.

The social structure of African countries has undoubtedly changed in the three decades since independence. All countries have become much more urbanized, and we know that urbanization affects social and power relations.[5] But we do not have a clear understanding of how these changes affect democracy. Now, as in the past, migrants to the cities may join new voluntary associations, thus strengthening the vibrant civil society that ideally provides the social underpinnings for democratization. But rural-urban migrants may also fall back on more traditional means of survival, seeking access to power through patron-client relations or organizations mobilizing village, ethnic, or religious identities—mechanisms that facilitate the survival of individuals in the new urban settings but do not promote social change favorable to democracy.[6] High rates of rural-urban migration urbanize individuals but also "villagize" the cities.[7]

There certainly is a civil society capable of maintaining its autonomy from even repressive states in Africa. Recent studies are unanimous in underlining the fact that years of political repression and state-centric politics have not succeeded in obliterating the population's capacity to organize. Neither did colonial repression, as witnessed by the emergence of voluntary associations that eventually coalesced into liberation movements in all countries. Yet independence did not bring about democratization. There is no evidence at this point that would allow us to conclude that the civil society in Africa is stronger today than it was thirty years ago and thus that democratic transformation is bound to occur this time. Indeed, in Chapter 4 Jennifer Widner shows that organizations of civil society in African countries have little impact on political parties and elections.

If social conditions are probably no more favorable to democracy now than in the past decades, economic conditions are definitely worse. Studies of democratic transitions point out that an expanding economy and economic policies that address the interests of the major mobilized constituencies facilitate the change.[8] Far from experiencing a period of growth, African economies are in deep crisis or barely initiating a recovery, with no hope for a quick turnaround leading to sustained, high growth rates. Furthermore, structural adjustment programs (SAPs) leave African governments little maneuvering space in which to address the demand of mobilized constituencies. If the process of democratization is to continue now, it will have to do so under unfavorable economic conditions. At best economic recovery and democratization will go hand in hand; at worst they will impede each other—Nicolas van de Walle and Carol Graham discuss these issues in Chapters 2 and 5, respectively.

None of this means that democratization in Africa is an impossibility at present. What it means, though, is that the change will have to be led by politics—in contrast, for example, to democratization in rapidly developing countries like Taiwan or South Korea, where the process of political change has been preceded, and at least partially led, by socioeconomic change.

If the process of democratization is to continue now, Africans will need once more to seek first the political kingdom, as they did at the time of independence or in the attempted Marxist-Leninist transformations of the 1970s. The issue of power becomes paramount.

■ Democratization and the Problem of Power

The problem of democratization, particularly in a purely political transition, is the problem of power. At one level, this means redistribution. The incumbent leaders or parties must accept that power will not be concentrated and monopolized as before, but that it will be shared, according to certain agreed-upon mechanisms, among political parties, interest groups, and formal governmental institutions. They also have to accept institutionalized uncertainty. Power will be limited by the activities of a loyal opposition. Winners will have to further weaken their grip by allowing a tension to develop even within their own ranks between the executive and the legislative—a dialectical relation at best, leading to compromise and stability, but possibly a deeply conflictual relation leading to stalemate. The winners must also allow some of the institutions to remain autonomous—not only the judiciary but also the military, which should obey orders from the government but not become the militia of a particular party. The complex problems entailed in the transformation of the military are discussed in Chapter 3 by Eboe Hutchful.

It is this aspect of power—its redistribution—that worries incumbent leaders facing the challenge of democratic transformation. In most cases, they do their best to limit redistribution by putting obstacles in the path of opposition parties so that they will perform poorly in the elections and by trying to maintain their grip on institutions not subject to voting results, particularly the military and the judiciary. Resistance to democracy is first and foremost resistance to power redistribution.

At another, more fundamental level, however, the problem of power in a democratic transformation is how to generate it and how to do so in ways that are compatible with democratic norms. This problem is particularly acute in a transition rooted in politics alone rather than in socioeconomic change as well. Power, Samuel Huntington wrote many years ago, is not "something which may be laying around on the floor of the capitol or the presidential palace, and that a group of conspirators may sneak in and run off with it. . . . The problem is not to seize power, but to make power, to mobilize groups into politics and to organize their participation in politics."[9]

In an authoritarian system, power is generated through control of a repressive apparatus capable of excluding potential challengers. It is also generated through political parties and mass organizations capable of mobilizing people around the goals the government wants to attain and of preventing them from becoming mobilized around conflicting goals. Redistributing such power does not bring about democracy, but only results in a reshuffle of the ruling elite and perhaps a slight broadening of it.

In a democratic system, power by definition cannot be based on coercion or on mobilization from the top. Generating power requires orchestrating the interests of various groups, causing a number of constituencies to define their interests in a way that coincides with the goals of a particular political party, or shaping the party's goals so as to appeal to the interests of a large segment of the population. This requires a lot of dexterity on the part of the leaders but also an active rather than a passive population or, in the current parlance, an engaged civil society.

Beyond the problem of power redistribution, thus, democratic transformation entails a sea change in the nature of power and in the institutions needed to generate it. And this is the most difficult aspect of the transformation. As Jennifer Widner points out in her chapter, in the process of transformation many new groups emerge, but they are not necessarily integrated into the orchestration of interests that provides the support for political parties. Organizations of civil society, usually considered to be the key to democratic transformation, may remain surprisingly isolated from the process through which political power is generated.

The problem of generating sufficient power through democratic means remains largely unsolved in African countries at present, and it is not going to be solved easily. Paradoxically, the very change that triggered the present wave of democratic openings, the collapse of socialist systems, may prove to be a major obstacle to the consolidation of democracy, depriving politicians of the ideology that played a crucial role historically in the formation of powerful political parties capable of challenging incumbent regimes. Socialist parties destroyed democracy when they were able to seize power, but they promoted democracy when they remained in the opposition. In the absence of an ideology with broad appeal, African political parties form along ethnic and religious lines. Rather than promoting democracy, this increases the level of conflict.

■ Democracy and Institutions

Power is an abstract concept, difficult to pin down and measure in practice. The temptation for the social scientist, as a result, is to rely on the more tangible development of institutions as a measure of power. A democratic government has solved the problem of power when it has created the appropriate array of democratic institutions and these institutions have acquired the right characteristics.

The list of these institutions is well known: parliaments and independent judiciaries capable of curbing the ever-threatening authoritarian tendencies of the executive; efficient bureaucracies to provide without favoritism the services needed for the functioning of the modern state; professional armies willing to remain under civilian control, without taking advantage of their monopoly on the means of coercion to impose themselves on other institutions; well-organized political parties to aggregate and articulate interests; and an array of other intermediate organizations of civil society to strengthen the political role of the population beyond the ballot box and to provide a voice for the disparate interests political parties do not necessarily represent.

The existence of such institutions and the extent to which they resemble the model deemed to be characteristic of a modern democracy indeed provide an easy, formal measure of the extent to which a country can be defined as democratic. They do little, however, to help us understand the process of democratic transformation, particularly in the very early stages in which African countries find themselves at the present time. Above all, they may obfuscate the issue of whether countries are making progress toward democracy by imposing an unrealistic view of the process. The initial stages of a democratic transformation are most of the time all but democratic. Eventually, the above-mentioned institutions must emerge. In the process, however, progress toward democracy is likely to be the outcome of conflict, power struggles, possibly even violence, and of nondemocratic pacts among political organizations.[10] By focusing on the final outcome, we risk neglecting the importance of the changes that are taking place.

■ Democracy and Conflict

Democratic transformations have historically been complex and prolonged processes, often beset by violence in the initial stages, when the regime resisted change and a redistribution of power. They have also entailed long periods of political instability as the new regimes tackled the problem of generating sufficient power to govern the country. Democratization in France entailed a revolution and then long decades of political turmoil and deep socioeconomic change before political stability was reestablished. Democracy in the United States emerged from a war of independence, a civil war, and a slow process of evolution—and for much of its history the country would not have rated very high on the scale by which democracy is measured today. In Germany and Japan, it took a major military defeat before democratic transformation occurred. The list could continue.

There are, to be sure, more benign examples of democratic transformations. The cases of the southern European and Latin American countries studied by Guillermo O'Donnell and Philippe Schmitter (*Transitions from Authoritarian Rule: Tentative Conclusions About Uncertain Democracies*, 1986) show that it is possible for democracy to come about through less dramatic and violent processes—indeed they conclude that violence does not augur well for the success of a democratic transition. But even these cases demonstrate the difficulty of the transformation and underline the fact that change does not take place all at once. No democracy is perfect, but new democracies are particularly imperfect as well as extremely unstable.

The process may be particularly difficult in those countries where external pressure was an important factor in forcing a political opening. Policymakers in countries like the United States inevitably envisage their role as that of engineering reform, not of promoting violent upheavals with uncertain outcomes. Yet attempts at engineering democracy through an orderly process of reform may not only prove impossible but also become counterproductive when fear of violence and instability leads donor governments to tacitly accept lack of democracy as the best alternative. Such a policy conundrum is not easy to solve.

■ The African Record

In addition to the evidence about how difficult the process of democratic transformation was even in successful countries, Africa's postindependence record also suggests that the current political openings are not necessarily the beginning of a straightforward process but may only be an episode in a long and tortuous process of political transformation.

This is not the first attempt at democratic transformation in Africa. The majority of countries reached independence after holding multiparty elections and with democratic constitutions, but most abandoned the system within a short period. A frequent explanation for this early failure of democratic systems is that they had been imposed by the colonial powers. This idea needs rethinking. The role of the colonial powers was of course important, and this was reflected in the difference between the political systems of the former British and former French colonies. It is also true that most African constitutions were written by foreign experts. But this does not mean that they were imposed. In most countries, there existed several political parties that wanted a chance to compete, as well as other organizations, from labor unions to cultural societies and sports clubs, that had played a part in the decolonization process, aspired to a role in the postindependence period, and welcomed the protection afforded by a democratic constitution. What led to the abandoning of the democratic political institutions was not a revolt by Africans against an alien imposition but an act of force by the incumbent leaders or the military trying to protect themselves against all opposition by banning political parties and organizations of civil society as well.

To be sure, the abandoning of Western-style democratic institutions was given an ideological justification with the argument that the system neither fitted the African tradition of solidarity and consensus building nor satisfied the need for unity and nation building of the newly independent states. There is no reason to doubt the good faith of many intellectuals who formulated these ideas. But what emerged was not reconciliation systems based on African traditions. For the most part, it was authoritarian regimes based on personal power, military control, or a centralized single party, and more interested in repressing opposition than in building consensus. These regimes did not try to build different kinds of linkages between civil society and the state on the basis of an African political culture. They simply sought to demobilize civil society.

The rediscovery in the last few years that even the most repressive regimes did not succeed in demobilizing civil society completely has given rise to considerable optimism about the prospects for democracy. In view of the previous observations, this optimism may be exaggerated. There are unfortunately no serious studies that would allow us to compare the degree of organizational strength of civil society now and in the immediate preindependence period. But certainly there was a rich organizational life in Africa at that time, although some kinds of organizations that are appearing in Africa today, such as human rights organizations or women's groups, were absent as they were in most of the world thirty years ago. The multiplication and strengthening of voluntary organizations that is taking place in many countries at present is certainly relevant to the emergence of more democratic political systems in the long run. It should not be forgotten, however, that the existence of voluntary organizations in the past has not been sufficient to foil the authoritarian transformation of the state.

There are, however, some significant differences between the situation that prevails now and that of the early postindependence period. The international context has changed and with it the political climate. With the disappearance of the socialist countries, the appeal of socialist ideologies has waned, at least for the time being. The segment of the urban population that articulates political ideas in Africa as a result now appears more committed to democracy than in the past, when socialist ideals strongly influenced intellectuals and politicians. On the other hand, there still remains a large degree of skepticism about the validity of Western representative institutions and a desire for a more African solution to the challenge of democracy, although it remains as unclear as ever what form such democracy should take in practice.

The position of the general public toward democracy remains ambiguous. On the one hand, there is widespread discontent with existing systems, both political and economic, and thus a strong desire for change. "Change" has been the central political slogan in many recent African elections, as Carol Graham shows in the case of Senegal (Chapter 5). On the other hand, desire for political change is no more synonymous with support for democracy than desire for economic change is synonymous with support for structural adjustment. It is a fact that Africans have turned out to vote in great numbers in recent multiparty elections in most countries, but this cannot be interpreted as support for democracy, because Africans have also turned out to vote in great numbers in previous single-party elections. Popular attitudes toward democracy are divided and often quite confused and contradictory, as much recent research shows.[11]

We know a little more about how African politicians view democracy—with enthusiasm when they are in the opposition, and with caution when they are in power. Few leaders have embraced the cause of democratization unambiguously. Most have been forced to accept competition by a mixture of mounting internal opposition and pressure by aid donors. Until the second round of multiparty elections takes place, it is impossible to judge whether the new elected leaders' commitment to democracy will prove to be greater than that of their predecessors, now that they are the ones who have more to lose than to gain from democracy.

Indeed, a number of African leaders—former and newly elected—are beginning to articulate anew the same objections to democracy that were popular among their predecessors in the early years of African independence. Even some of the leaders most acclaimed in the United States for the change they have brought to their countries fall in this category. Yoweri Museveni in Uganda has repeatedly declared that multiparty competition is too disruptive for his country but that democracy can be safeguarded through no-party competition—a disturbing argument to a student of African politics who heard it many times before and who watched the subsequent consolidation of authoritarian regimes. And President Jerry Rawlings of Ghana, now considered to be a democratically elected president after having led two successful military coups d'état, still sees military government as a preferable alternative to instability under a civilian government.

Finally, there is growing ambiguity in Africa—an ambiguity to which the United States contributes—as to whether democracy in Africa should mean majoritarianism or power-sharing. Two experiences in particular have colored the discussion on this issue, the negative one of Angola and the positive one of South Africa. In September 1992, Angola held multiparty elections under a majoritarian constitution that prescribed, not surprisingly, that the party winning the majority of votes would form the government. The result is well known. The leader of the opposition, Jonas Savimbi, trailing behind the incumbent Eduardo Dos Santos in the first round of elections, pulled out of the second, and the war resumed. South Africa, on the other hand, held elections under a provisional power-sharing constitution in April 1994 and election results were accepted by all parties— although the Inkatha Freedom Party's commitment to the system of which it had become part remained marginal at best.

The lesson derived from these examples, by many Africans but also by policymakers in this country, is that democratic transitions require power-sharing rather than winner-take-all systems. Such an idea is either tautological or highly misleading. A winner-take-all system is by definition not democratic. However, a majoritarian system is not winner-take-all, as the experience of all industrial democracies shows: Power is divided among governmental institutions, opposition parties play a major role even between elections, organized interest groups allow citizens to influence the government even between elections, and individual rights are safeguarded. Power-sharing political systems, on the other hand, are not automatically democratic. Although there are examples of democratic power-sharing systems, as Arend Lijphart has shown in his studies, there are also many examples of undemocratic power sharing.[12] Some of the politically more astute African leaders, like Jomo Kenyatta of Kenya, bought political stability by offering their adversaries a share of the spoils. Many single-party regimes in Africa were essentially nondemocratic power-sharing systems. The growing emphasis on power sharing may turn from a facilitator of the process of democratization into an obstacle to its continuation.

There is nothing in this record to suggest that either conditions or attitudes toward democracy have changed much from the early days of African independence to the present time. It is not clear that there are real differences in the degree to which civil society is organized. Democracy continues to be advocated with greater enthusiasm by the opposition than by incumbent leaders, suggesting that opportunism is still much more important than principle. The old, self-serving objections to the suitability of liberal democracy to Africa are being voiced again, and even Western countries have some doubts—as seen in the recent criticism of majoritarian systems. To a long-time observer of African politics, the continuity appears much more striking than the change.

■ The Study of Democratic Transformation

The chapters in this book address the salient problems that emerge after the initial political opening and that will determine whether such an opening is the beginning of a process of democratization or a brief interlude between authoritarian regimes. They also examine the question of whether the United States can help democratic transitions, or whether structural constraints and political considerations prevent it from doing so effectively.

The book focuses neither on the initial political opening nor on the consolidation of democracy, because it is too early to talk of consolidation in most countries. Rather, it considers the dangerous in-between period, when incumbent governments and opposition groups have to settle down for the long haul that will determine whether African countries will enjoy lasting political transformation or revert to authoritarianism.

First, this book looks at major issues that arise in the transition. Jennifer Widner explores the difficult problem of establishing linkages between political parties and organizations of civil society. Nicolas van de Walle and Carol Graham examine different aspects of the relation between economic reforms and democratic transitions. Eboe Hutchful looks at the thorny problem of transforming the military so it can accept democracy.

Second, two authors provide case studies of countries where the democratic transition has suffered serious setbacks: Michael Schatzberg looks at the problem in Zaire, and Peter Lewis analyzes the failure of the transition in Nigeria.

Linking the activities of civil society to those of the political parties, carrying out simultaneously political and economic reform, and ensuring the political neutrality of the military in the long run are all issues of great complexity. Each is difficult in itself; the linkages among them are even more intricate and poorly understood.

If the task of the analysts seeking to understand the problems of democratic transitions is difficult, that of U.S. policymakers is even more daunting, as the last chapter of this book shows. It involves not only understanding the process but also manipulating it. And manipulating, furthermore, while also safeguarding the broader interests of the United States.

The Clinton administration and earlier the Bush administration embraced the cause of democracy in their policy toward Africa. David Gordon was involved in the formulation of U.S. policy to promote democracy in Africa as a Congressional staff member. His contribution to this book reflects the concerns and dilemmas faced by U.S. policymakers.

■ Notes

1. Adam Przeworski, *Democracy and the Market* (Cambridge: Cambridge University Press, 1991), p. 51.
2. Guillermo O'Donnell and Philippe Schmitter, *Transitions from Authoritarian Rule: Tentative Conclusions About Uncertain Democracies* (Baltimore: Johns Hopkins University Press, 1986), p. 11.
3. Schmitter and O'Donnell point out that in a transition, the rules of the political game are not defined but are hotly contested, since all parties know that the rules will contribute to determining winners and losers in the future. In a premature closure, the rules are defined unilaterally by one side, thus precluding further contestation. What distinguished these premature closures from a reversal to authoritarianism is that, on paper at least, the rules are reasonably democratic—except that they block the transformation under the circumstances. See O'Donnell and Schmitter, *Transitions: Tentative Conclusions*, p. 6.
4. To mention only some very prominent statements on the preconditions for democracy, Barrington Moore, Jr., *The Social Origins of Dictatorship and Democracy* (Boston: Beacon Press, 1967), p. 418, declares "no bourgeoisie, no democracy"; Seymour Martin Lipset, "Some Social Requisites for Democracy: Economic Development and Political Legitimacy," *American Political Science Review* 53, no. 1: 69–105, focuses on economic development; Samuel Huntington, *The Third Wave: Democratization in the Late Twentieth Century* (Norman: University of Oklahoma Press, 1991), also stresses the importance of economic development; Robert Putnam, *Making Democracy Work: Civic Traditions in Modern Italy* (Princeton: Princeton University Press, 1993), singles out a historically developed pattern of associational life, which he calls "social capital," as the substratum that makes democracy possible. Pioneering work on the concept of civil society in the African context is found in Donald Rothchild and Naomi Chazan, *The Precarious Balance: State and Society in Africa* (Boulder, Colo.: Westview Press, 1988).
5. Studies of African urbanization, largely neglected by students of democratization, offer considerable evidence concerning both the extent of social change and its limits. They also provide an important reminder that the emergence of voluntary organizations, too often regarded as a recent phenomenon that augurs well for democracy, is not a new phenomenon at all, and that it has not prevented the consolidation of authoritarian regimes in the past. See, for example, Kenneth Little, *West African Urbanization: A Study of Voluntary Associations and Social Change* (Cambridge: Cambridge University Press, 1967) and *African Women in Towns* (Cambridge: Cambridge University Press, 1973); Akin Mabogunje, *Urbanization in*

Nigeria (New York: Africana Publishing, 1968); Joseph Gugler and William Flanagan, *Urbanization and Social Change in West Africa* (Cambridge: Cambridge University Press, 1978).

6. See Abner Cohen, *Custom and Politics in Urban Africa* (Berkeley: University of California Press, 1969); Howard Wolpe, *Urban Politics in Nigeria* (Berkeley: University of California Press, 1974); A. L. Epstein, *Politics in an Urban African Community* (Manchester: Manchester University Press, 1958); Joan Nelson, *Access to Power* (Princeton: Princeton University Press, 1979).

7. This theme was developed in the 1960s in Janet Abu-Lughod, "Migrant Adjustment to City Life: The Egyptian Case," *American Journal of Sociology* 67: 22–32; and Herbert Gans, *The Urban Villagers* (New York: The Free Press, 1962).

8. John Sheanan, "Economic Policies and Prospects for Successful Transition from Authoritarian Rule in Latin America," in Guillermo O'Donnell, Philippe Schmitter, and Laurence Whitehead, eds., *Transitions from Authoritarian Rule: Comparative Perspectives* (Baltimore: Johns Hopkins University Press, 1988), pp. 154–164; and Schmitter and O'Donnell, *Transitions: Tentative Conclusions,* pp. 45ff.

9. Samuel Huntington, *Political Order in Changing Societies* (New Haven: Yale University Press, 1968), p. 144.

10. The willingness to recognize the role that violence and nondemocratic maneuvers play in democratic transformations is directly inverse to the time perspective of the different authors and their degree of involvement in policymaking. Thus, at one extreme Barrington Moore in *Social Origins* has no problem in recognizing the role of violence in an analysis of democratization that is retrospective and spans several centuries. Schmitter and O'Donnell, whose historical perspective is much shorter and case studies much more recent, recognize the importance of nondemocratic pacts and compromises in democratic transitions, but take a pessimistic view of the impact of violence in *Transitions: Tentative Conclusions.* Michael Bratton and Nicolas van de Walle, in "Neopatrimonial Regimes and Political Transitions in Africa," *World Politics* 46, no. 4: 453–489, downplay the possibility that democracy may come from a sharp, violent break with a past, thus arriving at the conclusion that democratization is more likely to succeed in countries where participation and competition in formal political institutions were already routinized.

11. See, for example, National Democratic Institute for International Affairs, "Imagining Democracy: A Report on a Series of Focus Groups in Mozambique on Democracy and Voter Education," (Washington, D.C.: National Democratic Institute, 1993).

12. Arend Lijphart, *Democracy in Plural Societies: A Comparative Exploration* (New Haven: Yale University Press, 1977); and *Democracies: Patterns of Majoritarian and Consensus Government* (New Haven: Yale University Press, 1984).

2

Economic Reform and the Consolidation of Democracy in Africa

Nicolas van de Walle

Recent political changes have given rise to a growing scholarly literature on regime transitions, both for nations in other areas of the world[1] and increasingly for those in Africa.[2] What remains poorly understood are the problems relating to the consolidation of democratic rule, particularly in countries such as those in Africa that lack a democratic past and pluralist institutions.

This chapter assesses one of the biggest threats to the consolidation of democratic regimes in Africa, the intense economic crisis facing most of the nations in the region, and the politically difficult policy reform programs that must be implemented to overcome it.[3] It was in fact partly the inability of the previous authoritarian regimes to find solutions to their economic conundrums that led to their downfall. The economy the democratic forces inherited was often in serious risk of complete implosion, with massive deficits, hyperinflation, capital flight, and a crumbling infrastructure.

Economic crisis is generally unfavorable to officeholders, and political stability depends on national economic performance. If the new democracies in Africa do not make significant progress on at least minimal economic stabilization and begin to reverse the recent deterioration in the quality of life, they are unlikely to remain in power long. The severity of the current economic crisis poses special threats; in some cases, the very existence of national political institutions will be threatened, either because they are undermined by subnational identities or because they lack the fiscal basis to function effectively. In a continent that has already spawned the complete breakdown of the state in Somalia, Liberia, and Rwanda, this is a real threat. In fact, the economic crisis is so bad in some countries that what the donors call "structural adjustment," or the implementation of structural reforms that aim to transform the country's economic institutions, is arguably unrealistically ambitious for the near future. Instead, achieving basic macroeconomic stabilization and restoring a semblance of fiscal balance would already be remarkable and a tremendous test of the capacities of most governments in the region.

In this chapter I seek answers to the following questions: How can the new democratic regimes address economic problems their predecessors found intractable? What factors will increase their chances of success? A caveat is in order: I do not address the problem of long-term economic growth and the construction of *developmental* states in sub-Saharan Africa of the kind existing in East Asia. Long-term structural transformation of the region's economies will require considerably more effective state institutions than currently exist, except perhaps in South Africa. An entire other chapter would be needed to examine the relationship between democracy and the construction of developmental states in Africa. I focus instead on the problems relating to short-term economic stabilization; I assume that current institutional, financial, and ideological endowments are fixed and cannot easily be changed.

I adopt an entirely procedural and minimal definition of democracy. Africa's posttransition regimes are defined to be democratic as long as they schedule multiparty elections on a regular basis and as long as the government more or less observes the political and social rights of the vast majority of the population. Such a definition recognizes implicitly that day-to-day politics in these countries will continue to tolerate, if not engender, tremendous social inequalities, abuses of power, and weak pluralist institutions.

This chapter is divided into four sections. The first section argues briefly that regime type does not explain well the ability to pursue economic reform. There is no intrinsic reason to believe that the new democracies will prove any less able to undertake economic reform than previous authoritarian regimes. Democratization may actually facilitate the implementation of reform, but in general these regimes will have to overcome many of the same types of constraints with roughly the same resources as their authoritarian predecessors.

The second section analyzes the factors that are likely to determine the ability of the new regimes to promote successful economic stabilization. Stabilization is defined as restoring a sustainable equilibrium of the balance of payments, a government budget of between 0 and 3 percent of gross domestic product (GDP) and low to moderate inflation. A third section briefly discusses the recent history of three African nations that have undergone democratic transitions: Madagascar, Mali, and Zambia. Finally, a fourth section draws lessons from the case studies and sets out a research agenda.

■ Regime Type and Economic Reform

The economy that the new democratic elites inherit in most African countries has typically suffered from two decades of mismanagement, exogenous shocks, and inappropriate policies, resulting in a growing debt crisis and a semipermanent process of negotiations and debt rescheduling with international creditors. In addition, the democratic transition itself has occasioned large economic costs, either because of extensive civil unrest and sometimes violence, or because of the fiscal recklessness of authoritarian leaders trying to hold onto power. Thus, the governments that emerge from the process of democratization face the daunting tasks of consolidating pluralist institutions and undertaking urgent economic reform simultaneously.

For the fledgling democratic states, speedy stabilization of the economy is almost certainly a sine qua non of both sociopolitical stability and longer-term economic success. In its absence, the economy will continue to drift, and policy will continue to be dictated by crisis management and the immediate requirements of quarterly International Monetary Fund (IMF) missions and Paris Club negotiations every twelve to eighteen months. Public infrastructure and services will not improve, and the government will not be able to create the conditions that attract private investment and pave the way for long-term growth. It must be emphasized that there are no alternatives to stabilization for the new democracies. Little foreign direct investment or African capital repatriation can be expected as long as the economic climate is so uncertain. For one thing, the high and variable inflation present in many of these countries scares away all but short-term speculatory investments. Thus, short of simply printing money, governments have to generate their own revenues or convince the West to grant public finance.[4]

The dilemma for the new democratic governments is that they risk losing legitimacy if they do not quickly restore economic stability, but the policies required to bring about stabilization may well be extremely unpopular, at least until they bring about results.[5] New governments typically enjoy a honeymoon period during which the population will blame their predecessors for their hardships. But in the absence of progress, sooner or later the government will be held accountable and begin to lose its popularity; the very stability of democratic rule will eventually be threatened, with a return to popular unrest and a greater likelihood of military intervention. That was indeed the pattern for countries like Ghana, Nigeria, or Sudan in their previous brief democratic experiments.

What will determine the ability of the new African democracies to stabilize the economy? The predominant view in the political economy literature has been that there are various economic policymaking advantages for nondemocratic regimes.[6] In brief, constituency pressures on democratic governments are believed to result in policies that sacrifice investment to promote current consumption. Likewise, the main obstacle to economic reform is believed to be political pressures on the government to maintain these policies in exchange for popular support.[7] Indeed, scholars from different ends of the ideological spectrum have argued that there is a natural affinity between market liberalization and political repression.[8] Deepak Lal expresses this view well when he writes that "a courageous, ruthless and perhaps undemocratic government is required to ride roughshod over these newly-created special interest groups."[9] If this conventional wisdom is correct, few of the new African democracies will survive. The absence of progress on the economic front will undermine their popularity and erode support for democratic rule, increasing the possibility of a slide back toward authoritarian rule.

Recent empirical work on Latin America has found little evidence to suggest that democratic governments are less capable of undertaking stabilization policies, however.[10] There is unfortunately no comparable study for Africa, but the economic performance of the handful of competitive regimes before 1989 (Botswana, Mauritius, The Gambia, Senegal) certainly does not support the proposition either, since Botswana and Mauritius have enjoyed the highest sustained growth of any states in Africa over the last twenty years, while The Gambia and Senegal have not performed worse than their authoritarian neighbors in the Sahel region.

In fact, there are reasons to believe that, on balance, democratic governments in Africa may actually have some advantages in promoting economic reform.[11] First, while institutional checks and balances within the state as well as increased participation by nongovernmental actors slow down the speed of decisionmaking and may make it more chaotic, they can also improve policymaking by lessening the chances that policy will be undermined by state incompetence and corruption or that misguided policies will be adopted without debate.[12] A free press and the presence of opposition parties in the legislature help to curb governmental corruption, for instance. Second, democratic governments may be better able to impose economic austerity on their citizens because they have greater popular legitimacy than do authoritarian governments. Elections have provided a mandate for the policies that are carried out, and opponents know that they can undo the damage if they mobilize in time for the next election.

Thus, on balance, it can be argued that the benefits of democratization will outweigh the costs. But I would not exaggerate the impact of political change in Africa: Past state repression and cooptation have weakened or eliminated nongovernmental actors such as the independent press and civic, union, and professional associations, and they will require time and effort to grow as institutions. These groups may be empowered somewhat by the new political climate, but they are likely to overcome the authoritarian legacy as well as financial and organizational difficulties only slowly and incompletely; their ability to pressure the government—for or against progrowth policies—will continue to be limited for some time.[13]

Moreover, even if Africa's democratic transitions constitute significant political openings, the institutionalization of democratic practices will inevitably take a long time. It requires the development of a democratic political culture and the strengthening of mechanisms of transparency and accountability, which cannot take place overnight. In the meantime, many of Africa's democracies will constitute what Terry Lynn Karl has called *hybrid* regimes—states in which formal democratic practices coexist with the persistence of authoritarian practices, a clientelist political culture, and other legacies of the pretransition regime.[14] In these states, many of the past obstacles to economic reform will remain unchanged.

■ Economic Stabilization in New Democratic Regimes

Several factors are likely to prove important in predicting whether the new African democracies will be able to stabilize the economy. Some apply to all governments that undertake economic reform, whether or not they are new, and/or democratic.[15] Perhaps the most important of these is the state's institutional capacity. To predict the likelihood of successful reform, we would want to know how effective and professional the civil service was and how well developed the state's extractive capacities. Undertaking significant economic policy reform in a short period obviously requires considerable administrative skill, regardless of the nature of the political regime. In the long run these capacities can change, but in the short run they are more or less fixed, even if the uncertainty and chaos of the transition may have in some cases resulted in their temporary decline. Relative to the industrialized West, or even to the states in East Asia, all African states could be said to have low capacities, but there are nonetheless significant differences among them: Most Africanists would recognize, for example, that Kenya's state institutions are stronger and more capable than those of Burkina Faso or Sierra Leone.[16]

This institutional capacity is particularly important to the new democratic governments in Africa, whose leaders have typically relatively little recent experience of government. To take as an example the heads of state of the three countries discussed later, Zambian president Frederick Chiluba spent three decades in the labor movement and never held public office, and the Mali and Madagascar heads of state, Alpha Oumar Konaré and Albert Zafy respectively, had been out of government for twenty years or so. In such situations, the capacities, internal discipline, and apolitical nature of the permanent civil service is critical to the success of the new leaders, who need to be able to make the machinery of government work for their new programs and objectives.

Other factors help explain specifically the ability of new democratic governments to undertake reform. Three such factors are hypothesized to be particularly important: the speed with which a reform program can be implemented after the transition, the degree of consensus within the political class about the need for reform, and the strength of the majority political party.

☐ The Speed of Implementation

A first key factor is the speed of implementation of the reform program after the transition. There is evidence across a wide spectrum of regimes that new governments are more likely to bring about substantial economic reform than old ones. In other words, governments can take advantage of the honeymoon period they will inevitably enjoy at the outset of their tenure in power to make significant progress on reform measures. The longer they prevaricate, the less likely reforms will be implemented because stabilization policies are likely to be unpopular, given their impact on people's short-term welfare. Initially, austerity is blamed on the previous government or can be attributed to the disruptive impact of the transition. Populations are more tolerant of the government they recently put into power and may well not expect immediate improvements in their living standards, particularly if conditions have been deteriorating for some time and the new government can persuade them that a crisis exists that requires drastic action.[17] In sum, governments need to move quickly and implement stabilization policies soon after coming to power, especially new democratic governments because the primary resource available to them is probably the goodwill and popularity generated by the transition from authoritarian rule. It is crucial that they exploit it fully by moving fast, before they lose the special prestige they acquired by restoring popular sovereignty. I hypothesize that democratic governments that do not make significant progress on stabilization of the balance of payments or the budget in the first year of office face a much lower probability of doing so subsequently.

Some new governments will not take advantage of the honeymoon period because they come to power lacking a firm commitment to reform, or because, as I discuss in the next section, not all the members of the ruling coalition share a consensus regarding the best way to address the economy's problems. But even among the sample of governments that are firmly committed to stabilization, wide differences exist in the ability of governments to take advantage of the honeymoon. First, as discussed above, some governments may be hampered by a weak state capacity: The state is simply not able to undertake the stabilization measures that require great administrative capabilities and discipline.

Second, the nature and length of the transition serve to reduce the effective length of the honeymoon. If the transition is long and drawn out and there is no government in place for a year or so after the old government is removed, the popular mood and the legitimacy of democratic rule may have severely eroded by the time a permanent government is installed and turns its attention to economic stabilization. Observers of democratic transitions usually argue that the length of the transition is positively correlated with its chances of political success; long-drawn-out transitions are more likely to result in stable democratic politics.[18] The argument developed here qualifies this generalization. At least in Africa's more chaotic and protest-driven democratizations, the economic consequences of long transitions can seriously compromise the emergent regime.

☐   *Policy Consensus*

Second, the degree of consensus within the political class about the need for reform is a critical factor. A key characteristic of democratic regimes is their inclusiveness and competition. As a result, democratic governments cannot rely on intimidation and repression to enforce the implementation of policies but must rely to a greater extent on dialogue and persuasion. Debates in parliament, in the press, and during electoral campaigns are likely to have a significant impact on whether the government's program is politically sustainable, and democratic governments will have less control over these public debates than authoritarian ones. In turn, this implies that stabilization is more likely to succeed when there is a broad consensus within the political class and state elites about the nature of economic circumstances and the appropriate policies.

This includes, first, general agreement within the permanent civil service, the political opposition, and civil society. They need not agree with the manner with which the government proposes to undertake stabilization, but it is important that the basic principles of sound macro policy be widely accepted across the political spectrum. Thus, for example, the exact manner in which the budget deficit is tackled is not important, but there should be broad agreement that printing money to cover the deficit is not acceptable, and that there is need to accomplish a combination of increases in revenues with decreases in expenditure. The less common ground there is on basic principles of macroeconomics, the more polarized politics will be and the more difficult it will be for the government to escape widespread opposition, let alone persuade the population of the need for tough medicine. If, however, there is recognition of the dimensions of the economic problems facing the government, then stabilization policies will be legitimated and the opposition more easily contained.[19]

Second, the presence of broad agreement within the leadership of the ruling party or within the ruling coalition of parties is important as well. Lack of cohesion will undermine the government's credibility and will weaken the government's position, notably within parliament, as the opposition will be able to drive a wedge between different members of the majority, undermining their willingness to continue supporting what are unpopular measures. As important, it will weaken the government's ability to mobilize support through its political party, a factor that needs to be further singled out.

□ *The Presence of a Strong Party*

Even when consensus emerges regarding the economy, there will be plenty of room left for disagreement and polarization. This suggests the importance of the new government's ability to persuade key social constituencies of the need for reform or at least to delegitimate and isolate opposition. To win the public debate, a strong and unified political party is essential. Such a party will make effective control of the legislature more likely and also mobilize public opinion, defuse criticism by servicing constituents' special needs during periods of austerity, and alert the government to emerging political problems. As difficult policies are put into place, the ability of the party in power to explain their objectives and expected benefits will be key to popular support. In addition, a strong and cohesive party will help increase the capacity of the government to carry out the policies as they are designed. It is important that all members of the new government support the general thrust of the reform measures and work toward their success or at least do not openly express their misgivings. A strong, unified party will help maintain that discipline.

■ **Three Case Studies**

A brief review of the cases of Madagascar, Mali, and Zambia will help illustrate the arguments already presented and draw out further implications. All three states undertook democratic transitions in the early 1990s. Each is a desperately poor African state, in which a new democratically elected government was faced with seemingly similarly disastrous economic situations.

□ *Madagascar*

An early attempt at rapid state-led industrialization, under the *Tous azimuths* economic policy,[20] had resulted in a balance-of-payments crisis and the rapid accumulation of debt, necessitating recourse to the IMF as early as 1981. During the 1980s, President Didier Ratsiraka progressively replaced his regime's Marxist rhetoric with a more market-friendly discourse and accommodated the international financial institutions (IFIs) sufficiently to be considered one of their success stories.[21] Nonetheless, progress on policy reform was actually quite uneven, with draconian cuts in the public sector wage bill,[22] but an inability to sustain reductions in the budget and trade deficits during the 1980s.[23] Trade and marketing liberalization measures were undermined by strong rent-seeking pressures within the administration, which the regime did little to correct. Despite various promises to pursue privatization aggressively, over 100 parastatals remained in place in 1990 and continued to weigh on the budget. Over time, the real efforts made to decrease public expenditures were negated by the government's inability to increase revenues sufficiently. The budget deficit decreased from 18.4 percent of GDP in 1980 to 4 percent in 1986 but was back up to 7 percent by 1989; a combination of corruption and incompetence accounted for revenue shortfall and expenditure overruns. International debt continued to increase, reaching $3.6 billion at the end of 1989. Private investors were not impressed, and foreign direct investment slowed to zero or negative totals in the late 1980s and amounted to only $6 million net in 1989.[24] Analysis by Frederic Pryor, based on rather spotty data, suggests a pattern of increasing inequality and poverty throughout the 1970s and 1980s.[25]

In sum, by the beginning of the 1990s, the country had a decade of donor-enforced austerity under its belt with relatively little to show for it. The IMF and World Bank were increasingly pushing for tougher measures to promote liberalization, and the government was promising a renewed effort, albeit without much conviction.[26] The presidential elections of March 1989 had returned Ratsiraka to office for a third term, with 62 percent of the votes cast. Nonetheless, widespread disillusionment with the government existed within urban groups and intellectuals because of the widespread corruption of the Ratsiraka government as well as growing economic hardship.[27] The regime had never been able to create a unified, vanguard single party, relying instead on a weak coalition of parties to maintain support, and Ratsiraka ruled through the civil service and careful clientelist management of the economy, which in the long run undermined the capacity of the state and weakened the economy.

In March 1990, the government formally allowed opposition parties to form, partly as a response to events in the rest of Africa. In fact, a number of groups, led by the associations linked to the Christian churches, had already begun to mobilize popular support on behalf of political liberalization.[28] The opposition, soon united in an informal and unruly alliance of over fifteen parties, church groups, and associations called the Forces Vives (FV), began to press the government for constitutional reform, using strikes and protest marches.

The government's unwillingness to accept more than limited political liberalization put it on a collision course with the opposition.[29] In July 1991, the FV upped the ante by declaring the 1989 elections nondemocratic and therefore null and void and by appointing its own provisional government, with retired general Jean Rakotoharison as president and Albert Zafy, head of a small party in the FV, the Union Nationale pour le Développement et la Démocratie (UNDD), as prime minister.[30] With the cooperation of the civil service and the passive complicity of the police, the ministers of FV's "insurrectional government" began occupying ministry buildings. Ratsiraka offered various face-saving compromises, but the opposition now insisted on his unconditional resignation. A pivotal event was the FV's march on the presidential palace on August 8, at which a hundred protesters were killed when the presidential guard fired on the crowd. Soon thereafter, the French embassy suspended its military assistance and publicly appealed to Ratsiraka to resign.

Nonetheless, the stalemate continued for several months longer, with the FV maintaining an effective general strike but Ratsiraka surviving and increasingly able to manipulate the internal divisions within the FV. A denouement came finally on October 31, 1991, thanks to pressures on Ratsiraka, from the donors and particularly the army, to reach a settlement. An interim agreement signed that day established a transitional government for eighteen months, pending the adoption of a new constitution and the convening of elections. In the meantime, Ratsiraka became a figurehead president, and executive power was transferred to a thirty-one-member Haute Autorité de l'Etat (HAE) under the leadership of Zafy. Nonetheless, Prime Minister Guy Razanamasy remained as head of a "transitional government," in which several FV members were now included. In addition, a consultative body of 130 members, the Conseil de Redressement Economique et Sociale (CRES), replaced the National People's Assembly. The agreement had the political advantage of providing well-paid positions for many of the politicians of the different factions but inevitably generated institutional duplication and competition.

The next couple of months were characterized by confusion, much political posturing, and little effective governance, while the country was prey to growing violence and the economy continued to deteriorate.[31] A referendum in August 1992 approved the new constitution. It weakened the presidency and strengthened parliament significantly and was somewhat ambiguous about the relative powers of the prime minister and the president.[32] In the first round of presidential elections held November 25, 1992, Zafy received 45 percent of the vote, followed by the former president with 29 percent.[33] In a runoff ten weeks later, Zafy confirmed his popularity with a large majority. Nonetheless, the transitional government remained in place until legislative elections, scheduled for June 1993, permitted the formation of a new government. Several parties had by that point defected from the FV, but the remainder of the alliance, known as the Cartel HVR, managed to secure some forty-five seats, making it the biggest single parliamentary group.[34] Francisque Ravony, who had served as deputy prime minister in the transition government, was invested by a narrow margin as prime minister and formed a government in late August 1993.

The transition from the end of the Ratsiraka government to this first Zafy government had thus lasted some three years. During that time the economy had lost any momentum gained during the 1980s. GDP had declined by an estimated 6.8 percent in 1991 and .2 percent in 1992. The current account deficit had increased from $82 million in 1989 to 192 million in 1991 and 290 million in 1993, while inflation had crept up to 22 percent. Arrears on servicing foreign debt had reached $773 million or more than twice the annual level of exports.

At the beginning of the transition back in 1990, the country was benefiting from an IMF program, and the World Bank was preparing its first structural adjustment soft loan of some $100 million after a number of sectoral adjustment loans during the previous decade. The transition put these programs, as well as significant balance-of-payments support from France, on hold, even though the Ratsiraka government continued to meet its debt-service payments through 1991. The new government sent an important delegation to Paris and Washington as early as October 1993 to try to negotiate new loans.[35] But through mid-1995, the government had still not reached agreement with the IFIs for new lending, despite having floated the Malagasy franc in May 1994, as they had required.

Part of the problem lay in the government's declining popularity in the face of continuing economic crisis; for instance, the World Bank's insistence on an ambitious civil service reform, with the loss of 30,000 civil servants and a pay freeze for the remaining ones, resulted in a forty-eight-hour strike by the civil service on January 22–24, 1994, officially to oppose the "authoritarian tendencies" of the government. In addition, the population had become cynical about the petty factionalism of the political class and its corruption as their own welfare continued to deteriorate.[36] The endemic corruption that had characterized the previous regime had not disappeared with the transition, and the government was embarrassed by a series of revelations involving the skimming of millions of dollars in public funds by high-level civil servants.[37]

But the inability to agree on a reform program also reflected disputes within the governing coalition itself. The intense factionalism of the transition now moved into the parliament and government. Despite the government's publicly stated intention to pursue free market reforms once it took office, there was no consensus on economic policy issues within the Cartel HVR: Some of its members enjoyed economic rents that liberalization threatened, while others retained an ideological aversion to reform, and yet others simply felt opposition to the IFIs to be good politics.[38] By 1994, such debates increasingly centered around the growing rift between President Zafy, hostile to reform and playing the populist card by darkly blaming the country's economic ills on "economic sabotage by foreigners,"[39] and Prime Minister Ravony, in charge of day-to-day governance and the leading proponent of agreement with the IFIs. Zafy undermined the negotiations by openly seeking "parallel financing," miraculous commercial loans that would lessen the need for official donor support. In the event, several such loans turned out to be fraudulent schemes that cost the government large sums of money as well as considerable embarrassment and annoyed the donors.[40] Zafy's nationalist credentials were reinforced, however, and when he proposed a national referendum to change the constitution so that he could dump Ravony, the population sided with him. By the end of 1995, the future of economic reform was in doubt.

□ *Mali*

Moussa Traoré came to power as the head of the military coup that toppled the regime of Mobido Keita in 1968. Over the years, he "civilianized" his regime and after 1976 ruled through a single party, the Union Démocratique du Peuple Malien (UDPM). Traoré initially continued Keita's ambitious state-led development strategy, which included an annual growth rate of 11 to 12 percent in administrative expenditures between independence and 1968, the development of a large and unprofitable parastatal sector, and a series of costly subsidies and services designed mostly for the urban population of the capital, Bamako.

By 1981, a growing balance-of-payments crisis convinced the Traoré government to go to the IFIs for financial support, beginning a cycle of partial reform and debt rescheduling not unlike the one just described for Madagascar. The restructuring and liquidation of parastatals, the liberalization of agricultural marketing, and controls on recurrent expenditures were all agreed to but then at best partially implemented. The budget deficit in 1988 remained at the unsustainable level of CFA 49.5 billion, some 9 percent of GDP. The policy dialogue with the IFIs was rocky, and they actually suspended all disbursements for a time in 1987–1988 for noncompliance. The renewal of IFI lending in 1989 resulted in a more aggressive austerity program by the government, including an attempt to eliminate the long-standing policy of guaranteed jobs for all college graduates, in order to reach a budget deficit of no more than CFA 15 billion in 1990, or 2 percent of GDP.

This new wave of austerity was partly responsible for the emergence of prodemocracy protests that began to destabilize the regime in 1989. Several political parties began to organize in the second half of 1990, including the Alliance pour la Démocratie au Mali (ADEMA), a coalition of several smaller parties, and the Comité National d'Initiative Démocratique (CNID).[41] Also noteworthy was the creation during this time of the Association des Etudiants et Élèves Maliens (AEEM), a student organization that supported both democratization and the protection of students' purchasing power and was to play a critical role in the transition. Personal rivalries between the leaders of these groups prevented their consolidation but were muted in this early phase for the sake of the struggle against the Traoré government.

Late 1990 and 1991 were characterized by growing protest and unrest.[42] Initial government tolerance soon gave way to the violent suppression of protests and attempts to intimidate opposition leaders. Events came to a head on March 22–24, 1991, when violent student protests and the setting on fire of some government buildings were harshly repressed by the police, resulting in between 100 and 150 deaths. On March 25, Traoré was arrested by parachutists commanded by Lt. Col. Amadou Toumany Touré. The government, parliament, and constitution were dissolved, and a military Conseil de Réconciliation Nationale (CRN) took power, soon replaced by the Comité de Transition Pour le Salut du Peuple (CTSP), enlarged to include members of the opposition as well as the military. Touré headed the CTSP but made it clear its role was strictly temporary and promised elections before the end of 1991. A transitional government was created in April 1991 to manage day-to-day operations.

A national conference convened in late July and adopted a new constitution, which was ratified by referendum on January 12, 1992.[43] Various delays pushed back the electoral calendar, and legislative elections were eventually held on February 23 and March 8, with ADEMA securing a comfortable majority (76 seats out of the 129 contested). Ten of the 21 parties contesting the elections won seats. The elections were marred by a low participation rate and allegations that ADEMA had benefited from considerable fraud.[44] The leader of the ADEMA alliance, Alpha Oumar Konaré, similarly won the presidential elections, held in two rounds on April 12 and 26, 1992. Touré continued to be probably the most popular man in the country but remained on the sidelines as he had promised.

The transitional government promised to continue the economic reform program already underway, and an enhanced structural adjustment facility

(ESAF) loan was in fact signed in August 1992 with the IMF right after the inauguration of the new government. President Konaré pledged his support for the reform program, despite the fact that ADEMA had had little input in the negotiations. Although he expressed resentment at the short deadlines in the IMF's program, in a number of public pronouncements in late 1992 and 1993 he admonished Malians of the need for sacrifices in the months ahead. Unfortunately, the transition had exacted a huge cost on the economy. Damage to the downtown business district of Bamako during the riots of early 1991 alone was estimated at between CFA 10 and 25 billion.[45] The Traoré government had also accumulated significant arrears on debts to various domestic creditors and had engaged in extensive embezzlement in the waning days of the regime.

Konaré's efforts to address these daunting issues were hampered by political problems. He did not benefit from much of a honeymoon, with several issues fueling an increasingly acrimonious political climate in Bamako almost as soon as he took office. First, the trial of former president Traoré and thirty-two of his closest associates, accused of both economic crimes and of "blood crimes" against the democratic protesters in 1991, resulted in opposition claims that the government was too soft on the previous government.[46] The Association pour la Défense des Victimes de la Répression (ADVR), an association created specifically to push for financial compensation to the victims of the struggle against the Traoré regime, adopted a highly critical attitude toward the government.[47]

Second, violent student protests against the government's education policies erupted in early 1993. The agreement with the IMF included promises to cut the cost of student grants in half, to CFA 4 billion (then worth some $13 million). This policy proved unsettling and divisive for ADEMA, which had found it useful to egg on the students against the Traoré regime, including on the issue of student grants. In any event, violent student protests in March and April resulted in at least one death and numerous injuries as well as the destruction of public property. Student protests erupted again in February 1994, following the devaluation of the CFA franc. By then, public opinion seemed to be turning against the students,[48] and the government promised to hold firm to its policies, even if it had to be acutely aware of the students' role in the downfall of the previous regime.

Third, personal rivalries within ADEMA almost immediately began to undermine its unity and Konaré's position. Konaré had chosen to include several other parties in the government, despite their poor showing and the opposition of his own backbenchers, as part of his ambition to develop a "Republican Pact." At the Alliance Congress of July 1993, Konaré's leadership was severely criticized. In November, ADEMA's vice president, Mamadou Lamine Traoré, left with his party, the Parti Révolutionnaire pour un Mali Démocratique (PRMD); thus Konaré's own party, the Parti Malien du Travail (PMT), was the only important organization left. This fragmentation of ADEMA led to accusations by the opposition that Konaré now lacked the legitimacy to rule. Parties that had been included in the Republican Pact rather uncharitably joined in the criticism, including the CNID, which left the government in early 1994. Even within what remained of ADEMA, Konaré was contested, notably for having given too many important ministerial positions to non-ADEMA members. Because of pressure from ADEMA Konaré replaced Prime Minister Abdoulaye Sekou Sow, an independent technocrat, with Boubacar Keita, a leader of ADEMA, in February 1994. Keita was the third prime minister in less than 2 years.[49]

Finally, the persistence of the Tuareg rebellion in the north was a financial burden to the government and a source of further divisiveness in Bamako political circles. Konaré's management of ongoing peace talks allegedly annoyed senior military officers.[50]

Remarkably, in view of these political problems, as of mid-1995 the government remained committed to stabilization and could report limited progress. The budget deficit declined from about CFA 83 billion in 1994 to CFA 54 billion the following year, although it remained about a tenth of GDP. The government claimed it would achieve budgetary balance by 1997. Its efforts to raise revenues by clamping down on customs and tax evasion enjoyed limited success, and a rebound of agricultural commodity production following the devaluation further helped increase revenue. The IFIs increasingly lauded Mali as a success story and were predicting 5 to 6 percent growth in 1995, if the favorable weather continued.

☐ Zambia

The regime of Kenneth Kaunda promoted economic policies of state-led growth that promoted rent seeking, inefficiency, and little economic development.[51] As the economic crisis worsened and private capital flows turned negative, Zambia turned to the IMF and World Bank for financial support and received a series of loans in the late 1970s and early 1980s.[52] A serious attempt at reform was initiated in October 1985 with the beginning of the Radical Reform Program (RRP), supported by the World Bank and IMF. By then, Zambia was the most indebted country in the world relative to its GDP, and economic conditions had dramatically deteriorated.

The 1985–1987 RRP envisaged thorough liberalization of the economy as well as fiscal and monetary stabilization. In particular, the maize consumer subsidies that weighed heavily on the budget were to be drastically reduced and maize marketing liberalized completely. However, the ensuing sharp rise in the price of mealie meal in December 1986 led to mass rioting in the Copperbelt, and the government rescinded the subsidy removal.

Partly as a result, Kaunda canceled the RRP in May 1987, causing the suspension of most donor assistance. The country would go it alone, he argued, rather than accept the diktat of the IFIs.[53]

An alternative, heterodox program was put into place, but within two years, amid growing inflation and a runaway budget deficit, the government renewed its policy dialogue with the donors. The IMF approved Zambia's Policy Framework Paper (PFP) in September 1989, and a three-year IMF shadow program was put into effect in January 1990, with a plan to address the servicing of arrears to the IFIs in order to requalify the country for renewed lending. Progress was fitful, however, and another attempt at the removal of the maize subsidies was aborted because of urban rioting in June 1990.

Kaunda's popularity shrank over the years because of his government's disastrous economic performance. Kaunda increasingly maintained political stability by relying on the patronage and rent seeking afforded by the preeminent role of the single party, UNIP, and by state intervention in the economy. By one estimate, for example, Kaunda disposed of some 40,000 patronage positions controlled by the United National Independence Party (UNIP) in Lusaka alone during the mid-1980s.[54] These practices were difficult to reconcile with the fiscal austerity and economic liberalization increasingly demanded of the regime during the 1980s.

Open criticism of the one-party system emerged in 1989. In particular, the Movement for Multiparty Democracy (MMD) was formed in July 1990 as a pressure group to fight for the return to multiparty politics in Zambia. The MMD would soon gain the support of organized labor, various human rights activists, most of the business community, and many disgruntled UNIP politicians who had fallen out of favor with Kaunda. Frederick Chiluba, the president of the Zambian Congress of Trade Unions (ZCTU), quickly became the co–vice president responsible for organization and operations of the interim executive. He would later emerge as the presidential standard-bearer for the party. Although other small political parties would emerge, the transition soon turned into a contest between UNIP and MMD.

In May 1990, Kaunda bowed to the growing pressure and scheduled a national referendum on the single party. It soon became clear that UNIP would lose the referendum, however, and on September 24, 1990, he decided to forgo the referendum in favor of direct multiparty elections to take place in October 1991. The election proceeded with remarkably little trouble, as Kaunda appears to have believed to the end that he would prevail in a free and fair election. In November 1991, however, Kaunda and UNIP were soundly defeated, as Frederick Chiluba won 76 percent of the presidential vote, and his party, the MMD, won 125 out of 150 parliamentary seats. Kaunda chose to respect the results and ensured a peaceful transfer of power to the MMD.[55]

The new MMD government came to power with the economy facing unmanageable external debt-servicing difficulties, severe shortages of foreign exchange, a budget deficit hovering between 6 and 10 percent of GDP, a triple-digit rate of inflation, and severely deteriorating infrastructure and social services. Moreover, the economic situation had worsened dramatically in the second half of 1991, when Kaunda forsook the reform program agreed to with the donors in a doomed attempt to win reelection. Thus, civil service salaries had been increased by 100 percent right before the election, and the state had provided UNIP with billions of kwacha for discretionary spending for the campaign. As a result, the fiscal situation was worsening rapidly, and inflation was picking up speed. Estimated at some 37 percent in 1985, inflation had climbed to 93 percent in 1990 and was running at some 190 percent when the MMD entered power.

It was thus important for the MMD to move quickly to control the economy. Luckily, the previous government had already negotiated a complete reform program with the donors, which remained essentially viable despite its suspension in September 1991. As a result, the donors resumed lending to Zambia within a couple months of Chiluba's arrival in power on the basis of the 1990 PFP.[56] Belying his past as a trade unionist, Chiluba put a reform-minded team of technocrats in charge of economic policy and promised rapid change. These technocrats included a number of officials who had been in government in the mid-1980s and came to power with a clear strategy for action. In part as a result, the MMD's first year in power was characterized by significant progress on macroeconomic stabilization. An extremely tough monetary policy coupled with tight fiscal austerity was put into place. The key to the government's fiscal effort was the removal of maize subsidies. By the end of the Kaunda regime, it was widely believed that trying again to remove them would amount to political suicide. The MMD government was nonetheless able to remove all maize subsidies immediately without any political turmoil.

As a result of these policies, the economy was well on its way toward macroeconomic stabilization within a year of MMD's entry into government. In 1991, the budget deficit had stood at 7.4 percent of GDP. Thanks to the MMD's efforts, it had declined to 2.2 percent in 1992, and by early 1994, the government was able to predict a budget surplus for the year. How sustainable is this effort in the near future? There remains a strong consensus within MMD to pursue the policies needed to keep inflation low. However, a number of political problems have emerged. First, the MMD alliance has been fragmenting since early 1993, with several key defections. Over time, Chiluba has strengthened his control of MMD, at the expense of a number of its original leaders, men like Emmanuel Kasonde or Arthur Wina who have since joined the ranks of the opposition. For the time being, nonetheless, MMD's position in parliament remains unassailable and Chiluba's control over the party complete. Indeed, the legislature remains as weak and ineffective as during the Kaunda regime, and backbenchers have found it practically impossible to influence government policy.

Second, the regime has been bedeviled by accusations of high-level corruption and involvement in drug running. This led the donors to threaten to suspend their extremely generous support of the regime at the end of 1993. Domestically, several extremely damaging newspaper stories have embarrassed key members of the government. There is little doubt that Chiluba has lost much of his enormous initial popularity as a result of both these scandals and the continuing lack of real progress in improving people's welfare. Scandals directly delegitimate the process of economic reform, moreover, as they give the impression that liberalization policies benefit the political class even as they impose austerity on the population.[57]

Third, the government's more ambitious long-term program of structural reform has made little progress. Civil service reform and privatization both have stalled, for example, and agricultural marketing liberalization has lost ground after a promising start. In some cases, implementation difficulties are to blame, but in others, opposition to reform within the state itself is responsible. This is the case notably for privatization, where rent-seeking interests close to the presidency have succeeded in slowing down the process and lessening Chiluba's commitment to reform. It appears that the longer the Chiluba government remains in power, the more it finds appealing some of the power maintenance strategies of its predecessor, even when they are not compatible with economic reform.

This dynamic intensified as the October 1996 elections approached, with no further progress on economic reform and growing polarization of the political class. Kaunda came out of retirement in 1995 and announced his intention to enter the presidential contest. Few observers gave him much of a chance, even if a clearly rattled Chiluba began a campaign of petty harassment against the former president. More seriously, 1995 witnessed a growing challenge to Chiluba within the increasingly divided MMD. Several of the party's young turks were purged in mid-1995 for contesting Chiluba's leadership and promptly created their own party.[58]

■ Explaining Outcomes

These three case studies are extremely suggestive in terms of the hypotheses laid out above, even if few firm conclusions can be drawn without increasing the number of cases. In addition, neither political nor economic reform is complete in any of the countries. Yet some patterns do emerge from our brief overview.

First, and most obvious, the three regimes have pushed for economic stabilization at least as effectively as their authoritarian predecessors, sometimes in very difficult circumstances. The nightmare of a populist explosion following democratization has not been borne out; the leaderships in all three countries have been forced to realize the absence of a real alternative to accommodation with the IFIs, at least in the present international context. Even when the leaders do not fully believe in the virtues of orthodox stabilization policy, the experience of power leads them to the conclusion that the advantages conferred by donor finance outweigh the political disadvantages of their conditionality. As Zafy found out in the parallel financing episode, there is no sustainable alternative to IFI financing. I will return to this issue below; here suffice it to say that all three states are officially committed to stabilization, thanks to which a large proportion of the national budget is paid for through IFI loans and grants.

Second, all three cases suggest the daunting nature of Africa's current dual transitions. In each case, progress on economic and political reform is a thankless task for the foreseeable future; extremely painful economic reforms need to be sustained for years before they will result in appreciable per capita growth and the alleviation of poverty; and democratization has not eliminated long-standing problems of corruption, low state capacity, and weak political organizations. Even in Zambia, where the dual transition was the smoothest, there is little margin for error in the coming years.

The three cases contrast sharply, however, especially regarding the ability of the new government to take advantage of the honeymoon to implement reform measures. Comparing the first year of the posttransition government, the MMD in Zambia was able to achieve significant progress, whereas the government of Konaré in Mali achieved little and of Zafy in Madagascar even less. Several reasons emerge quite clearly. The honeymoon effect in Mali and particularly Madagascar appears to have been dissipated by the length of the transition. If we take the first significant organized domestic demands for multiparty democracy as the beginning of the transition and mark the end by the entry into office of a popularly elected executive, we get the transition lengths described in Table 2.1.

The length of the transition has several implications. First, the longer the transition, the more the popular goodwill generated by the democratic movement has dissipated by the time a new government is securely in place and able to address economic issues. This is most clearly the case in Madagascar, where the factional infighting during the long transitional government tried people's patience. By the time Zafy gained control, the

Table 2.1   The Length of the Democratic Transition

	Mali	Madagascar	Zambia
Start	March 1990	April 1989	May 1990
End	June 1992	March 1993	Nov 1991
Length	27 months	47 months	18 months

democratic forces, rather than the Ratsiraka government, were getting blamed for the state of the economy.

In addition, the cost to the economy of the transition grows dramatically with its length. The outgoing government has few incentives to govern well. Not only is it tempted to employ deficit financing to remain in power, but also corruption and other forms of malfeasance are bound to increase as it becomes clear the transition is near and control from the top weakens. In all three countries, fiscal and monetary imbalances increased dramatically in the last days of the outgoing government. In Zambia, Chiluba took over the reins right away with a team determined to pursue reform, but many months were lost with transitional governments in Mali and Madagascar, in both cases headed by well-intentioned technocrats who had a mandate to oversee the economy but not to engage in any major new initiatives. In both cases, the economy continued to drift for months, with the accumulation of arrears and a decline in the state's fiscal discipline. Significantly, lending from the IFIs was not renewed until after the permanent democratic government was in place.

Thus, the length of the transition appears to be an important factor in whether or not the new government can undertake reform as soon as it enters office, but it is not the only factor. In addition, clear differences appear in the readiness of the new governments to undertake reform. The MMD in Zambia appears to have been more committed to economic reform than the prodemocracy alliances in the other countries. Certainly, the reformers in the MMD in Zambia were more influential within the party than was the case for either the FV or ADEMA. The Zambian business community was an early and powerful supporter of the MMD, whereas in neither Mali nor Madagascar was the business community a significant voice in the party.[59]

Moreover, the MMD reformers developed a clear agenda for reform well before November 1991 and were ready to take action when they entered office. The MMD's number-two person and first minister of finance, Emmanuel Kasonde, had numerous meetings with the World Bank and IMF in Lusaka and Washington in the months before the election.[60]

Similarly, the MMD's electoral platform, thrashed out and agreed to by the different factions in the party, spelled out in detail the measures it would take and enjoyed broad support within the party. By way of comparison, both Konaré and Zafy spent much of the transition vigorously criticizing the reform program.

Second, the degree of consensus about the need for reform also explains why the three countries differed in their ability to take advantage of the initial honeymoon period to restructure. It does seem in hindsight that the MMD government benefited from broader public and elite support for rapid stabilization. In part, this support reflected the importance of the business community and other proreform elements in the democratic coalition. Perhaps more important is the history of reform efforts in the country and the relationship between the donors and the previous regime. Kaunda had long publicly fought against the donors and had staked his reputation on a heterodox experiment without the donors between 1987 and 1989. The failure of that experiment made orthodox reform supported by the donors somewhat more attractive to policy elites in 1991. As Robert Bates and Paul Collier have argued, considerable policy learning had taken place in Zambia in the late 1980s,[61] reducing the hostility to orthodox stabilization measures. Very different policy lessons had been learned in Mali and Madagascar, where authoritarian governments had followed the diktats of the IFIs, however insincerely. Because Ratsiraka had aggressively defended the need for orthodox stabilization, the opposition crystallized against it, even though, ironically enough, Ratsiraka had maintained the various rent-seeking networks and patronage that real economic liberalization would have eliminated. Finally, and more speculatively, the fact that alone of the three Zambia suffered from extremely high inflation levels may have convinced the political class there of the need for extreme action. With inflation running at over 200 percent, the perception that a crisis existed that posed a real threat to the economy may have provided legitimacy to the stabilization effort. In Mali there was virtually no inflation thanks to its membership in the Franc Zone, whereas in Madagascar inflation levels remained a sustainable 15 to 30 percent during most of the transition. As a result, political elites in those two countries may have believed that the situation was essentially manageable.

Third, the roles of political parties in the three cases are sharply dissimilar. It is true that in all three countries, parties appear to share broadly similar views on policy issues and are not sharply distinguished by ideology. The sometimes acrimonious disputes between parties reflect mostly personal rivalries and short-term strategic considerations. Nonetheless, the ability of opposition parties to disrupt the government is clearly much larger in Mali and Madagascar than in Zambia, where the opposition parties have been more or less marginalized and the MMD remains unrivaled. In

the former two countries, an extremely contentious and fragmented political life saps the government's energies and its popular legitimacy. Every
policy decision is mocked or lambasted in the legislature, and the government must laboriously recreate a majority from its own backbenchers to
pass any bill.

In all three countries, the party of government is relatively weak in
organizational terms and unable to mobilize voters or legislators. None
appears able to provide effective support to the government at the grassroots level, for example, a factor I argued would be important to the ability
of a democratic government to sustain economic reform. At the same time,
however, the MMD appears somewhat more disciplined and cohesive than
either the FV or ADEMA. The latter are essentially alliances of smaller factions, always threatening to burst apart and requiring constant attention
from the top leadership. Keeping ADEMA together has led Konaré to
change prime ministers every six months, for example, and Zafy has to perform a constant juggling act to keep the different partners of his Cartel
HVR reasonably content. MMD has not been without divisions. Many of
its most prominent members have left the party, which appears considerably weaker than it did in the early posttransition period. The MMD
includes many old UNIP apparatchiks that remain opposed to reform and
lobby against it. Nonetheless, in contrast to his counterparts in Mali and
Madagascar, Chiluba retains a majority in parliament and does not need to
fear a revolt by his backbenchers.

■ Conclusion

Based on this evidence, the prospects for economic recovery and for the
consolidation of democracy appear better in Zambia and worse in Mali and
Madagascar. Of the three, the Chiluba government was the only one to take
advantage of the honeymoon and to push through reforms. Zambia still has
many problems. Democratic values have clearly not developed deep roots,
and as long as there are few effective checks and balances on the MMD
government, there is a risk that the present democratic order disguises what
is becoming in effect one-party rule dominated by the executive. Chiluba's
willingness to play by the new democratic rules has weakened as the 1996
elections approach.

Even so, Zambia emerged from its transition in better shape than Mali
and Madagascar, where the length and complexity of the transition resulted
in the near total suspension of economic policymaking for over a year. The
governments that then emerged did not have a clear strategy for dealing
with the crisis and proved largely passive and reactive. Interest groups such
as students in Mali took advantage of government indecision to press their

claims on the public purse. The political class was highly fragmented and driven by personal disputes that could in time only discredit democratic politics. In Madagascar, the military has remained resolutely on the sidelines, but general support for the regime is waning. Calls for federalism, exacerbated by Ratsiraka to try to hold on to power, today weaken the Zafy government and delegitimate the current constitution.[62] In Mali, the threat of military intervention remains high, particularly given Touré's continuing popularity and the appeal to many of a Ghanaian-style denouement to current problems.

By mid-1995, all three governments had lost much of the popular enthusiasm that had swept them into office, but each seemed likely to survive until the end of their electoral term, no mean accomplishment in postcolonial Africa. The governments in Mali and Madagascar seemed more vulnerable, however, to some kind of regime breakdown. Ironically, they had lost more of their legitimacy than the Chiluba government in Lusaka and yet had achieved considerably less to restore the bases of long-term economic growth.

■ Notes

I would like to thank Chris Barrett, Michael Bratton, Jonathan Hartlyn, Marina Ottaway, and Mamisoa Rangers for their comments on earlier drafts of this paper.

1. Among a large literature: Samuel P. Huntington, *The Third Wave: Democratization in the Late Twentieth Century* (Norman: University of Oklahoma Press, 1991); Nancy Bermeo, "Rethinking Regime Change," *Comparative Politics* 22, no. 3 (1991): 357–377; Guillermo O'Donnell and Philippe Schmitter, *Transitions from Authoritarian Rule: Tentative Conclusions About Uncertain Democracies* (Baltimore: Johns Hopkins University Press, 1986); Karen L. Remmer, "New Wine or Old Bottlenecks? The Study of Latin American Democracy," *Comparative Politics* 23, no. 4 (July 1991): 479–98.

2. For example, Michael Bratton and Nicolas van de Walle, "Popular Protest and Political Transition in Africa," *Comparative Politics* 24, no. 4 (July 1992): 419–442, and "Neopatrimonial Regimes and Political Transitions in Africa," *World Politics* 46, no. 4 (July 1994): 453–489; Samuel Decalo, "The Process, Prospects and Constraints of Democratization in Africa," *African Affairs* 91 (1992): 7–35; Christopher Clapham, "Democratization in Africa: Obstacles and Prospects," *Third World Quarterly* 14, no. 3 (1993): 423–438; René Lemarchand, "Africa's Troubled Transitions," *Journal of Democracy* 3, no. 4 (October 1992): 98–109; and Peter Lewis, "Political Transition, and the Dilemma of Civil Society in Africa," *Journal of International Affairs* 46, no. 1 (summer 1992): 31–54.

3. Different perspectives on Africa's economic crisis include Ajay Chhibber and Stanley Fischer, *Economic Reform in Sub-Saharan Africa* (Washington, D.C.: World Bank, 1991); Benno Ndulu and Nicolas van de Walle, eds., *Agenda for Africa's Economic Renewal* (Washington D.C.: Overseas Development Council, 1996); Thomas Callaghy and John Ravenhill, eds., *Hemmed in: Responses to Africa's Economic Decline* (New York: Columbia University Press, 1993); Paul

Collier, "Africa's External Economic Relations, 1960–1990," in Douglas Rimmer, ed., *Africa, 30 Years On: The Record and Outlook after Thirty Years of Independence* (London: James Curry, 1991); Giovanni Andrea Cornia, Rolph van der Hoeven, and Thandika Mkandawire, eds., *Africa's Recovery in the 1990s: From Stagnation and Adjustment to Human Development* (New York: St. Martin's Press, 1993); and William Easterly and Ross Levine, "Africa's Growth Tragedy," unpublished manuscript (Washington, D.C.: World Bank, November 1994).

4. See the fine essays by Janine Aron, "The Institutional Foundations of Growth," in Stephen Ellis, *Africa Now: Policies, People and Institutions* (London: James Currey, 1996), and by Ibrahim Elbadawi, "Consolidating Macroeconomic Stabilization and Restoring Growth in Sub-Saharan Africa," in Ndulu and van de Walle, *Agenda for Africa's Economic Renewal.*

5. Stephan Haggard and Robert Kaufman, eds., *The Politics of Economic Reform* (Princeton: Princeton University Press, 1992), pp. 338–341.

6. This is argued notably by Jagdish Bhaghwati, who says there is a "cruel choice" to make between democracy and rapid economic growth. See p. 204 of his monograph, *The Economics of Underdeveloped Countries* (New York: McGraw-Hill, 1966). Two recent thoughtful discussions of this literature are provided by Adam Przeworski and Fernando Limongi, "Political Regimes and Economic Growth," *Journal of Economic Perspectives* 7, no. 3 (summer 1993): 51–69; Larry Sirowy and Alex Inkeles, "The Effects of Democracy on Economic Growth and Inequality: A Review," *Studies in Comparative International Development* 25, no. 1 (spring 1990): 126–157.

7. See, for instance, Deepak Lal, "The Political Economy of Economic Liberalization," *World Bank Economic Review* 1, no. 2 (January 1987): 273–300; Mancur Olson, *The Rise and Decline of Nations* (New Haven: Yale University Press, 1982).

8. John Sheahan, "Market Oriented Policies and Political Repression in Latin America," *Economic Development and Cultural Change* 28, no. 2 (January 1980): 267–292; Bjorn Beckman, "Empowerment or Repression? The World Bank and the Politics of African Adjustment," in Peter Gibbon, Yusuf Bangura, and Arve Ofstad, *Authoritarianism and Democracy and Adjustment* (Uddevalla, Sweden: Nordiska Afrikainstitutet, 1992), pp. 83–105; and Atul Kohli, "Democracy Amid Economic Orthodoxy: Trends in Developing Countries," *Third World Quarterly* 14, no. 4 (1993): 671–689.

9. Deepak Lal, *The Poverty of Development Economics* (London: IEA Hobart Paperback, 1983), p. 33.

10. See, for example, Karen Remmer, "The Political Economy of Elections in Latin America, 1980–1991," *American Political Science Review* 87, no. 2 (June 1993): 393–406.

11. These arguments are more fully developed in my essay, "Political Liberalization and Economic Reform in Africa," *World Development* 22, no. 4 (April 1994): 483–500.

12. World Bank, *Governance and Development* (Washington, D.C.:World Bank, 1992).

13. See Robert H. Bates and Annie O. Krueger, "Generalizations Arising from the Country Studies," in Bates and Krueger, eds., *Political and Economic Interactions in Economic Policy Reform* (Oxford: Blackwell, 1993): pp. 455–456, for a similar conclusion, based on slightly different arguments. Rather than repression, they emphasize the uncertain environment in which economic agents are unsure about the welfare impact of policy reforms.

14. Terry Lynn Karl, "The Hybrid Regimes of Latin America," *Journal of Democracy* 6, no. 3 (July 1995): 72–86.

15. There is now a broad literature on the politics of adjustment. See Joan M. Nelson, ed., *Economic Crisis and Policy Choice: The Politics of Economic Adjustment in the Third World* (Princeton: Princeton University Press, 1990); Joan M. Nelson, "The Politics of Economic Transformation: Is Third World Experience Relevant in Eastern Europe?" *World Politics* 45, no. 3 (April 1993): 433–463; Haggard and Kaufman, *The Politics of Economic Reform;* Merilee S. Grindle and John W. Thomas, *Public Choices and Policy Change: The Political Economy of Reform in Developing Countries* (Baltimore: Johns Hopkins University Press, 1991).

16. Again, among a large literature on state capacity in Africa, see David Leonard, "The Political Realities of African Management," *World Development* 15, no. 7 (1987): 899–910; Goran Hyden, *No Shortcuts to Progress: African Development Management in Perspective* (Berkeley: University of California Press, 1983).

17. Grindle and Thomas, *Public Choices and Policy Change.*

18. See, for example, Samuel Huntington, *The Third Wave.*

19. John Williamson, "Democracy and the 'Washington Consensus,'" *World Development* 21, no. 8 (1993): 1329–1336.

20. This roughly translates as "all out" or "all at once."

21. See, for example, S. Rajcoomar, "Madagascar: Crafting Comprehensive Reforms," *Finance and Development* 28, no. 3 (1991): 46–48.

22. Public sector wages were compressed in real terms by almost a third between 1980 and 1983.

23. The process of economic reform in Madagascar is chronicled in Gilles Duruflé, *L'Ajustement Structurel en Afrique: Sénégal, Côte d'Ivoire, Madagascar* (Paris: Karthala, 1988); Michael Griffin, "Madagascar: Ratsiraka's Volte-face," *Africa Report* (May-June 1987): 50–52; Christopher Barrett, "Understanding Uneven Agricultural Liberalization in Madagascar," *Journal of Modern African Studies* 32, no. 3 (1994): 449–476; Paul Dorosh and Rene Bernier, "Staggered Reform and Limited Success: Structural Adjustment in Madagascar," in David E. Sahn, ed., *Adjusting to Policy Failure in African Economies* (Ithaca, N.Y.: Cornell University Press, 1994), pp. 332–365; and Adrian Hewitt, "Madagascar," in Alex Duncan and John Howell, eds., *Structural Adjustment and the African Farmer* (London: James Currey, 1992), pp. 86–112.

24. *Economist Intelligence Unit Country Report,* no. 1, 1991, p. 20.

25. Frederic L. Pryor, *Malawi and Madagascar: The Political Economy of Poverty, Equity and Growth* (New York: Oxford University Press for the World Bank, 1990).

26. See "Madagascar: The Ultra Liberals," *Africa Confidential* 32, no. 4 (February 22, 1991).

27. The growing instability and conflict of the end of the Ratsiraka regime is covered in Eliphas G. Mukonoweshuro, "State Resilience and Chronic Political Instability in Madagascar," *Canadian Journal of African Studies* 24, no. 3 (1990): 376–398.

28. The critical role played by the churches is analyzed in Sylvain Urfer, "Quand les Eglises Entrent en Politique," *Politique Africaine,* no. 52 (December 1993): 31–39.

29. Three careful accounts of the transition have informed the following paragraphs; see Jean Claude, *Willame Gouvernance et Pouvoir: Essai sur Trois*

Trajectoires Africaines, Madagasacar, Somalie et Zaire (Brussels: Institut Africain-CEDAF, 1994), especially pp. 161–180; and Philip M. Allen, *Madagascar: Conflicts of Authority in the Great Island* (Boulder, Colo.: Westview Press, 1995), chapter 3; and Françoise Raison-Jourde, "Une Transition Achevée ou Amorcée," *Politique Africaine,* no. 52 (December 1993): 6–18.

30. Zafy was a university professor who had served in cabinet briefly as minister of health between 1972 and 1974 but had been out of government since. Within the FV, he was essentially a compromise candidate who was not viewed as a threat by the other aspirants to FV leadership. See Allen, *Madagascar,* and personal communication, Leslie Fox.

31. See "Madagascar: A Clergyman's Coup," *Africa Confidential* 33, no. 16 (August 14, 1992).

32. Charles Cadoux, "La Constitution de la Troisième République Malgache," *Politique Africaine,* no. 52 (December 1993): 58–66.

33. The presidential election is well analyzed in Jean Pierre Raison, "Une Esquisse de Géographie Electorale Malgache," *Politique Africaine,* no. 52 (December 1993): 67–75; in the same issue see also the essay by Yvan Razafindratandra, "Mission d'Observation du second Tour des Elections Présidentielles à Madagascar," pp. 89–101.

34. These legislative elections pitted some 4,000 candidates in 121 parties for 139 seats under a system of proportional representation. Some 25 different parties won seats.

35. See *Marchés Tropicaux,* October 1, 1993, p. 2448.

36. News that members of the HAE had earned salaries some thirty times the minimum wage plus various other perks, for the length of the transition, increased people's cynicism.

37. See *Marchés Tropicaux,* February 17, 1994, p. 319.

38. See "Madagascar: A Clergyman's Coup."

39. Quoted in *The Economist Intelligence Unit Country Report,* third quarter, 1994, p. 20.

40. See "Madagascar: Money Missing? Who Cares?" *Economist* (October 14, 1995).

41. Richard Vengroff, "Governance and the Transition to Democracy: Political Parties and The Party System in Mali," *Journal of Modern African Studies* 31, no. 4 (1993): 541–562. In addition, this period would witness the reappearance of the US-RDA, the party of Mobido Keita, originally founded in 1946 and now headed by Tieoulé Konaté.

42. Jane Turrittin, "Mali: People Topple Traoré," *Review of African Political Economy* 52 (November 1991): 97–103.

43. It was approved by 99.76 percent of the voters, with an abstention rate of 57 percent.

44. See "Mali: Personalities Before Politics," *Africa Confidential* 33, no. 4 (February 21, 1992). In both the legislative and presidential elections, the participation rate was estimated at only around 20 percent of the electorate.

45. *Economist Intelligence Unit Country Report,* no. 1, 1993.

46. In February 1993, Traoré and four of his associates were sentenced to death. Konaré then commuted the sentences.

47. The government would in fact spend as much as CFA 350 million for this purpose (see *Economist Intelligence Unit Country Report,* no. 1, 1993).

48. See the analysis in "Difficile Apprentissage de la Liberté," *Jeune Afrique* 1735 (April 7, 1994); and *Economist Intelligence Unit Country Report,* second quarter, 1994.

49. See *Marchés Tropicaux,* February 11, 1994, p. 260.

50. The Tuareg rebellion is described in "Mali: Personalities Before Policies" and in "Mali: Talking Peace Again," *Africa Confidential* 36, no. 10 (May 12, 1995).

51. This section draws extensively from a longer analysis in Dennis Chiwele and Nicolas van de Walle, *Democratization and Economic Reform in Zambia,* a report presented to USAID-Zambia (Zambian Democratic Governance Project, Michigan State University), 1994.

52. A large literature exists on Zambia's attempts at economic reform in the 1980s. See, for example, Thomas Callaghy, "Lost Between State and Market: The Politics of Economic Adjustment in Ghana, Zambia, and Nigeria," in Joan M. Nelson, ed., *Economic Crisis and Policy Choice: The Politics of Adjustment in the Third World* (Princeton: Princeton University Press, 1989); and Robert H. Bates and Paul Collier, "The Politics and Economics of Policy Reform in Zambia," in Robert H. Bates and Anne O. Krueger, eds., *Political and Economic Interactions in Economic Policy Reform* (Oxford: Blackwell, 1993); John Loxley, "The IMF's Structural Adjustment Programmes in Zambia and Ghana: Some Issues of Theory and Policy," *Leeds Southern African Studies, No. 12* (University of Leeds, Leeds, 1990); Ravi Gulhati, "Impasse in Zambia: The Economics and Politics of Reform," *Analytical Case Studies No. 2* (Washington, D.C.: IBRD, 1989); Jeffrey J. Hawkins, Jr., "Understanding the Failure of IMF Reform: The Zambian Case," *World Development* 19, no. 7 (1991): 839–849.

53. The best account of the events leading to the break with the IFIs is provided in Tina West, "The Politics of the Implementation of Structural Adjustment in Zambia, 1985–1987," in Center for Strategic and International Studies, *The Politics of Economic Reform in Sub-Saharan Africa* (Washington, D.C.: CSIS, March 1992); see also Callaghy, "Lost Between State and Market"; and Bates and Collier, "Politics and Economics of Policy Reform."

54. Bates and Collier, "Politics and Economics of Policy Reform," p. 391.

55. The election is well described in Michael Bratton, "Zambia Starts Over," *Journal of Democracy* 3, no. 2 (April 1992): 81–94; and Caroline Baylies and Morris Szeftel, "The Fall and Rise of Multi-Party Politics in Zambia," *Review of African Political Economy* 54 (1992): 75–91; and Keith Panter-Brick, "The Prospects for Democracy in Zambia," *Government and Opposition* 29, no. 2 (spring 1994): 231–247.

56. An updated PFP was prepared in February 1991, forming the basis for an Economic Recovery Credit from the World Bank, the first tranche of which was disbursed in March.

57. On this point, see Julius O. Ihonvbere, "From Movement to Government: The Movement for Multi-Party Democracy and the Crisis of Democratic Consolidation in Zambia," *Canadian Journal of African Studies* 29, no. 1 (1995): 1–25.

58. See "The Market Democrats," *Africa Confidential* 36, no. 10 (May 12, 1995).

59. In Madagascar, for example, the business community tended to side with the Mouvement pour le Progrés du Madagascar (MFM) and its leader, Rakotonirina Manandafy, rather than the FV. The MFM was a member of the FV coalition but joined the opposition to Zafy. See "Madagascar: The Ultra Liberals."

60. This is well documented in Chiwele and van de Walle, *Democratization and Economic Reform in Zambia.*

61. Bates and Collier, "Politics and Economics of Policy Reform."

62. Personal communication, Leslie Fox.

3

Militarism and Problems of Democratic Transition

Eboe Hutchful

In recent years, democratization and political liberalization have transformed the political landscape in Africa. Nowhere is this more evident
than in southern Africa, where sweeping political changes—the peace
accords and the elections in Namibia, South Africa, Zambia, Malawi, and
Mozambique—have transformed the region from a zone of war to one of
incipient democracy. Elsewhere in Africa, military regimes in Mali, the
Central African Republic, Benin, the Congo, Ghana, Mauritania, Burundi,
Burkina Faso, and until recently Niger have made a transition to some form
of electoral democracy. Unalloyed military government continues only in a
few countries (Nigeria being the most prominent example). Authoritarian
one-party regimes in the Côte d'Ivoire, Kenya, Gabon, Cameroon, Cape
Verde, Tunisia, and elsewhere have submitted themselves to elections.
Similar steps toward multiparty democracy have recently been completed
or are underway in Ethiopia, Eritrea, and Tanzania.

Although these transitions add up to important political changes, their
magnitude and significance should not be exaggerated. The forms of
"democracy" that have emerged on the continent differ greatly in quality
and depth, and considerable caution is required in assessing their significance. First, in few of these countries (Benin, Zambia, Malawi, Mali, and
South Africa among them) have elections actually unseated incumbent governments or shifted power decisively from the preexisting political class. In
a large number of cases, elections have merely "constitutionalized" existing
authoritarian regimes, military as well as civilian, with former dictators
donning a thin mantle of democracy. In formerly single-party states such as
Kenya, Côte d'Ivoire, Gabon, and Cameroon, the official party has re-
emerged as the dominant party within the framework of multipartyism; the
military regimes in Ghana, Burkina Faso, and Mauritania have been
replaced by a *parti militaire* that exploited the advantages of incumbency,
winning elections the rules of which were set, by and large, by the governing regime. Some democratic freedoms have been realized (mainly in the
area of the press and the independence of the judiciary), but these are still

fragile and circumscribed and depend on the continued goodwill of the political leadership. In several of these transitions (Kenya is again a good example), after a brief period of liberalization the regime has returned to its old repressive style of rulership.

In all these countries, furthermore, important pillars of the authoritarian structures that undergird African states continue to survive irrespective of the nature of the political leadership. This is particularly true in relation to the control and functioning of the security agencies. Hence we may speak of regime rearrangement rather than political transformation or democratization; even so not all regimes have proved successful in this process of self-transformation. Finally, the number of coups and military political actions that have occurred since 1993 suggest the ominous possibility that the pendulum may well be swinging back toward at least limited forms of remilitarization.

In this chapter, I will focus on the transitions from military rule and (to a lesser degree) other manifestations of militarism. A Council for the Development of the Social Sciences in Africa (Codesria) network on "The Military and Militarization in Africa" has investigated the permutations of militarism in Africa over the last few years, in my view greatly enhancing our understanding of the phenomenon.[1] The research of the network, however, did not focus specifically on the dynamics of the transitions to democracy. Nevertheless, valuable insights do emerge on issues of democratic transition from military rule in the Codesria volume. Although it is possible to concur with Robin Luckham that military regimes should be viewed within the perspective of the general phenomenon of authoritarianism, with Henry Bienen that so-called military regimes do not constitute a generic regime type, and with Claude Welch that it is virtually impossible to differentiate military and civilian regimes on the basis of their structures, ideologies, and practices, transitions from military rule nevertheless differ from those commencing from civilian forms of authoritarianism in several respects.[2]

First, they raise the problem of the subordination of the military to democratic control by civilians following an active political role and the associated problem of how to prevent reentry into politics by the military. In this sense transitions from civilian authoritarian regimes have the crucial advantage of building upon already existing traditions (however fragile) of military subordination to civilian rule. Second, at least in Africa, military dictatorship has had particularly corrosive effects on military institutions, professionalism, and efficiency, posing tricky problems of military order for incoming civilian administrations. Third, the struggle against military authoritarianism has often spawned not democracy, but particularly vicious and debilitating new forms of militarism and militarization. Virtually all the outbreaks of civil war and warlordism (Somalia, Liberia, Chad, and

Ethiopia) have commenced in armed struggles against military dictatorships. Fourth, in these transitions the posture of the military institution is
clearly a crucial determinant of the outcome of the struggle against the dictatorship. The military (although never completely united on the score of
democratization) may lean in a proregime direction (as in Togo, Zaire, and
Nigeria) or may decide in favor of neutrality and acquiesce in democratic
change; more rarely, the military may even decide to intervene actively to
terminate the regime itself and facilitate the transition to democracy, as it
did in Mali.

■ Pathways from Military Rule

For these and other reasons, among them the highly variable terrain of militarism itself, the outcomes of transitions from military authoritarianism
have been particularly fluid and diverse. In brief, these have included

1. complete demilitarization and the emergence of an elected democratic dispensation, as in Benin, Mali, the Congo, Central Africa
   Republic, and Sierra Leone;
2. regime rearrangement, as in Ghana, Burkina Faso, and Mauritania.
   For example, the Provisional National Defence Council in Ghana
   mutated into the National Democratic Congress (NDC); the Conseil
   Militaire du Salut National in Mauritania won the 1992 elections as
   the Parti Republicain Démocratique et Social, and so on;
3. aborted transitions in Algeria and Nigeria, with the transition
   process (laboriously crafted but also cynically manipulated in the
   latter case) being called off at the last minute when the "wrong"
   political party appeared poised to win (and in the case of Nigeria
   actually won) the elections, followed by the reimposition of military rule and regression into even more vicious repression;
4. successful regime resistance and deflection of democratic pressures,
   most prominently in Zaire and Togo, followed in the latter case by
   regime consolidation and constitutionalization (with General
   Gnassingbé Eyadema winning the presidential elections);
5. transitions involving collapse of the existing central state and emergence of new state entities in Ethiopia, Eritrea, and Somaliland;
6. transitions in which disintegration of the central state has been followed by the emergence of warlordism (Somalia and Liberia); and
   finally, on a different plane,
7. peace pacts followed by the electoral victory of the former leadership of the liberation movements in South Africa, Namibia, and
   Mozambique.

This movement away from the militarization of politics in some African countries has coincided or overlapped with new manifestations of militarization (or remilitarization). Examples are the coup in The Gambia, long a cornerstone of democracy in West Africa, and the relapse to repressive rule in Nigeria and Algeria noted earlier. More worrisome is the pattern of military political actions following upon initially successful transitions. These have ranged from a series of limited "trade union" actions linked to pay and other disputes (Lesotho in January and April 1994, Guinea in February 1996, Central African Republic in April 1996) to complete displacement of the new regime in Niger and Burundi. (Burundi's "creeping coup" commenced with the killing of President Melchior Ndadaye in October 1993 and ended with the takeover of the government again by former Major Pierre Buyoya in July 1996. It coincided with the second "return to democracy" the same month in Niger, in which General Ibrahim Mainassara Bare, the leader of the January coup, "won" the elections to become the new president.) If anything, the tempo of remilitarization seems to have accelerated in 1996. However, there is encouraging evidence of democratic survival and even consolidation, with Benin (the pioneer in militarization in the 1960s and 1970s and demilitarization in the 1990s) once again leading the way with its second peaceful democratic succession in the 1990s (for good measure even returning power—through the ballot—to the very military dictator removed in the earlier democratic revolution). This diversity suggests that it is impossible to generalize about these transitions and the political and ideological calculus of the military in them without a close scrutiny of specific local factors and developments. Unfortunately, detailed analysis of this kind is beyond the scope of this chapter.

Although the record of transition from military rule appears incomplete and even disappointing, it nevertheless needs to be placed in historical context to be evaluated properly. Before the recent round of democratization, only a few military regimes in Africa had dissolved and actually handed over power (as opposed to civilianizing or constitutionalizing it in some way). Invariably, the new civilian regimes were short-lived. The best-known examples were Sudan (1964 and 1985), Ghana (1969 and 1979), and Nigeria (1979); there were also "arbitrator" transfers of power in Benin in 1963 and 1965. Seen from this historical standpoint, the present processes of democratization represent some evidence of progress.

What is less readily apparent is the depth of the political transformation that has taken place even in those situations in which the military continues to cling to the shadow of power. This is manifest in the intensity of the popular pressures that forced the political openings, the changes in the international and geopolitical context, the extent of the political liberaliza-

tion these autocrats have had to endure (including real concessions to multipartyism and freedom of the press), and the extent of the legitimacy crisis
facing both military rule and military institutions. Unlike earlier liberaliza-
tions and constitutionalizations, which were carefully calculated to adorn
the structures of authoritarianism and render them more palatable, this time
the emperor has been shown to be indeed lacking in clothing. In fact, that
more has not been accomplished along the road to democracy must be
blamed as much on the incompetence of the political opposition as on the
wiles of the dictatorship.

The most important lesson is the fact that military dictators can no
longer flout the popular will with impunity. The incapacity of the military
to ignore popular pressures is the most striking indicator of the profundity
of the political transformation that has occurred in Africa. In Uganda,
Ethiopia, Somalia, and Liberia, the refusal of military dictators to institutionalize peaceful political change led to armed rebellions that resulted in
the overthrow or disintegration of the existing political order; both Nigeria
and Algeria were rendered ungovernable following the failure of the regime
to respect the verdict of elections that it had itself instituted; and although
in Zaire and Togo the stubbornness of incumbent dictators and their cynical
manipulation of the transition process have succeeded in disorganizing and
exhausting the democratic opposition, the political costs have been
extremely high.

These developments seem to point to the fact that at least for the foreseeable future the classic form of military dictatorship may no longer be a
viable proposition. Its basis, the unquestioned political domination exer-
cised by a professional army fed by imports of foreign arms, has disappeared under the weight variously of the democratic surge, the diffusion of
the instruments of violence, the desacralization of weaponry, and the erosion of the charisma associated with the bearers of institutionalized violence.

These gains may again prove short-lived, however, if the new democracies are unable to subordinate their militaries to the authority of the elected civilian institutions. And indeed, many elected governments have gotten
off to an unpromising start in this regard. Confrontations between the
prodemocracy movements on the one side and the military and security
agencies on the other suggest that democratic governments may have come
to power with a weak base in the military. Rebellious military units
besieged the transitional governments in the Congo, Niger, and Togo and
twice attacked the new government in Lesotho in 1994.

These clashes were most serious where leadership of the democracy
movement and that of the military or the authoritarian leadership have fall-
en into the hands of rival ethnic, racial, or regional groups. In Burundi,
political power after the 1993 elections came to repose in the hands of a

Hutu-dominated political party, while the military continued to be dominated by Tutsis, helping to lay the foundation for the events culminating in the coup of July 1996. In Nigeria, the decision of the northern-dominated military oligarchy to abort the transition and to refuse to hand over power was in part the consequence of the election victory of a Yoruba candidate from the southwest. In both of these cases, the military had become the unofficial political party of a particular ethnic alliance.

Outcomes of this kind should be blamed less on ethnic conflict than on the systematic attempt by incumbent dictators to play up ethnic differences in order to deflect demands for democratization and forestall political change, and to validate their claim that the only alternatives to authoritarianism are "tribalism" and "chaos" and that democracy is contrary to the culture and existential conditions of Africa.

This was most clear in the role played by the government of Daniel arap Moi in fomenting the violent "ethnic" disturbances in the Rift Valley of Kenya and in the attempt by Somali President Mohammed Siad Barre to build up a clan-based political structure to shore up his power, a tactic that backfired tragically.[3] Nevertheless the frequency with which the media are already reporting popular disillusionment with democracy suggests that this strategy has not been entirely unsuccessful.[4]

The erosion of the political power and repressive ability of the military is positive and indeed necessary for the laying of democratic foundations, but it does not in itself guarantee democracy; indeed it can pose several dangers for the democratization process as a whole. National security in the true sense (not, as is often the case in Africa, regime security) and the assurance of law and order are legitimate and indeed essential aspects of democracy, and they can only be ensured by states that are both strong and responsive. Weak and traumatized armed forces are not only incapable of safeguarding national security, they may directly threaten it; as important, they are often incapable of maintaining their own corporate solidarity and conception of long-term corporate self-interest required for effective bargaining in the process of extrication from power.

Hence the most likely consequence of a political defeat of the military is not its permanent political effacement and the establishment of stable democratic rule but the iteration of weak and unstable civil regimes and military juntas or putsches. The alternative to repression by the rogue state is thus not always democracy but any of a number of possible conditions of anarchy, warlordism, and banditry. These constitute a far greater danger to personal security and democracy than authoritarian rule based on the central state. The dilemma of democracy is that it demands a well-armed military establishment that is at the same time subordinate to civilian control.

■ Bringing Security Agencies Under Democratic Control

Despite its importance, the issue of how to bring the armed forces and security and intelligence agencies under democratic control has not been treated with any depth or consistency in most African transitions. This is in dramatic contrast to Latin America, where the issue has spawned a growth industry among academics, political parties, and strategic research centers.[5] This chapter attempts to contribute to our understanding of this aspect of democratization and of the roles played by the various players and actors: the authoritarian regime, civil society and democratic institutions, the military, and finally the international community.

The motivation and policies of the incumbent authoritarian regime are the most transparent, and they determine to a large degree the transition process, shaping the future prospects of civil-military relations. The interest of the dictatorship is to undermine the professionalism of the military, to isolate the institution from democratic currents, frustrate the possibility of retribution, dominate whatever "reforms" are undertaken in the military arena, and entrench its own allies and doctrines in the military forces.

Often, the political posture adopted by the military results from a particular ethnic coloration fashioned by the dictatorship, which leads to the erosion of social and professional autonomy. In several cases incumbent dictators have virtually privatized the army (Togo and Zaire are both examples of this). Military dictatorships have also introduced deep-rooted dysfunctionalities into the military institution. This is done deliberately because the less professional the military is, the less likely it is to act in pursuit of a coherent institutional interest, to distance the interests of the institution from those of the regime, or to strike compromises designed to protect long-term professional objectives.

Typically, in these transitions the authoritarian regimes have sought to exercise tight control over security-related issues in order to protect their base in the security forces and to isolate the democratic movement and the security forces from each other. This kind of censorship was manifest, for instance, in the transitions in Ghana and Nigeria. Although in both instances attempts at military reform preceded the transition to democracy, the military regime retained tight control over reform, permitting no discussion or participation by civilians. The process of self-reform allowed the military to retain the initiative (or at least to preempt the possibility of unwelcome initiatives by incoming civilian governments) and to incorporate the interests of both regime and military institution, but not those of the public, into the reform process.

■ The Role of Civil Sectors and Democratic Institutions

Success in crafting viable civil-military relations in the democratic transitions will depend very much on the roles of civil society and the democratic forces and, less obviously, on the military institution itself. The first requirement is the existence of civil sectors both organized and united enough on basic issues of principle to negotiate new relationships and guarantees with each other and with the military.

One of the main sources of the political power of the military regime is the ability to manipulate to its advantage the fragmentation of civil society and the ideological splits among political organizations. Julius Ihonvbere documents the devastating consequences of the disunity and opportunism of the Nigerian political class in making possible the continuance of military rule, and he demonstrates how this facilitated the Abacha coup and the reimposition of military dictatorship.[6] To forestall this possibility Alfred Stepan suggests the revalorization of democracy pacts: All democratic groupings need to commit themselves to the defense of democratic rights and processes and to desist from inviting the military to intervene in political conflicts.[7]

Organizations of civil society also need to develop autonomous military intelligence and the ability to challenge the claims of the military establishment to the right to secrecy and exclusive expertise over military affairs; if necessary, they need to help restructure the prevailing security doctrine. This requires redefinition of the very concept of security so that it ceases to be the exclusive preserve of the military; this can be done, for instance, by drawing a distinction between military and nonmilitary aspects of security or between "security" (which is the responsibility of the citizenry as a whole) and "defense" (the legitimate area of the armed forces).

One of the key difficulties in the African transitions is the lack of interest and expertise among African publics with regard to military governance as well as strategic and security issues. Prodemocracy movements have also frequently made tactical and substantive errors in confronting these questions during the transitions. Defense- and security-related issues should be a major arena of democratic struggle, and the democracy movements must have a strategy for forcing these issues onto the public agenda.

The possibility of resistance by the military itself to such an initiative should not be discounted or underestimated. A remarkable example of the attempt of the military to protect its claim to secrecy and exclusive competence even during the democratic transition is offered by Tanzania, where recently an account of the 1964 mutiny of the Tanganyika King's Africa Rifles by a local historian, Nestor Luanda, was declared "confidential," and the entire first printing (1,000 copies) was acquired by the Tanzanian People's Defence Force. That this could happen to a book on a mutiny that occurred three decades ago does not suggest much progress in bringing security issues into the public domain.

I have argued elsewhere that much also rests on how reforms are approached and that for obvious reasons it is necessary to avoid the impression either of complete military autonomy and self-direction or of civilians dictating unpopular reforms to the military.[8] Forging a clear consensus between the military and civilians on such issues as force levels and mission and on the overall direction of reform should alleviate much of this danger by giving broad legitimacy to the reforms. The military reform movement will have to take the appearance of a military-civil coalition, conveying the message that the military is reforming itself but in a process approved and legitimized by civilians. This satisfies at the same time the twin principles of military expertise and civilian supremacy.

Civilians should of course be aware that within the military itself there is usually more than one reform position. Indeed many of the issues affecting the military that have been mentioned here, including mission doctrine and corporate structure, are being debated within the military itself, and the prevailing orthodoxy on some of these questions is often challenged by sections of the military, particularly among the subaltern ranks. The best possible approach for civilians may be to identify and ally with the forces in the military that advocate reform directions most supportive of democracy. These include reprofessionalization and respect for civilian supremacy.

The new democratic institutions are a second, crucial actor in crafting viable civil-military relations. Legislative self-empowerment with regard to military issues and policies is key to effective civil and democratic control. It includes the ability to review effectively military budgets and affairs; the development of the legislature's own research, information, and monitoring expertise; and an appropriate committee system and congressional staff.[9]

Democratically elected authorities must take the lead in reshaping strategic concepts and ways of thinking. This in turn means, as argued by Virgilo Bertran, that the "education and training of a staff of qualified civilians in military planning and administration, logistics, etc., is one of the first priorities" of any civilian governments seeking the ability to "formulate, execute and control Defence and Military Policies."[10] In most African countries, institutions and agencies for strategic studies are nonexistent in the civil sector, an important problem considering the low capability of the military sector in this area also. But the executive must intervene actively in revising the existing security doctrine, force mission, goals, and structures and in establishing the content and curriculum of service schools. The executive must similarly play an active role in the internal stabilization of the military.

There is as yet little research into what mechanisms, if any, are emerging to ensure democratic oversight and control over the military in the newly democratizing countries of Africa. In many countries, legislative oversight of military and defense issues was one of the early casualties of independence; many African constitutions still make formal provisions for such oversight in relation to the armed forces (or more appropriately, to budgetary matters pertaining to the armed forces), but they are usually silent on the intelligence and other special security agencies that often form the underpinnings of authoritarianism and human rights abuses. Traditionally, these mechanisms have been heavily concentrated around the presidency, with the president rather than the minister of defense exerting powers of control.

The little information that exists does not suggest that much has changed under the new democracies in this respect. The available evidence is far too sparse to allow firm conclusions, however. An anecdote will illustrate my point. While in Washington in 1995 to attend a conference on "Civil-Military Relations in Latin America: Lessons Learned," I bumped into two visiting senior parliamentarians from a "newly democratized" African country. As luck would have it, both were members of the committee overseeing defense issues in the new parliament. I was told that the committee had just passed its first defense budget. The description of how the "passing of the budget" was done was instructive. According to the legislators:

> On the day in question the Minister of Defense came to the National Assembly. He explained that as this was a confidential security document, it could not be discussed by the Assembly. In accordance with tradition therefore we passed it [the military budget] without debate.[11]

This appeal to tradition as an excuse for failing to debate the military budget was in itself curious, since even a short perusal of the record would show that in this country previous parliaments had in fact vigorously debated the defense budget, particularly in the early years following independence. It should be pointed out that the minister of defense was a holdover from the previous government, having been in the post for almost a decade, and the president was a former military man. The chairman of the parliamentary committee was also a retired officer (as were two others on the nineteen-member committee), and he had come to the position virtually by default because the parliamentary committee in charge of such appointments felt that he was the only member of parliament (MP) who knew anything about the military. Indeed, except for the initiatives of this officer (which included arranging a visit to the military barracks, found to be in "deplorable" state), the committee was virtually moribund. Furthermore, although the parliament had oversight over the military and police, it had none over the intelligence services and the secret police, which remained under the presidency and were also inherited unchanged from the previous regime. The secret police included both the official secret police and a second—even more secret—police unit that officially did not exist. With these outfits it continued to be "business as usual" (my informant's words).[12] Not only did this situation not appear anomalous to the new members of the legislature, the information also suggested that they themselves lacked any notion of the requirements of their new position as members of oversight committees on the defense and security forces.

This is not an isolated example. In relation to Lesotho, Khabele Matlosa argues that the Defence Commission, which under the 1993 constitution and the Lesotho Defence Force Order No. 17, 1993, is responsible for the appointment, discipline, and removal of the members of the Defence Force, was structured (essentially by the previous military regime) in order to ensure that the military would dominate defense policy and run its own affairs.[13] Such domination went well beyond the requirements of "professional autonomy" as conventionally understood. The powers of the Defence Commission as detailed in the constitution and the Lesotho Defence Force Order effectively shifted decisionmaking and policymaking on critical military matters away from the existing parliament to what was in effect a security elite. The almost complete domination by the commanders of the security forces is the most striking aspect of the Defence Commission, with the prime minister, who also doubled as the defense minister, as the sole civilian member of the commission.

Fortunately not all the new legislatures are abdicating their responsibility for defense and security issues so easily as the two cited here. Faced with similar prompting by securocrats to look the other way, the committee responsible for defense in the new South African parliament said "no thanks" and decided to scrutinize the budget.[14]

■ Role of the Military Institution

The third actor is the military itself, specifically those military forces coherent and far-sighted enough to be willing to negotiate their corporate and professional interests with the new governments and democratic forces. One of the key problems for democratization is the weakened state of African armies. The internal condition of many African armies borders on anarchy, with declining discipline and esprit de corps and inadequate and outdated equipment and support services. Intramilitary conflicts, of an ethnic, generational, rank, and ideological character, have often spilled over in turn to threaten the political order. Unlike in Latin America, where armies have shown greater ability to act as professional forces over time and through this to dominate the political process, in Africa the lack of professionalism and institutional stability—exacerbated by involvement in poli-

tics—is the greatest danger associated with the militaries. Military capabilities have been sufficient to establish—if not sustain—political dominance,
but they are not credible even for minimal tasks of national defense.
Nevertheless, many of Africa's weak armies are involved in a large variety
of internal security operations (against Islamic fundamentalists in Algeria,
the Casamance rebels in Senegal, the Tuaregs in Mali, the Revolutionary
United Front [RUF] rebels in Sierra Leone, and so on). Several African
armed forces have been locked for years in unwinnable wars (a good example of this is the Sudanese army in its war against the Sudan People's
Liberation Army [SPLA] rebels); others have gone down in defeat and disappeared altogether (Uganda, Somalia, Ethiopia); yet others (such as the
Chadian and Liberian armies) have been reduced to just one warlord fragment among others. This high rate of military failure threatens both democracy and national security.

Ironically, the ruin of the military can be laid right at the door of the
military dictators. I have argued elsewhere that the political dynamics and
cleavages characteristic of military regimes have often had devastating
effects on the military institution and on military professionalism (arguably
civilian dictators do not have nearly the same ability to devastate the military). Deliberate deescalation of the fighting capabilities of military units is
one of the strategies employed by these military dictators to subordinate the
military to the regime; while national security demands military competence, regime security often requires military weakness. This would explain
the tendency for African armies to be "declawed" (disarmed) in normal circumstances, and the equal tendency for such armies, once rearmed to fight
a war or conduct an operation, to turn their guns on the regime instead, as
in Sierra Leone. In the event, both national security and regime security are
compromised.

The negative effects of authoritarianism have often been best articulated by the military leadership itself. In the case of Nigeria, General Salihu
Ibrahim, a "legalist" officer who tried to reprofessionalize the armed forces
but was retired before he could succeed, delivered the following comments
in his valedictory statement:

> I make no pretence of my disdain of the involvement of the military in the
> political affairs of this country. I hold the strong view that any military
> organization that intends to remain professional and relevant to its calling
> has no business meddling in the political affairs of its country. . . . It is
> quite an open secret that some officers openly preferred political appoint-
> ments over and above regimental appointments no matter the relevance of
> such appointments to their career progress. The inability of us to make the
> desired progress in our professional orientation during my tenure is
> explained by this political interest group, who though very small in num-
> ber, constituted themselves into a very powerful pressure group, unfortu-

nately to the detriment of the service, and, of course, their colleagues. The end result of the collective actions of this pressure group was the visible decline in professionalism, morale and discipline in the Nigerian Army. For example, we suddenly found ourselves operating the Nigerian Army with disregard to existing rules and regulations. . . . We became an army whereby subordinate officers would not only be contemptuous of their superiors but would exhibit total disregard to legitimate instructions of such superiors.[15]

This view is confirmed by General Emmanuel A. Erskine, a Ghanaian officer who led UN peacekeeping forces in Lebanon, who in discussing the case of Ghana observed that military intervention in politics had "created problems for the armed forces as an institution. Most military interventions have resulted in a fall in the standard of discipline of the armed forces."[16]

These statements suggest the recognition that the military can continue to resist democratization and democratic control only at the expense of its own professionalism and ultimate survival (Haiti is a case in point). Furthermore, they suggest a key opening around which the new democracies can fashion a strategy for subordinating the military. The consensus that the dictatorship has been disastrous not only for democracy but also for the military institution and for professionalism should constitute the basis for an alliance between the democracy movements and the officers favoring a return to professionalism and also the crux of a strategy to detach the military institution from the dictatorship. By the same token it can be argued that democracy, with its insistence on civilian subordination and political noninvolvement of the military, may well form the best foundation for military professionalism and specialization.

This issue of the professionalism of the military is a crucial one because the ability of the military institution to read the emerging political terrain and to develop a coherent strategy to negotiate protection of its core and legitimate professional interests is an essential aspect of the transition process. The South African Defence Forces (SADF) represent one of the few examples of a military force that clearly anticipated the need to remake itself in order to adapt to rapidly changing political circumstances. The SADF has been strikingly successful in attaining such a goal, particularly considering the apparently intractable issues that control over military and intelligence resources were thought to pose in this particular transition.

South Africa is unique among brokered transitions because of the size and complexity of its armed forces, the existence of a large and sophisticated military-industrial complex, and the fundamental role occupied by force in the historical reproduction of the apartheid system. It was the closest approximation to a national security state in Africa. During the period of the "Total Strategy," the boundaries between the military and civil spheres became deliberately blurred in order to facilitate mobilization against the perceived "total onslaught" by the domestic and international enemies of apartheid. South Africa was placed under the rule of the securocrats. The State Security Council, initially only one of four cabinet-level standing committees, fell under the domination of the security forces and displaced the cabinet itself to emerge as the center of national decisionmaking and official power. According to Herbert Howe, "By the mid-1980s, the National Security Management System (NSMS) and its 500 local Joint Management Centres (JMC) accountable to no elected body had deepened the security establishment's rule of South Africa to the extent where the Cabinet usually rubber-stamped their decisions."[17] However, in light of the reassessment of the SADF's role following the defeat at Cuito Cuanavale, the independence of Namibia, the "End Conscription" campaign, and the opening to the African National Congress (ANC), the objectives and language of the SADF changed from that of subordinating all national institutions and resources to the pursuit of the "national security" of South Africa to a stress on professional standards (promotion and command through seniority), subordination to and autonomy from the civil authorities, and "restructuring." The redefinition of the strategic conceptions of the SADF was carried out at the level of specialized military and civil research institutes (including some at the universities), which, as argued by Horace Campbell, outstripped in sophistication any intellectual and ideological movements extant on the side of the ANC and the democratic forces.[18]

The proactive stance of the former SADF and its allies in South African society is apparent in the extent to which its strategic vision has shaped that of the new government, to the extent that scholars like William Gutteridge can assert the existence of a "fundamental identity of interest" between the ANC and the SADF.[19] Restructuring became a substitute for a more fundamental transformation of the relations of force and the conversion of the military-industrial complex to serve popular needs and to demilitarize the region. Instead of undertaking a program of defense conversion, the Mandela government, and the defense minister in particular, regard Armscor (the largest exporter of manufactures in South Africa) as a key tool of export expansion and economic recovery. Within the region and abroad Nelson Mandela and his entourage have made a pitch for South African arms exports. In turn, Armscor seeks to portray itself as a promoter of the government's program of job creation, welfare, and social justice. However, force integration has run into several difficulties, as former MK fighters have objected to the terms of their absorption into the military. Hundreds of former MK fighters were dismissed when they went AWOL from the SADF military camps to protest treatment by the military command. A protest by black South African police was brutally suppressed by their white counterparts.

The loss of legitimacy of the military has grave implications both for democracy and for the humane and efficient conduct of war. The dramatic collapse of state armies on the field of battle can be attributed in large measure to the "legitimation deficit" they suffer, a problem in turn rooted in the fact that they seek to defend regime security rather than national security, as Sunday Ochoche argues.[20] A politically irresponsible army is also liable to be irresponsible on the battlefield. For instance, I am convinced that the excesses of the Nigerian army and air force in Liberia are related to the callousness with which civilians are routinely treated at home by these same forces.

Although the security implications of weak armies are clear, the implications for democracy are much more complex. Military forces were crucial ingredients in the process of state formation in Europe. Strong states, secure in their ability to exercise effective military and police force, in turn negotiated democratic freedoms with their citizens. In Africa, however, the processes of state formation and democratization are occurring simultaneously, posing issues that we have yet to conceptualize properly.

■ Restructuring the Military and Defense Framework

The previous discussion suggests that the challenges facing democratic forces in respect to the armed forces as well as security and intelligence agencies cannot stop at redefining the military's future relationship with the political process, but must also extend to a rethinking of the role, mission, and doctrine of the armed forces. Reform must integrate both operational and political objectives, never one to the exclusion of the other. These objectives call for a fundamental reassessment not only of force doctrine, mission, and structures but in some cases even of the existing military models. Entirely new military structures and relationships may have to be explored.

The prospects in this area depend to some degree on the form taken by the transition itself. In theory, the defeat on the battlefield of the armies of the dictatorship presents the most favorable option for democracy, because this allows the victorious forces to reshape security organs in ways that make them more consistent with accountability and democratic control. In practice, however, these military victories by guerrilla forces, exacted at great cost, can lead to tremendous problems of military disorder and to the dispersal of large quantities of armaments among the population. In the most extreme cases, such as Somalia, the result can be the collapse of the central state. It is not at all clear that these irregular forces will initiate some qualitatively new form of military institution, rather than remake themselves into conventional military forces, as occurred with the former liberation armies in Zimbabwe and Mozambique. In any case, few African democracies will have the opportunity radically to reconstruct their armed forces.

Both military privileges and the determination of military mission in turn raise the issue of military budgets, a key issue in democratic transitions. As Nadir Mohammed's contribution to the Codesria volume suggests, the size of real military outlays varies quite substantially among the individual African countries and bears little consistent relation to economic means.[21] The main determinant of the level of military expenditure is the presence or absence of hostilities. In general, real military outlays declined substantially in most African countries throughout the 1980s and early 1990s. While real military spending in many African countries has stagnated or declined to the point at which many armies are barely able to perform essential functions, it nevertheless remains too high in most cases in relation to the country's GNP.

Military budgets cannot be discussed without placing them in the context of ongoing economic reforms. We have little information or knowledge as to how militaries and military expenditure perform under conditions of stringent economic reform. One problem is that neo-orthodox reforms have nothing specific to say about defense issues. In general, military expenditure is regarded as an unwelcome residue in the budget process. Ironically, however, the military is a key player in resolving the issues of political stability that drastic economic reforms are likely to bring to the fore. Although China has demonstrated that it is possible and conceivable, in the process of economic reform, to both contract military spending and increase military efficiency and capital intensity,[22] the indications are that in most countries economic reform has had a serious and negative impact on military operations, morale, and effectiveness. Undoubtedly, the best example of this is the former Soviet Army, a classic case of how political transformation and economic reform can together gut armies and potentially destabilize both civil-military relations and democracy itself.

Outcomes like the post-Soviet debacle are most likely to happen where budget cuts have occurred without a supporting program of fundamental military restructuring. For instance, although Ghana is usually considered the most successful case of adjustment in Africa, the finance minister, Kwesi Botchwey, had this to say about the state of the armed forces: "[Ghanaian] soldiers live in dilapidated quarters and their hardware is obsolete. The situation is so bad that Ghana might not be able to defend itself in some circumstances."[23] This statement could well be applied to many African armed forces and indeed proved almost prophetic when the Ghanaian army was asked to quell ethnic conflicts in the north of the country in 1994. In 1993 (coincidentally the year of the restoration of democratic government) the food budget of the armed forces was cut by one-third and the fuel budget by almost 50 percent.

This is not to argue that falling military expenditures can be attributed solely to structural adjustment. In the case of Ghana, the substantial external inflows that followed from adjustment policies, though not available for military spending, could well have released domestic sources of funding for military purposes. Other factors may need to be examined to explain why military spending failed to rise correspondingly with the dramatic improvement in the state's fiscal situation. Whatever its causes, a decline in military spending that further deprofessionalizes the military threatens democratization. Faustian bargains[24] with the military may be required to stabilize democratic rule, and this may well include increased defense expenditures, which may in any case be required to underwrite the needed reforms suggested above. This is a major dilemma for countries undergoing structural adjustment.

The reestablishment of links between military and civil institutions should be part of the process of military restructuring in particular and democratic transformation in general. George Biddle, calling for "interaction and communication" between the military and civilian sectors, argues that:

> The military must not be isolated and insulated from civil society. Rather the two must have an active and ongoing exchange. If the military is exposed to the diverse interests and forces within pluralistic civil society, the armed forces begin to understand that their role is not to dominate or influence the civil sector but to be subordinate to it and to protect it from foreign threat. If the military learns to appreciate the broad spectrum of interests that exist, it intuitively realizes that its function is to remain neutral and thus serve democracy. Therefore, civil society and the armed forces must be constantly exposed to one another and maintain an open and transparent dialogue.[25]

■ Regional Security Arrangements

With Africa's small nations, weak and small armies, and limited defense budgets, regional defense arrangements and mutual defense pacts seem essential for rationalizing defense costs. However, progress in this area has been slow to materialize in part because of the OAU's (Organization of African Unity) principle of noninterference in the affairs of member states and because some African states (particularly Francophone states) have sought security under the military umbrella of a major foreign power. Thus, although African armies have long been involved in international peacekeeping, it is only now that they are becoming involved in regional peacekeeping (and even more recently that they are doing so under their own steam). In the absence of similar self-imposed constraints, most foreign interventions have been carried out or coordinated by foreign powers or the United Nations, even when they involved African troops. However, there is evidence that this reticence is breaking down and that African states, whether unilaterally or collectively, are looking more seriously at the possibility of intervention across neighboring borders in extreme situations. The Economic Community of West African States Monitoring Group (ECOMOG) intervention into Liberia is a landmark in this respect. A particularly significant dimension of this development may be an emerging willingness to use collective intervention to frustrate coups (and protect democracy) in neighboring countries, such as the reversal of the 1994 attempted coup in Lesotho, the pressures on the military regime in Niger to restore power to civilians after the January 1996 coup, and the current threat of sanctions against Burundi by regional trade partners. Because of the long collaboration between the Frontline States and the historical absence of coups, southern Africa provides the best opportunity for this kind of coordinated action. However, the events cited here have also shown that the necessary consensus and coordination may not always be forthcoming among regional partners or between regional and international ones (the same Western nations that leaned heavily on the regime in Niger to hand over power have been much more lukewarm about supporting the sanctions against Burundi). Regional integration of military forces may also make it more difficult to execute a coup against a national government.

■ The Problem of External Linkages and Dependence

Military and intelligence agencies may not only constitute a state within a state but also maintain extensive and specialized contacts across international boundaries and constitute global networks parallel to, and usually autonomous of, those of the political and diplomatic authorities. This poses another challenge to democratic forces. As the Senate Intelligence Committee and the White House recently discovered regarding the Central Intelligence Agency (CIA) in Guatemala, these contacts and the messages they transmit may contradict those of the official authorities but are almost impossible to monitor effectively. (For years the CIA conducted its own foreign policy in Guatemala out of the U.S. Embassy, maintaining links and conducting operations with Guatemalan military officers independently of—and usually unknown to—both the U.S. ambassador and the national government, and funneling aid to the Guatemalan military for several years after Congress voted to suspend such aid.) Because of their covert and extralegal character, the extraordinary reach of modern surveillance and intelligence-gathering techniques, and their lack of public accountability, intelligence agencies present particular challenges to democratic freedoms, especially in their ability to circumvent the legal protection and restraints associated with democracy.

In Africa (as in Latin America) the military has been dependent on external forces, which has proved particularly corrosive for democracy. First, the military has tended to act with reference to geopolitical concepts shaped by the interests of foreign powers. Second, the lack of linkages with civil organizations deprives the military both of the ability to develop a rational calculus toward the domestic political and social order and of the means to exercise influence through broad-based linkages and alliances. This increases the military proclivity to coup activity. At the same time, it must be conceded that mutual defense pacts with foreign powers (France in particular) have provided effective protection against coups by national militaries and, rightly or wrongly, underwritten regime survival and continuity (the latest example of this is the French intervention to defeat a mutiny over wages in the Central African Republic in June and November 1996).

On a more positive level this dependency provides one explanation as to why the reshaping of the geopolitical map in the post–Cold War period has been so important in securing the withdrawal of the military from politics. External forces also can and have played a crucial role in military restructuring, particularly in brokering peace agreements and providing military retraining and financial and technical aid to accelerate the resettlement of demobilized military personnel. And although major powers have shown much less interest in the specifics of reshaping civil-military relations in Africa than they have in Latin America, several agencies such as the U.S. Agency for International Development and the National Democratic Institute for International Affairs are helping to promote national policy and policy dialogue on such issues. In one of the earlier instances of such external support the National Democratic Institute helped to sponsor an international conference in Montevideo that brought together military and civilian experts from Argentina, Uruguay, Brazil, and other countries to address issues of defense and control of the military in a democratic society and produced the "Montevideo Declaration" of July 1989, with its valuable guidelines on the role of the legislature.[26] At a less formal level other European governments such as those of Scandinavia are evolving programs that may focus on nongovernmental organizations' actions to help sustain demilitarization and institutionalize stable civil-military relations. Recently both the International Monetary Fund and the World Bank have begun openly to address issues of military spending and reform of defense budgets.[27]

■ Dealing with Human Rights Abuse

How should new democracies deal with atrocities and human rights abuses by government and security agents or with those who overthrow constitutional governments through force of arms? Should the emphasis be placed on justice and accountability (if not retribution) or on national reconciliation? This question has been posed in several of the current transitions—the Truth Commission in South Africa; the trials of the former Dergue in Ethiopia, Traoré in Mali, and Hastings Kamuzu Banda in Malawi; and the attempted prosecution of the perpetrators of ethnocide in Rwanda. As we already know from the history of Latin America, this issue can weigh heavily on the transition and color the prospects for civil-military relations. As with other issues, there are few routine or comfortable answers to such questions, and many compelling arguments can and have been made on both sides. The new Ugandan constitution states that anyone illegally overthrowing a constitutional government should and will be punished, no matter how far down the road. Until recently this would have seemed like quixotic self-indulgence. However, recent events in South Korea will probably change the terms of this debate. By convicting Chun Doo Hwan and Roh Tae Woo for their part in the Kwangju massacre and imposing severe sentences on them, Korea has sent a brilliant and unambiguous reminder—the more so since both culprits had been highly successful in leading the modern economic and political transformation of Korea—that history can always be revisited. If Chun and Roh, why not Mobutu Sese Seko and Eyadema?

■ Conclusion

One of the main dangers to democratic consolidation is the combination of weak civilian leadership with no experience of military affairs or base in the armed forces and factionalized armed forces capable neither of efficient performance of security functions nor of ensuring the undivided loyalty of the military. The new African democracies face an intertwining of the crisis of political authority and military authority. This situation confronts the fragile democratic power with the dual task of building and consolidating new political institutions in the civil sector and at the same time of facilitating the rebuilding of the authority of the military commanders, by no means an easy task for hard-pressed and inexperienced new governments.[28]

African militaries have not attempted to follow Latin American armies in their attempt to institutionalize their political role by constructing "protected democracies," however.[29] In Africa, the greater danger to democracy lies in the emergence of the authoritarian electoral regime and authoritarian democracies with their "new breed of strongmen" created by the multiple political and economic pressures under which the new democracies must attempt to function.[30]

■ Notes

1. See Eboe Hutchful and Abdoulaye Bathily, eds., *The Military and Militarism in Africa* (Dakar: Codesria, Forthcoming).

2. Robin Luckham, "The Military, Militarization, and Democratization in Africa: A Survey of Literature and Issues," *African Studies Review* 37, no. 2 (September 1994): 13–75; Henry Bienen, *Armed Forces, Conflict and Change in Africa* (Boulder, Colo.: Westview Press, 1989); and Claude Welch, *No Farewell to Arms? Military Disengagement from Politics in Africa and Latin America* (Boulder, Colo.: Westview Press, 1987).

3. On Kenya, see Frank Holmquist and Michael Ford, "Stalling Political Change: Moi's Way in Kenya," *Current History* (April 1995): 177–181; on Somalia, see Hussein Adam, "The Military and Militarism: Rethinking the Somali Political Experience," in Hutchful and Bathily, *Military in Africa*.

4. See "Democracy Brings Turmoil to the Congo," *New York Times,* October 14, 1994, p. 3, in which a Congolese economist is quoted as saying: "Democratic elections are the worst thing that ever happened to this country."

5. See, for instance, Brian Loveman, "'Protected Democracies' and Military Guardianship: Political Transitions in Latin America, 1978–1993," *Journal of Interamerican Studies and World Affairs* 36, no. 2 (summer 1994): 105–189; Jean Crugel, "Transitions From Authoritarian Rule: Lessons from Latin America," *Political Studies* 39 (June 1991): 363–368; and Richard Millet, "An End to Militarism? Democracy and the Armed Forces," *Current History* (February 1995): 71–75.

6. Julius Ihonvbere, "The Military and Nigerian Society: The Abacha Coup and the Crisis of Democratization in Nigeria," in Hutchful and Bathily, *Military in Africa*.

7. Alfred Stepan, *Rethinking Military Politics: Brazil and the Southern Cone* (Princeton: Princeton University Press, 1988).

8. Eboe Hutchful, "Military Issues in the Democratic Transitions in Africa," in Hutchful and Bathily, *Military in Africa*.

9. Stepan, *Rethinking Military Politics.*

10. Virgilo Bertran, "Some Lessons Learned in Civil-Military Relations in Latin America," (paper presented to the Conference on Civil-Military Relations in Latin America, the Democracy Project, School of International Service, American University, May 4–6, 1995).

11. Personal communication, Washington, D.C., 1995.

12. Ibid.

13. Khabele Matlosa, "Military Rule and Withdrawal from Power: The Case of Lesotho?" in Hutchful and Bathily, *Military in Africa*.

14. I thank Robin Luckham for this piece of information.

15. General Salihu Ibrahim, Chief of Army Staff, September 15, 1993. Cited in Olusegun Obasanjo, "Leadership and Accountability," *TELL* (Lagos), December 20, 1993, and quoted in Ihonvbere, "Military and Nigerian Society," in Hutchful and Bathily, *Military Africa*. Although Ibrahim was unable to effect his reforms, his agenda of reprofessionalization has been picked up by other officers. According to Major-General Alwali Kazir, an overhaul of the Nigerian army is in the works. Curiously, even as the military regime once more tightens its grip on political power in Nigeria, Kazir in a speech in early 1995 "reaffirmed the subordination of the army to civil and democratic structures," providing further evidence of the distanc-

ing of the institution from the regime. *West Africa,* January 30–February 5, 1995, p. 147.

16. Interview with the British Broadcasting Corporation (BBC) on Focus on Africa program, February 3, 1992.

17. Herbert Howe, "The SADF Revisited," in Helen Kitchen and J. Coleman Kitchen, eds., *South Africa: Twelve Perspectives on the Transition* (Washington, D.C.: Center for Strategic and International Studies, 1994), p. 81.

18. Horace Campbell, "The Dismantling of the Apartheid Military Machine and Problems of Conversion of the Military-Industrial Complex," in Hutchful and Bathily, *Military in Africa.*

19. William Gutteridge, *The Military in South African Politics: Champions of National Unity?* (Research Institute for the Study of Conflict and Terrorism, Conflict Studies 271, June 1994).

20. Sunday Ochoche, "Militarization and National Security in Africa," in Hutchful and Bathily, *Military in Africa.*

21. Nadir Mohammed, "Trends, Determinants and the Economic Effects of Military Expenditures in Sub-Saharan Africa," in Hutchful and Bathily, *Military in Africa.*

22. Keith Crane et al., *Economic Reform and the Military in Poland, Hungary and China* (Santa Monica, Calif.: Rand Corporation, 1991).

23. "Opening Statement to the Meeting of the Consultative Group for Ghana," Paris, June 24–25, 1993.

24. Robin Luckham, "Faustian Bargains: Bringing Military and Security Establishments Under Democratic Control," in Robin Luckham et al., *Democratization in the South: The Jagged Wave* (Manchester: Manchester University Press, 1996).

25. George C. Biddle, "A Principal Lesson of Civil-Military Relations" (paper presented to the Conference on Civil-Military Relations in Latin America, The Democracy Project, School of International Service, American University, May 4–6, 1995).

26. National Democratic Institute for International Affairs, *Toward a New Relationship: The Role of the Military in a Democratic Government* (Washington, D.C.: National Democratic Institute, 1990).

27. See, for instance, Geoffrey Lamb and Valeriana Kallab, *Military Expenditure and Economic Development: A Symposium on Research Issues* (World Bank Discussion Paper No. 185), and *IMF Survey,* December 14, 1992. Among current research projects at the World Bank are one dealing with the economic implications of the transition from war to peace and another dealing with the best ways to downsize armies.

28. Typically, this situation produces a temptation on the side of the incoming civilian authorities to consolidate their power by manipulating the cleavages in the armed forces. Such an attempt was an important factor in the overthrow of the new democratic governments in Ghana in both 1972 and 1981.

29. Loveman, "Protected Democracies and Military Guardianship."

30. See James Petras and Steve Vieux, "The Transition to Authoritarian Electoral Regimes in Latin America," *Latin American Perspectives* 21, no. 5 (fall 1994): 5–19; and Nathaniel Nash, "A New Breed of Strongmen in the South: Latin America's Authoritarian Democracies," *New York Times,* January 16, 1994.

4

Political Parties and Civil Societies in Sub-Saharan Africa

Jennifer A. Widner

The years from 1989 to 1994 witnessed nearly unqualified support for the reintroduction of multiparty rule from donors and African political reformers alike. The assumption was that party competition would increase governmental accountability to producers, deepen contacts between political elites and rural majorities, and broker compromises among the new interest groups and associations rapidly emerging everywhere, thus helping to contain the power of clientelist barons. In short, advocacy of multiparty systems was based on some clear, but controversial, hypotheses about the relationship between civil society and political parties.

Now many of the same people have started to worry that democratization, especially the legalization of opposition parties, may induce fragmentation—that it may destroy nations rather than build them. Instead of giving voice to farmers and businesspeople whose activities are central to economic growth, or facilitating reciprocity among these groups, the introduction of party competition has unleashed the politics of ethnic identity in some countries and failed to play any clear role in mediating claims against the state. Indeed, the hypotheses articulated in the 1960s by Tom Mboya, Julius Nyerere, and other advocates of single-party rule—and by the likes of Jerry Rawlings and Yoweri Museveni more recently—seem to find confirmation in current news reports out of Africa.

This chapter explores the difficulties of consolidating democracy when the interest groups that form the basis of coalition are small, fragmented, and without substantial legitimacy. The limited ties between emerging political parties and new interest groups or associations in many African countries present a striking paradox. In the wave of political liberalization that began in 1989, trade associations, law societies, civic organizations, and other nongovernmental groups assumed important roles in brokering the legalization of opposition political parties and forcing the conduct of competitive elections. They launched a new language of governmental accountability, rarely heard so strongly in the continent's formal politics. To many, this discourse promised a shift in the basis of political organization—the creation of a new public, or a civil society, constructed and appropriated by residents of African countries instead of imposed from outside.

This happy scenario did not materialize, even in part, except in a very few places. In only a handful of countries have parties sought to appeal to the interests horizontal associations represent. Clientelist ties or ethnic differences have more often than not constituted the main lines of cleavage in the emerging party systems. Although there is important variation in the character of the new systems, the overwhelming impression conveyed by the first competitive elections of Africa's "second liberation" is one of extreme fragmentation and particularism.

There are several plausible explanations for this state of affairs, and they will be explored in this chapter. The paradox observed has its roots in two conditions: (1) nongovernmental organizations, including legal-sector NGOs, remain narrowly urban-based and highly fragmented and (2) the very limited extent of economic liberalization means that business and other potential funders of political parties remain hostage to the incumbent government. Where associations are many but small and interest group structure is decentralized, politicians find it expensive to try to win votes on the basis of economic policy positions. They are more inclined to rely on kinship or to build on old clientelist networks. Appealing to new associations as a vote-getting strategy is especially difficult where party leaders themselves are uncomfortable with the consultation and compromises required to reach out to horizontal associations or where financial control remains concentrated in the hands of single individuals or barons.

This chapter focuses on the character of civil society, economic reform, and the ways these shape the kinds of party systems that emerge. The analysis also permits generalization about the prospects for democratic consolidation. The first section of this chapter probes the significance of the topic for the concern with democratization, considering the assumptions about parties and pressure groups that underlie the advocacy of multiparty systems. The second section elaborates the paradox, offering an overview of changes in associational life and political party systems. The third entertains alternative hypotheses for the patterns observed. The fourth section links the discussion to the broader problem of whether there are preconditions for democracy and to a concern with state building. The conclusion addresses the policy implications of these different approaches, with special emphasis on the prescriptions that flow from the accounts that have greatest explanatory power. Although examples are drawn from various sources, the chapter touches frequently on the Kenyan case.

■ The Paradox

There are two dimensions to the paradox. One is the proliferation in Africa during the 1980s of new forms of association based on common economic interest, including trade associations, unions, consumer groups, transporters' organizations, parent-teacher associations (PTAs), student leagues, and so on. In many countries, these groups organized general strikes that forced incumbents to permit the drafting of multiparty constitutions and the legalization of opposition political parties. The second dimension is the emergence of political parties based not on economic divisions within societies or on these new groups but on the cleavages formed by ethnicity and old clientelist networks. The parties that emerged in many countries often failed to seek votes from members of the associations that preceded them. Their leaders made little or no effort to devise platforms that appeal to the interests these new groups represent, so as to win the votes of members.

☐ *Changes in Associational Life*

The dramatic changes that took place in the associational life of most African countries during the 1980s gave some reason to believe that new political parties would form along cleavages different from those of the independence era. The changes in civil society were so dramatic that they seemed likely to produce a realignment in party systems.

During the 1980s, associations of many different types proliferated. During the 1950s, there had been a similar organizational flowering, but most of the groups that formed did not endure. Some governments proscribed all but a handful of nongovernmental organizations; others sought to incorporate them into the ruling party; in all cases, the scope of these organizations' activities was reduced. Lack of resources and governmental ineffectiveness, combined with the impact of international price fluctuations, appeared to trigger a resurgence of independent organizations during the 1980s, initially in the form of new religious groups (spirit churches and syncretic beliefs) and informal sector marketing or credit associations.[1] Government-sanctioned trade unions and producers' associations began to witness restlessness in their ranks during the latter half of the decade, and by the late 1980s some of their members were instigating breakaway organizations or taking to the streets to protest policies they deemed deleterious. After incumbent governments took the first steps to open the political process, many more groups appeared. For example, by the early 1990s in Côte d'Ivoire the associational life included two major, competing umbrella federations of labor unions; multiple ,business lobbies; representatives of bank employees, veterinarians, informal sector entrepreneurs, and journalists; at least two organizational representatives each for telecommunications workers, electrical utility personnel, secondary school teachers, bus workers, primary school teachers, Catholic school teachers, doctors and pharmaceutical workers, and many other groups; two major farmers' unions as well as several minor farm lobbies; four transporters' associations; a PTA; a consumers' rights lobby; a Jeune Chambre Economique, and many other groups.

Many of these groups spoke the language of governmental accountability. They argued not just that government policies were hurting their interests but that incumbents were too often bad managers and not to be trusted. They often evinced strong distrust of public officials, although many of these groups were led partly by civil servants. They demanded better public management and threatened to demonstrate or organize strikes if the incumbents did not take positive steps to change their ways. A few dispensed with the language of neocolonialism and pinned responsibility for their countries' ills directly on present political leaders rather than on the colonial powers. For instance, during the early 1990s, an iconoclastic book by Axelle Kabou, *Si l'Afrique Refusait le Développement,* which argued that dependency theories were smoke screens propagated to hide mismanagement, was the most frequently demanded text at one of the university libraries in Abidjan.

This change in political discourse potentially signaled a larger shift in African societies. In a very thoughtful essay, Peter Ekeh once argued that colonialism had led to the emergence of two publics in Africa.[2] Westerners assumed that the public and the private realms had a common moral foundation, but Ekeh suggested another possibility: "In fact, there are two public realms in post-colonial Africa, with different types of linkages to the private realm." In one public realm, primordial groupings, ties, and sentiments influence the individual's public behavior. There is a second, civic realm, which has no linkages with the private. Behavior in the civic public realm, which was created by colonialism and independence settlements, is in no way related to underlying norms. Hence, there can be no accountability in this sphere. The new language being spoken on the streets of African capitals by the members of associations and by students appeared to signal a new appropriation of this civic realm, a grounding of the civic public in a private morality forged over thirty years.

Many of the new associations actively tried to influence public policy. Unlike many (but not all) of the religious groups, most of the trade associations, unions, and consumers' groups perceived themselves not as self-contained communities or even as firms but as lobbies. They sought a role in decisionmaking, and many used what little leverage they had to gain entry to discussions of economic policy. For example, throughout the 1980s in both Kenya and Côte d'Ivoire, many strikes were launched by transporters' groups, *matatu* (informal-sector taxis) owners' associations, and truck drivers' unions on the grounds that government regulation dramatically increased the costs of their activities. Unlike kin-based groups, then, these organizations sought not to overturn formal structures of authority or operate in parallel with them, but to influence decisions within government—albeit government they had reconfigured.

The extent to which these new associations were distinct from sectarian interests or old client networks varied. In the Côte d'Ivoire, the government tolerated the expansion of participation in these activities but created its own associations alongside those that formed independently, dividing opinions and engendering a certain amount of infighting within each sector. In other cases, relatives of the chief of state or important barons in these communities saw in the creation of NGOs a way to attract financing from foreign donors. They rushed to create their own NGOs, which perpetuated the power of clientelist networks under a new guise. In still other instances, memberships of these groups derived heavily from particular regions or ethnic communities. Often the internal governance of the associations reflected the same hierarchical, seniority-based norms the clientelist networks displayed, and organizations suffered frequent discord and division as a result of competition between leaders of the same generation. This was particularly the case with women's groups in Kenya, for example. These aspects of associational life varied across countries, although the absence of systematic documentation makes it impossible to adequately ground such generalizations at this point.

☐ *Parties and Party Systems*

The kinds of relationships observers assumed would develop between the new associations and political parties have not materialized in most places. With some important exceptions, parties have made little effort to win the support of trade associations, unions, and other economic groupings. Instead, they are highly particularistic, offering broad attacks against official corruption but utilizing kin-based or clientelist networks to build constituencies.

The point is not that the associations should be affiliated with parties; to hold governments accountable, autonomous associations are more valuable. For new democracies to function as theory suggests, however, party leaders must consider these groups sufficiently important to listen to their demands and the concerns their officers and members express. Indicators of such responsiveness include incorporation of interest group demands in party platforms and campaign speeches, as well as attention to whether a party's votes come from segments of the population whose interests these associations represent.

Theory and reality diverge in many places. In the period 1989–1997 parties and associations have made relatively little effort to contact one another in most countries. Communication among them has been limited. Often, leaders of interest groups have contemplated cultivating a rapport with opposition parties but have retreated from offering an audience, much less the possibility of electoral alliance, out of fear that partisan political activity would divide their memberships. In Côte d'Ivoire, for example, the Syndicat National des Agriculteurs de Côte d'Ivoire (SYNAGCI, a farmers' union) initially received organizational assistance from Laurent Gbagbo's Front Populaire Ivoirien (FPI) but later diversified its ties and retreated from relationships with party officials, directing its lobbying efforts directly to ministers and members of the civil service. Even unions created by former ruling parties in order to divide the new interest groups have tended to become independent rather quickly, limiting their relationships with their organizers.

Although interest-group autonomy is a healthy trend for democratic consolidation, it often brings a reduction in the flow of information about member demands to party officials. For their part, political parties have paid scant attention to interest group concerns in the rhetoric of their candidates or in their platforms. Most opposition parties have attacked bad economic management by the incumbents in general terms, but few have made specific claims about which policies have proven problematic and to whom. When Kenneth Matiba and Charles Rubia in Kenya first made their demands for a return to multiparty competition in July 1990, they talked about the ways government policies made it difficult to conduct business or maintain agricultural production. They had formed these ideas in part through discussions with the members of trade associations in Kenya. This platform faded in importance after the legalization of parties, however. The election itself was largely fought on sectarian lines. Matiba's party, FORD-Asili, abandoned its leader's earlier stance and waged an election battle on communal, pro-Gikuyu terms.

The salience of horizontal associations or economic interests in party politics varied across democratizing countries during the first five years.[3] In one category are countries in which ethnic divisions appear to have relatively little impact on the party system: Zambia, Côte d'Ivoire, Namibia, Madagascar, Benin, and possibly Malawi. Opposition in Zambia initially consisted of a union-business-intellectual (teachers' union) alliance; in Côte d'Ivoire, of professionals and intellectuals; in Madagascar, of a variety of interests under the umbrella of the Forces Vives; in Benin, of civil servants and a broad-based social and economic coalition. In Namibia, the South

West African Peoples' Organization (SWAPO) remained a multiethnic organization, with over 50 percent of its candidates not Ovambo.[4] Although lawyers for some of the opposition parties emerging in Malawi say that it has been difficult to prevent ethnic appeals, the lines of division are far less clearly communal there than in many other countries. Aleke Banda is a businessman with private sector support, and Chakafwa Chihana, former trade union president, has a union base (as well as regional votes). Ethnicity is socially salient in these instances and surfaces in political infighting, but party systems have not (or have not yet) divided on such lines. In other countries, however—Cameroon, Congo, Kenya, Togo, Niger, Burundi, Rwanda, and Djibouti—ethnic, regional, or clientelist divisions dominate the party system.

The emerging party systems are characterized by a high level of fragmentation. Over 100 parties appeared in Ethiopia, more than fifty in Togo, forty-three in Guinea, and twenty-one in Côte d'Ivoire. In most countries the norm was between six and twelve. Actual levels of fragmentation in legislative and presidential elections were usually lower than initial numbers of parties would suggest.[5] Many parties chose not to sponsor candidates and gradually faded from existence for want of resources or adequate management. In other instances, one party—often but not always the incumbent—dominated the political scene. In a few cases, opposition parties forged alliances. An opposition coalition was most evident in Madagascar, where Albert Zafy won the election and his coalition of Forces Vives captured significant numbers of seats in the legislature. Coalitions were also formed in several other countries, including Togo, Niger, Guinea, Côte d'Ivoire, and Burundi.

Fragmentation may be partly a phenomenon of the transition. That is, initially many parties form, as they did in Poland, and then electoral competition weeds out the weaker ones, greatly reducing the numbers. But fragmentation may also be a function of the character of associational life and the ways political party leaders relate to interest groups in many African contexts.

■ Plausible Explanations

What explains the patterns displayed in the first multiparty elections? In the absence of extensive data, this section offers a range of hypotheses, not a definitive answer. The possible explanations of the paradox emphasize, variously, the socioeconomic background of new party leaders, the systemic consequences of ethnic parties, the vote-getting calculus of candidates under the conditions that currently prevail in most parts of Africa, the existence of functional alternatives to parties, and electoral rules. Of the various propositions set forth here, I conclude, it is a combination of two—the character of civil society and the limited extent of economic liberalization—that offers the greatest promise for explaining the overall paradox and also for explaining variation among countries.

☐ *Demographics*

One possible account for the patterns observed lies in demography. The largest cohort of voters in most countries is the 18 to 30 age group—the youth. Moreover, party headquarters and rallies are heavily populated by young men below voting age, for whom income-generating opportunities are few and dwindling in number. These youth do not have clear occupations, in most cases; thus they are not members of trade associations. Parents cannot help them and have little influence. Platforms that promise long-term policy reform favoring specific interest groups are not likely to gain the vote of this segment of the population. What matters is whether parties appear able to deliver short-term survival—and a sense of community or purpose—that party youth wings are designed to marshal or inspire. Mostly, "belly politics" prevails; votes go to those who provide rice or opportunity during the campaign period.

This explanation is often offered by those who are actively involved in the political changes taking place in their country. Even in a relatively successful, stable country like the Côte d'Ivoire, considerable concern and consternation about the country's political future derived from a breakdown in intergenerational ties. In a poignant but typical conversation, two doctors worried aloud that the country could easily go the way of its neighbor, Liberia. "Same causes; same effects," they said. Deteriorating economic conditions, coupled with increasing pressure on the land, meant that parents were increasingly unable to help their children establish themselves. Parents felt they could no longer influence their children's behavior. On the contrary, the youth were influenced by mass media that portrayed violence as part of daily life and a solution to problems. Young people could easily derail party politics by instigating street violence, they said. The cities had become powder kegs.

Church leaders in Kenya articulate similar concerns. In 1995, one church leader commented to me, "There is a culture of violence, certainly, but it is bred as much by economic conditions as by politics. There are many young people out of work. They stay out late. They drink. They become the warriors recruited by politicians to foment ethnic clashes."

The significance of demographics for the tenor of political life in Africa is less clear than it seems, however. It may account for the specter of violence that leads many to shrink from competitive politics. It contributes to felt levels of insecurity. But it cannot account for the variations observed between countries. It is better at capturing the regional particularities of political life than at accounting for intraregional differences.

☐ *Socioeconomic Backgrounds of Party Leaders*

Another set of possible explanations focuses on the attitudes and behavior of political elites. Lawyers and academics have played an especially large role in organizing opposition parties in Africa in the 1989–1994 period.[6] For example, lawyers have provided important leadership in both factions of the Forum for the Restoration of Democracy in Kenya and in some political parties in Togo, Cameroon, and Côte d'Ivoire. Laurent Gbagbo, leader of the opposition in Côte d'Ivoire, is a history professor.

Lawyers have relied on networks of their clients to create political bases. Attorney-client privilege, respected in many countries, protects communication between dissidents and their counsel. International nongovernmental associations monitor the treatment the lawyers receive and publicize harassment, lowering the risks of opposition activity in some cases. In theory, these women and men are in a position to build coalitions that escape the identity politics of the past.

The reality is different. Professionals often lose their ties to rural relatives. Their networks tend to be urban and therefore limited in capacity to reach out to voters, most of whom live in the countryside. Without the help of religious leaders, who are the only association leaders with broad rural bases, lawyers and other professionals often have a hard time getting their messages heard. They struggle with weak support or they rely on the same ethnic or clientelistic networks of their predecessors.

If this argument is valid, there should be no relationship between the occupational backgrounds of leaders or their deputies and patterns of party cleavage. At this time, there are few systematic data available to assess this hypothesis, but it is notable that Gbagbo, an intellectual, formed a coherent, if rather unsuccessful, coalition that eschewed ethnic bases for the first multiparty presidential race in Côte d'Ivoire; whereas Kenneth Matiba, a businessman presumably used to cutting deals, was unable to maintain his business-agriculture appeal in Kenya and resorted to the ethnic card.

☐ *Effects of Ethnic Parties on Party Systems*

Another cluster of explanations focuses on the consequences of ethnic diversity. Donald Horowitz is probably the best expositor of this perspective. He makes two claims. First, ethnic divisions in society are largely incompatible with others and rarely produce the kind of multilayered cleavages that have fostered the kinds of political party systems found in Europe. "The features of an ethnically divided society conspire to impede the development of the full range of social relationships among ethnic groups," he writes, "and this affects [the party's] organizational structure in and out of politics."[7] Where ethnic cleavages predominate, party leaders have little latitude for diversifying their base of support, and this produces both instability and a politics of threat instead of a politics of compromise.[8] Second, Horowitz notes, "Once ethnic politics begins in earnest, each party, recognizing that it cannot count on defections from members of the other ethnic group, has the incentive to solidify the support of its own group."[9] If this argument is valid, then we should expect to observe an increasing tendency for ethnic cleavages to prevail over time, where even one party out of six, or a dozen, has ethnic roots.

Although intuitively compelling, these arguments do not stand up especially well in the face of evidence. Fragmentation along ethnic lines does not occur everywhere ethnicity is socially salient. In Zambia, for instance, ethnic identity is important to many people in very many aspects of their lives. It is important in politics, in some settings. It has not yet produced party fragmentation along sectarian lines, however. Most countries in sub-Saharan Africa are ethnically divided; not all are host to ethnically based political parties. Clearly, there are intervening variables at work. Moreover, although we may indeed find that where ethnic parties emerge, they drive out others, that hypothesis does little to explain why such parties become important initially.

☐ *Existence of Functional Alternatives*

Another type of explanation is implicit in many of the discussions of party realignment in Europe. Scholars who study industrial democracies noted that during the late 1980s the character of political life changed in these countries. The political parties previously important began to lose their vote bases to extremist groups and the Greens. Many conflicts moved outside of party politics to the street, and there was an upsurge in alternative forms of political expression. Some researchers suggested that corporatist systems of interest representation had assumed many of the functions previously filled by parties and that parties had become anachronistic. Under these conditions, extremist and ethnic parties began to proliferate.

An analogous argument can be made in the African cases. Parallel forms of political authority (kingships, emirates, etc.) are quite powerful in some countries such as Nigeria and Uganda. These groups often fulfill many of the functions commonly assumed by parties in other political systems. Under these conditions, economic interest groups and other horizontal associations may place relatively little stock in parties as vehicles for expressing or aggregating interests, mediating disputes, and brokering compromises. Fragmentation and the proliferation of small, sectarian parties result. If this explanation is valid, then where parallel systems of political authority are strongest, we ought to observe the greatest fractionalization in newly elected legislatures and the emergence of very small, highly specialized political groupings, most likely with ethnic, not economic bases and in all cases with fairly low legitimacy.

☐ Length of the Campaign Period

Where a sudden change in access to decisionmaking is imminent, politicians scramble to find secure vote bases. Because kinship obligations generally mean that the home community can be counted upon, the first networks activated are ethnic.[10] Rules of obligation within lineages still retain support and therefore generate predictable behavior. By contrast, norms of reciprocity in civil society are unstable, and politicians necessarily incur more risk in basing campaign strategies on them, especially if there is little time in which to negotiate relationships.

If this argument is valid, we should expect to see an inverse relationship between the amount of time that elapses between legalization of parties and elections—or the duration of the campaign period—and the degree to which a party system is based on ethnic or regional differences. The more time is available to build constituencies, the less evident are ethnic distinctions in the vote bases of political parties. In second-generation multiparty elections, appeals to ethnicity may feature less conspicuously than they did in the first.

A case that casts doubt on this proposition is that of Côte d'Ivoire's first multiparty elections, in which only eight months separated the legalization of opposition parties and the conduct of elections (one of the shortest lead times), but in which ethnic divisions carried little weight, despite grumbling that Gbagbo's people spoke Bété. By contrast, Kenya's opposition parties initially appeared to be interest-based and only split apart, with some taking on an ethnic coloring, later.

☐ Electoral Rules

A final category of explanations focuses on the importance of electoral rules for the character of party systems. The conventional wisdom among political scientists is that proportional representation (PR) systems produce higher levels of fragmentation and encourage formation of extremist parties to a greater degree than do majoritarian systems. Although proportional rules may reduce levels of distrust by ensuring that parties that receive more than 5 percent of the vote (most systems have a 5 percent threshold) are seated in the legislature, they may also encourage politicians to form parties on narrower bases than would otherwise be the case, drawing sectarian views into political life.

If this explanation is valid in the African cases, we would expect to see different patterns of fragmentation and cleavage in countries with majoritarian systems compared to countries with PR systems. Once again, however, the evidence draws the theory into question. Most of the new electoral systems put in place in Africa since 1989 have been modeled on the Anglo-American model, not on the PR systems of other European countries. The modal electoral system is one of single-member districts where the winner must hold a majority of the votes, if not in the first ballot, then in a second-round runoff election. Namibia and South Africa are among the few countries with a PR system, although a few Francophone countries provide for multimember districts. Cleavages in party systems have not correlated with differences in electoral rules in these instances. For example, both Zambia and Kenya used the Anglo-American majoritarian system, with single-member districts, yet witnessed the emergence of very different political party systems. In Kenya, ethnicity became politically salient, while in Zambia, in 1989–1994, it did not.

Explanations rooted in the character of electoral rules can be seductive. The notion of manipulating constitutions and rules of electoral contests appeals to the love of the "technical fix" so characteristic of U.S. advisers. It is especially attractive today because it also corresponds to analytic trends within the social sciences and thus holds out the prospect of professional advancement to those who spend their time studying and devising new systems. It is well to remember that constitutions and rules attracted much attention just before independence only to be subverted by human behavior, which appeared to abandon formal rules for the myriad informal ones.

■ A Political Economic Explanation

There may be a very large array of practical reasons political parties have not forged or maintained strong ties with the new associations and interest groups that helped precipitate the move to multiparty rule. Two are worth discussing here.

□ The Vote-Getting Calculus

There are five main reasons why in most countries party leaders find it costly to appeal for votes to the new associations, the very groups that pushed for their legalization.

1. Investing in appeals to civil society may be risky because legislation on the books in many countries gives the incumbent government the power to restrict association and assembly. For example, in Kenya, associations labor under the Societies Registration Act and the new NGO Coordination Act. Members of the NGO Council estimated that between

1993 and 1995 approximately 80 percent of the NGOs applying for permission to operate were not allowed to register.[11] In absolute terms about 100 applications were denied. At the time of the conversation, there were 437 registered NGOs. Though registered, associations are not safe either because they can be deregistered.

Legislation similar to Kenya's Societies Registration Act remains on the books in many other countries, including Uganda and Tanzania, which in general have proven more tolerant of criticism in recent years. Where these laws exist, it is risky for a political party leader to try to get votes by appealing to associations.

2. The number of new voluntary associations is large and rapidly increasing, but the membership of these groups is small. One distinguished Kenyan lawyer commented that the NGO sector in his country was so polarized that it was hard for pluralism to prevail. He noted that the structure of the NGO sector itself was an obstacle: "There is no real framework or forum for exchanging ideas within the sector. If development NGOs associate with the human rights NGOs in the current environment, then they risk being labeled opposition by the provincial administration that grants them license to work. They cannot take a bold stand, as a result."[12] Thus, the tendency is to fragment.

Under these conditions, to assemble a significant vote base, party leaders must "press the flesh" with members of many of these groups. This is a very time-consuming and costly prospect, and where appealing to other blocs promises to deliver a higher number of votes for the investment of resources, politicians will gravitate toward these. Moreover, the associations tend to have very short life spans, making appeals to these groups wasteful of the time and energy of senior party figures. If this argument is valid, we would expect to see a greater tendency to make nonethnic appeals where peak associations or other organizations exist to coordinate the activities of smaller groups or where the economic base of a country facilitated the formation of relatively encompassing groups. Certainly, Zambia, with its large, fairly centralized miners' union, initially avoided the formation of ethnically based parties.

3. Leaders have little ability to deliver the vote of their association's members. Their own legitimacy is often contested. The associations may not be highly representative of the groups or sectors they claim to represent. Further, their members are shy of becoming involved in the often dangerous realm of partisan politics. Where political party officials doubt the efficacy or legitimacy of association leaders, we would expect to see less effort to appeal to these groups.

4. Information about the positions associations take on policy issues is scarce, making it difficult for party leaders to fashion their message so as to appeal to specific groups. Journalists in many parts of Africa have not seen the activities of new associations and interest groups as worthy of attention.

Party publications, which exist in many countries, are more interested in criticizing the government than reporting the views of citizens. In the absence of information about the identities, views, and activities of the new associations, politicians are not inclined to consult with them and appeal to their members. If this argument is valid, the extent and form of ties with the nonethnic, nonregional groups that populate civil society should vary with the availability of information about these groups in the popular media. This hypothesis must remain untested for lack of information.

5. There are few associations that represent the interests of farmers in most countries. To reach the rural majorities, then, candidates or party officials must either visit villages individually, which is an extremely costly prospect, or they must use kin ties, hometown associations, and clientelist networks to influence rural voters. If this argument is valid, then we should expect to see less resort to ethnic ties where large farmers' associations exist.

The case of Côte d'Ivoire's first multiparty election lends some credibility to this argument. Côte d'Ivoire was home to two broad-based farmers' unions, which were used as vehicles by political parties, although the unions also sought to distance themselves from partisan politics and invited guests from both parties to speak at their gatherings in many areas. The country did not witness fragmentation of the party system on ethnic lines in that election.

In most countries, churches and teachers' associations are the only groups with networks that reach out into rural areas all over the country. But teachers are usually under the thumb of the incumbent government, however sympathetic they may be to opposition parties. Churches may be useful vehicles for civic education, but they are normally reluctant to take a partisan political stance. They are not interest-based horizontal associations, and they do not usually mobilize the vote for a party leader. They often champion broad principles instead. Furthermore, the churches themselves sometimes draw their members predominantly from a region or ethnic group, and in such circumstances their mobilization could reinforce the salience of ethnicity in politics.

□ Economic Structure and Party Systems

The political economy of party finance reinforces clientelism and personalism in Africa's new plural systems. Interest groups and associations have more clout with party leaders when they can offer some monetary support for campaigning. However, where businesses, farmers, and others depend on government for licenses and contracts in order to survive, the incumbent government has many ways to control their political giving. As a result, most new parties are heavily dependent on the resources of the party leaders and their relatives.

Opposition parties need money, particularly since the incumbent party often has the resources of the state behind it, but businesses and associations are reluctant to provide financial help. In Kenya, the firms and societies that channeled small contributions to the opposition during the first multiparty election are hesitant to do so now for fear of retribution. Certainly, the business community is extremely worried about the deterioration of the infrastructure and corruption and would like to see a change of government. But businesspeople are wary about developing ties with any group pushing for democracy because they are vulnerable to punishment by the government, one respondent said.[13]

The present system provides the incumbent party with both easy access to public resources and enormous capacity to intimidate the private sector, preventing it from financing the opposition. This in turn forces opposition leaders to rely on clients and kin for support rather than appealing to the new associations. Although painful in the short run, economic liberalization would thus be a boon to democratic politics in the longer term.

■ Conclusion

Preliminary evidence suggests that the most promising explanation of the paradox lies in a combination of two hypotheses. The cost calculations of political party leaders lie at the center of this account. Party leaders have a finite amount of time and money available with which to build voter support. There is little lore about campaign strategies that are effective in African socioeconomic contexts, given the rarity of multiparty elections in the postindependence period. A hard analysis suggests that where new civil societies are highly fragmented, made up of many new, small groups with unstable membership, attempts to win votes by building group demands into platforms is not a very efficient way of building a constituency. Where new civil societies include groups that are large and fairly encompassing or where associations ally with one another, appeals to the economic interests these groups articulate may prove a comparatively more efficient vote-getting strategy.

Exactly how easy party leaders find the effort to build bases among the new associations will also depend on their personal skills and aptitudes. Those who have experience in building coalitions, in working with people from diverse backgrounds, and in facilitating compromise are likely to perceive the costs of negotiating constituencies among these new groups as lower than those whose background and training emphasize litigation or accord great importance to status. The latter are more likely to draw on old kinship networks or clientelist ties, whereas the former are more likely to break with such ways and build broader bases.

If the political economic explanation offered here is supported by more systematic examination of the data, it suggests possible solutions to the problem of building a party system really capable of ensuring government accountability, deepening contacts between political elites and rural majorities, and brokering compromises among the new interest groups and associations rapidly emerging everywhere—the tasks the supporters of reform expected multiparty systems to perform in Africa.

Policies should aim at reducing the costs and risks associated with appeals to interest groups instead of kin ties and should reduce opportunities for incumbents to punish businesses and unions that provide financial support to the opposition. Economic liberalization is part of the recipe. To borrow a phrase from Albert Hirschman, there is a political argument for the triumph of capitalism, in Africa as in Europe.[14] Further, friends of a more tolerant, competitive political system should support measures to improve press coverage of new associations and their activities, bring party leaders and interest group officers together, and encourage NGO alliances on issues important to them. They should provide incentives for associations to build bases in the countryside and eschew ethnic exclusiveness. They should take aim at the registration of societal acts that remain powerful vehicles for control of political opposition. Such steps might prove the best antidotes to ethnic fragmentation in the party system.

It is important to note that some of the activities of donors at present may actually aggravate the fragmentation of party systems along ethnic lines. Providing financial assistance to indigenous NGOs can spur the formation of many very small groups, as their leaders, including those associated with old clientelist networks, seek to capture a share of the new resources. The proliferation of these groups, many of which are likely to have high rates of turnover among members, may actually discourage political party leaders from paying heed to the demands of civil society as opposed to kin networks and the barons of the old order. Sponsoring opportunities for association leaders to meet one another and discuss shared interests, supporting dissemination of information about new groups, and encouraging party leaders and legislators to meet with interest groups—all these may be more helpful than direct assistance.

■ Notes

1. Probably the earliest recognition of these changes appeared in Naomi Chazan, "The New Politics of Participation in Tropical Africa," *Comparative Politics* 14, no. 2 (1982): 169–189.
2. Peter Ekeh, "Colonialism and the Two Publics in Africa: A Theoretical Statement," *Comparative Studies in Society and History* 17, no. 1 (1975): 91–112.
3. Cleavages are typically evaluated according to the character of the votes received by a party in elections. At the time of this writing, systematic data about

these were not available to assess the appeal of African political parties. The author
has used observer-team assessments and news reports about the bases of parties
instead, an imperfect (but temporary) measure.

4. National Democratic Institute for International Affairs, *Report on Namibia*
(Washington, D.C.: National Democratic Institute, 1990).

5. The difficulties of assessing fragmentation and its significance are legion.
Typically, fragmentation is measured as the probability that two legislators chosen
at random will represent different parties; see G. Bingham Powell, Jr.,
Contemporary Democracies: Participation, Stability, and Violence (Cambridge:
Harvard University Press, 1982) and Douglas Rae, *The Political Consequences of
Electoral Laws* (New Haven: Yale University Press, 1967). This measure gives us
little leeway to distinguish between systems where there is one dominant party and
a highly divided opposition and systems where there is one dominant party and a
highly unified opposition. Where incumbent parties have an edge because of the
shortness of the period between legalization of opposition and elections, what may
be of interest to us is the fragmentation of opposition parties, which this measure
does not capture. In using the measure it is also important to distinguish cases in
which there are legislative runoffs from cases where there are no such contests.

6. This kind of argument has a significant heritage. In 1964, James Coleman
and Carl Rosberg argued: "The political culture of the new African elites has probably been the decisive factor in the general trend toward one-party rule, although the
contributions of traditional society and colonialism and the 'ripe situation' were
essential preconditions." They pointed to "three rather common elements in the
political culture of African party leaders: elitism, statism and nationalism." James S.
Coleman and Carl G. Rosberg, Jr., "Conclusions," in *Political Parties and National
Integration in Tropical Africa* (Berkeley: University of California Press, 1964), pp.
661–662.

7. Donald Horowitz, *Ethnic Groups in Conflict* (Berkeley: University of
California Press, 1985), pp. 293–294.

8. Ibid., pp. 298–301.

9. Ibid., p. 318.

10. René Lemarchand has used a version of this argument to account for the
fragmentation in Congolese politics during the early 1960s. See René Lemarchand,
"Congo (Leopoldville)," in Coleman and Rosberg, *Political Parties and National
Integration,* p. 573.

11. Reportedly, between March 1993 and November 1994 the process went
smoothly. The Kenya Human Rights Commission and Greenbelt encountered trouble during that period, but on the whole applications for registration were granted.
The more restrictive practices started after November 1994 and were probably related to the outcome of the Paris Club meetings. For three months after those meetings, churches, the press, and opposition political parties also encountered greater
harassment. The NGOs remain stalled, in the view of those interviewed, while
harassment of the press and the churches subsequently lessened.

12. Group interview with legal-sector NGO leaders, Nairobi, October 1995.

13. Interview with business leaders, Nairobi, October 1995.

14. Albert O. Hirschman, *The Passions and the Interests: Political Arguments
for Capitalism Before Its Triumph* (Princeton: Princeton University Press, 1977).

5

Democracy, Adjustment, and Poverty Reduction in Africa: Conflicting Objectives?

Carol Graham

After decades of debate about the effects of economic reform (adjustment) on the poor, there is increasing evidence that the poor fare worse in countries that fail to adjust.[1] And, despite its short-term costs, economic reform also can provide unique political opportunities for governments to redirect public resources to poor and previously marginalized groups. Safety-net programs that reach such groups and also incorporate their participation can enhance the political voice as well as the economic potential of the poor. In such scenarios, economic reform can have positive effects on the process of democratization as well as on poverty alleviation.

This is by no means the case in every country that adjusts, and to a large extent the impact of adjustment on democracy depends on the pace and scope of economic change. Rapid and far-reaching economic change, which undermines the positions of entrenched interest groups, creates new political opportunities for governments implementing reform. In contrast, stalled reform or more closed political systems allow established interest groups to protect their privileged access to state resources and to the political system.

In addition to the pace and scope of economic and political change, the manner in which adjustment policies are presented and communicated to the public will determine their public acceptability and sustainability. In the longer term, the sustainability of economic reform hinges on its achieving political legitimation beyond the governing elite and among a variety of social sectors. And the sustainability of new resource allocations to less privileged groups depends on how effectively their political voice has been enhanced.

I posit here that the processes of economic reform and political liberalization can be mutually reinforcing, that rapid progress in one arena often creates opportunity in the other, and that the pace and scope of reform makes a great deal of difference in determining its acceptability in the short term and sustainability in the longer term. Although such assumptions are not universally applicable to the African region, particularly as political freedom is still restricted in many countries, the contrasting experiences of Senegal and Zambia provide concrete examples to support them.

■ Political Opening in Africa

Recently there has been an Africa-wide trend toward pluralism and multi-party government, which has made the politics of adjustment more complex.[2] Yet it also has the potential to enhance the political sustainability of reforms. With increased pluralism, adjustment is no longer an issue for an elite group of policymakers but rather becomes the "willingness of the body politic more generally to accept a prolonged course of medicine."[3] Enhancing government credibility and public understanding makes this acceptance much more likely, as does building support outside the traditional body politic and public sector bureaucracy.

The new political climate also allows participation by previously marginalized groups, which affects the government's vulnerability to pressure from established interest groups. Political opening can signify the replacement of nonelectoral, one-party systems with participatory multiparty ones, as in the case of Zambia. It can also expose the need to increase popular participation in countries in which democratic regimes are representative but not necessarily participatory, as in the case of one of Africa's oldest democratic regimes, Senegal. Although Senegal holds regular and open elections, most of the population is marginalized from genuine participation, and the country is ruled by a closed political elite. In most rural areas and even in some urban ones, religious leaders still have a great deal of control over how the population votes. Party representation, meanwhile, is very limited.

The contrasting cases of Senegal and Zambia are illustrative. In Senegal, from the viewpoint of the poor and marginalized groups and much of the political opposition, adjustment policies are closely associated with entrenched interest groups, the "haves." In Zambia, in contrast, widespread public debate on the need for major economic policy changes and awareness of the extent to which the costs would be shared by the entire population has generated public acceptance of adjustment measures, at least in the first few years of the Chiluba government.

■ The Politics of Adjustment in Africa

In general, African policymakers agree on the need for adjustment or at least on the absence of alternatives but are understandably concerned about its political costs. This is further complicated by the failure of most political discourse to distinguish between the direct effects of adjustment and the more generalized effects of the prolonged economic crisis it seeks to correct. Gradual adjustment often seems more politically palatable, but gradual economic changes make it more likely that entrenched political interests will find means to protect their privileged positions. As a result, deeper structural reforms may be more difficult to implement in the long run, and it may take much longer for the poor to benefit.[4]

Many countries in Africa are caught "between state and market":[5] Political leaders lack the will or the institutional capacity to implement structural reforms in addition to stabilization; the roots of the economic crisis that necessitated adjustment remain unaddressed; and the poor, who suffered deterioration in living standards prior to adjustment, fare no better or even worse during the prolonged period of stalled reform.[6] In theory they should benefit from structural changes, such as improved rural terms of trade and a reorientation of social welfare spending to primary education and preventive health care. Yet they cannot benefit if reforms are stalled or poorly implemented.[7] And programs that are implemented to protect "poor" groups during adjustment often evolve into opportunities for rent seeking within the public sector. Prolonged economic decline can also result in a culture of poverty. With no foreseeable end to economic crisis or stagnation, expectations gradually give way to resignation.[8] Experience in various African countries indicates that significant political change or severe economic crisis may be a prerequisite to creating a reform movement so widespread that it can override the strength of entrenched interests.[9]

This is demonstrated by the cases of Senegal and Zambia.[10] In Senegal, adjustment has been an ongoing process for over a decade, with many of the most difficult reforms yet to be implemented. Although elections are held regularly, political change has been marginal, with the Parti Socialiste (PS) retaining majority control. As a result, established interests within the public administration continue to pose effective opposition to necessary structural reforms. Efforts to compensate the losers during adjustment have been directed primarily at these interests rather than the poor. At the same time, because the poor are largely marginalized from the formal political system, there is little public debate on poverty despite its widespread nature.

In Zambia, in contrast, the October 1991 elections led to the defeat of the existing regime, which had experienced difficulty in implementing measures that would have undermined the privileged position of its supporters in the inefficient and partisan public administration. This gave the new Movement for Multiparty Democracy (MMD) government the political opportunity—at least in the short term—to proceed with extensive reform. The MMD government was also better able to target available public resources toward the poor and vulnerable.

■ The Political Economy of Adjustment in Senegal

Senegal is one of Africa's few long-established multiparty democracies. Its experience with prolonged and postponed adjustment in the 1980s illustrates the difficulties of sustaining economic reform and of protecting vulnerable groups—much less the poorest—in the process. The slow pace of change and the resulting absence of positive results have made the implementation of reform far more difficult, allowing groups strongly opposed to adjustment to retain privileged positions within the public sector and governing party. As a result they have been able to monopolize the benefits of most compensatory efforts at the expense of the poor. Thus, despite the large amount of resources spent on compensation, there has been very little impact on poverty reduction, a particularly striking result in a country with as pressing a poverty problem as Senegal. This suggests that more rapid and extensive reform would have been more effective at undermining the political monopoly of the privileged on the one hand and at extending benefits to the poor on the other.

□ *The Political Context*

Senegal's long-lasting political pluralism and stability, rare on the African continent, have many complex explanations. A detailed review of these is beyond the scope of this chapter, but some are worthy of brief mention. Although political freedom has been revoked at times, in particular during the 1968–1974 period of one-party rule, Senegal has made impressive strides in the liberalization of the one-party state[11] and has managed to avoid the civil strife of many of its neighboring countries.[12]

Senegal's political system, like its culture, is a complex mix of tradition and modernity, religious fervor coupled with a high degree of tolerance, and a blend of internationally based ideologies marked by a high degree of nationalism and pragmatism. The absence of a violent struggle for independence and the experience of Senegalese elites in the French national assembly differentiated Senegal from most other colonies. Ethnic divisions are mitigated by the unity that the Islamic religion provides. The role of religious leaders—the marabouts—is very strong,[13] with the *ngidal*, or orders, that the marabouts issue prior to elections still determining rural votes and even having a role in some urban areas.[14]

Also prevalent in the Senegalese political context is a high degree of clientelism and clanism: Personal and family ties have an extraordinarily high degree of importance and are the foundations of the political-administrative system. The PS, the governing party and the predominant political party for decades, is in theory based on socialist ideology but in practice acts as a clientelist political machine. Its main rival, the Parti Démocratique

Sénégalaise (PDS), is equally mercurial in ideology, and also quite dependent on clientelist ties for its political base. Even unions, traditionally quite strong in Senegal, are linked to the clientelist system.[15]

The predominance of religious leaders and clientelistic politics provides stability for the regime, but they are not necessarily democratic nor are they conducive to reform of the economic and administrative system from within. Much of the political elite remains uncommitted to a reform process that threatens its base of privilege. The clientelistic system is conditioned by three groups: trade unions, civil servants, and students. Civil servants' ties to the PS have made them a key base of support for the government after independence. University students traditionally have been granted free tuition and a guaranteed job in the civil service, and they have proven to be formidable political opponents when these benefits are challenged. Trade union members have also held a privileged position relative to the average worker, adding to the inefficiency of both public and private sectors.[16]

To some extent, clientelistic politics also prevails at the level of the poorest groups and in part explains the relative stability and acceptance of the system. Competing factions of the PS, for example, have traditionally tried to control urban shantytowns by vying to provide services. Yet with prolonged economic decline and the state's decreasing capacity to deliver services, the effectiveness of clientelism as a source of political stability, at least at the level of the urban poor, has declined.[17]

Indeed, notably absent from the public debate in Senegal is the plight of the increasingly large numbers of poor in peri-urban areas, who have the least margin for absorbing changes in prices of consumer goods and have experienced greater declines in incomes during the adjustment period than have rural groups.[18] Like the rural poor, they have a weak political voice. Although it is not clear whether reaching the poorest of the poor is feasible or optimal in terms of resource expenditure and poverty alleviation,[19] it is surprising that little if any attempt has been made to distinguish between poor and nonpoor groups in the allocation of compensatory benefits.

The prevalence of clientelism does not augur well for efficient public administration and economic management. Civil servants who have lost status and income due to adjustment have been able to form a relatively effective political opposition, substantially slowing the pace of reform.[20] Indeed, the number of civil servants has continued to increase throughout the adjustment period, although real wages have fallen steadily.[21] In the economy, the clientelist-based influence of the marabouts has been cited as a major reason for the precarious condition of the banking system.[22] A related phenomenon is that most wage earners support several extended family members, which has negative effects on their ability to save, a major obstacle to economic growth.[23]

The links between the formal political-administrative system, with the elite that benefits from it, and the rest of society are limited at best. The majority of the population is marginalized and increasingly frustrated with a stagnating economy and shrinking economic opportunities. This was vividly demonstrated by the violence surrounding the February 1988 elections as well as by the campaign slogan of the opposition: *Sopi,* the Wolof word for change.[24] To the Diouf regime, change meant inviting six parties to join the government in 1991. The offer was accepted by the main opposition party, the PDS, as well as by one Marxist party, the Parti de l'Indépendence et du Travail (PIT). Yet to the majority of splinter parties as well as to those disaffected with the political system in general, the inclusion of the PDS did not spell change, as the PS and the PDS are seen as interchangeable.[25] The perception that the government's incorporation of the opposition did not significantly change the system or its policies is shared by those traditionally marginalized, the poor.[26]

In recent years, the marginalization of the majority of the population from the political system has increased the importance of nongovernmental institutions and autonomous grassroots organizations, a development that is fundamentally democratic in character and is the political analogue of the informal economy: Unable to meet their demands within the system, people resort to activities in a parallel or informal arena. As in the case of the informal economy, there are legal and institutional limits to the influence that such groups can have on the central government. These limits, particularly in the political arena, can lead to popular frustration, as in the case of the February 1988 violence, or result in people looking for alternative systems, such as the growth of religious extremism.

☐   *The Adjustment Process*

From the time of independence Senegal has had the slowest growth rate of any African country without extreme civil unrest, yet at the same time has received the largest amount of foreign aid per capita.[27] This aid, coupled with reasonably good economic conditions and deficit spending in the 1960s and 1970s, allowed the system to maintain stability largely through the distribution of resources. Indeed, many argue that high levels of donor aid have allowed Senegal to postpone necessary economic adjustments indefinitely, even now.

In the two decades after independence, gross domestic product (GDP) growth averaged at most 2.5 percent a year, which hardly kept pace with population growth. The economy was characterized by a stagnant and highly protected manufacturing sector, an agricultural sector plagued by drought and policy distortions, and a patronage-ridden and inefficient bureaucracy.[28] By the early 1980s, the costs of these policies became increasingly evident, and the newly inaugurated Diouf regime, with the support of the Bretton Woods institutions, sought to correct these distortions through the implementation of an adjustment program. Since then, President Abdou Diouf has been trying to implement reform from within the system. Yet the most important—and politically difficult—structural changes, such as reform of the public sector and a reduction in the unwieldy civil service, have been indefinitely postponed, severely limiting the potential of the policy measures that have been implemented.

Prolonged economic crisis and adjustment have both entailed social costs, such as rising prices for consumer goods and a decrease in employment opportunities. The government's initial response to the social costs of adjustment was to "take care of its own." Its first effort, the DIRE (Délégation à l'Insertion, à la Réinsertion et à l'Emploi), was clearly aimed at groups within the system: civil servants and university graduates who prior to adjustment would have been virtually guaranteed jobs in the civil service. Aided by large amounts of donor funds, the DIRE (discussed below) was an expensive sweetener to buy off these groups.

At least in the short term, this may not have been a bad political strategy, as those who stood to lose most directly from adjustment were the groups that provided support for the regime. Yet the strategy was not accompanied by an effort to explain or "sell" the concept of reform to these groups or to the party rank and file. And as the technical team in charge of the reforms was poorly organized and very insulated from the rest of the government, there was even poor understanding of the measures at the cabinet level.[29] Thus most groups within the public sector remained opposed to reform despite attempts to buy them off. A 1986 survey of Dakar residents singled out civil servants and salaried workers as the most dissatisfied categories.[30]

Less privileged groups also felt the negative impact of economic crisis and adjustment and gradually became more vocal. In the February 1988 elections and their aftermath, the opposition, united behind the Alliance Sopi, was able to tap into the frustration of the urban poor, particularly unemployed youth, and mobilize them against the government. There was a major increase in unemployment in the 1980s: By 1991 unemployment in Dakar stood at 24 percent.[31] Underemployment was higher, but it is more difficult to measure. Unemployment was due to a gradual reduction of new civil service jobs and to the general economic downturn. It was exacerbated by migration from drought-ridden zones in the late 1980s, which increased the number of workers relying on a saturated informal economy.[32] This also placed an increased burden on an already inadequate urban infrastructure, which had deteriorated visibly in the 1980s.

The opposition was led by Abdoulaye Wade of the PDS, which is in theory a neoliberal party but in practice a center-left one. Wade criticized the adjustment process as being imposed from the outside and made a series of unrealistic promises, including the halving of the price of rice if elected.[33] Yet his message found a great deal of sympathy among the urban population. The Alliance Sopi was constituted on the eve of the 1988 election campaign by the PDS, the Ligue Démocratique/ Mouvement pour le Parti du Travail (LD/MPT), and the PIT in an attempt to capture the popular mood in favor of change. Wade and the PDS in particular made inroads in urban areas, capturing 24.74 percent of the national vote, almost 40 percent of the vote in Dakar, and over 45 percent of the vote in the region of Zinguinchor.[34]

Violence broke out on the eve of the elections after the government prevented PDS supporters from demonstrating, and protests spread to several cities. Official election results were heavily disputed by the opposition. Wade claimed that there was massive fraud and that he had won the election. The government response was to declare a state of emergency and to imprison Wade for "inciting insurrection." Wade was released in April, but a situation of civil unrest and political stalemate continued for twenty months.[35] The Alliance Sopi was expanded into a larger and more organized movement, CONACPO, that included most of the sixteen parties other than the governing PS.

The events surrounding the February elections had significant political impact both at home and abroad. During the course of the next few months the government embarked on a major attempt at "dialogue" with the opposition, making major concessions and giving in to virtually all of its demands by January 1991. The government accepted a change in the electoral code,[36] agreed to allow the opposition more access to the media, and invited several parties to join the government. The accord seemed to buy peace with the majority of the opposition, at least temporarily, and even played in the government's favor in resolving the insurrection in the Casamance, where the PDS had strong support. Although the opposition that remained outside the government accused the PDS and the PIT of being co-opted, the CONACPO alliance lost the primary reason for its existence. Wade, who was given the third most powerful position in the government, took on the role of the preeminent statesman and received far more media attention than he did as the leader of the opposition. Yet even from within the government, Wade remained critical of policies he said were imposed by the International Monetary Fund (IMF) and the World Bank and of privatization in particular.[37] The process of political liberalization, meanwhile, actually increased the strength of Diouf vis-à-vis the party old guard who were opposed to adjustment.[38] In parliamentary elections held in May 1993, the PS retained the national majority that it had in 1988. Of 130 parliamentary seats, the PS obtained eighty-four seats and the PDS twenty-seven seats.[39]

In the aftermath of the February 1988 violence, the government made the social costs of adjustment its first public and political priority.[40] It focused its efforts on a group that had played a critical role in the postelection unrest, the urban unemployed youth. The Agence d'Exécution des Travaux d'Intérêt Publique Contre le Sous-Emploi (AGETIP) was to provide rapid, visible, short-term employment to a frustrated and potentially destabilizing group and demonstrate the government's concerns with the social costs of adjustment at the same time. Yet due to the slow pace and limited scope of reform and the limited nature of democracy in Senegal, the benefits of the AGETIP, like those of the DIRE, remained concentrated among vocal, relatively privileged, and primarily urban groups.

☐ *The Safety Net Programs*

The first safety net program, the DIRE, was introduced in 1987 and received increased public attention after the political unrest of 1988. The DIRE was aimed at laid-off parastatal sector workers; civil servants who voluntarily retired; and university graduates who, previous to adjustment, would have found jobs in the civil service. The DIRE thus benefited relatively privileged civil servants rather than the poor, was run totally according to patronage criteria, had an extremely high rate of default on loans, and wasted an enormous amount of scarce public funds. It is thus widely regarded as a failure.[41]

The AGETIP was a semi-autonomous government agency designed to fund proposals from municipal governments and NGOs for labor-intensive public works, which were then subcontracted out to private sector companies that hired unemployed and primarily unskilled youth. The AGETIP, through rapid, transparent, and efficient management, has created a revolution of sorts and has even been cited as a model for the reform of Senegal's notoriously inefficient public administration. Insulation from the highly partisan and clientelistic public sector has been a determining factor in the AGETIP's ability to operate efficiently. However, although AGETIP has built a great deal of infrastructure that has benefited poor areas and has created temporary jobs for poor and unskilled youth in the process, it is clearly not a program that is specifically targeted at the poorest groups.

Despite its design and efficiency, the AGETIP could not overcome the problems related to the limited nature of democracy in Senegal. The program accepts proposals from municipal governments and a few nongovernmental organizations (NGOs). But because the opposition boycotted the 1990 municipal elections to protest electoral fraud, all municipalities are controlled by the PS, and the AGETIP's main beneficiaries have therefore been members of the governing party. In addition, AGETIP's relations with NGOs, which primarily are not affiliated with the governing party, have been very weak. Benefits have been concentrated in the limited segment of the population that supports the government or has ties to the public sector. The experience of Senegal demonstrates how the effects of slow or stalled economic reform and limited pluralism can be mutually reinforcing by allowing entrenched interest groups to dominate the political system and the public administration, thus institutionalizing the obstacles to political and economic change. Public institutions remain weak and their benefits more regressively distributed, and the poverty problem remains extensive.[42]

■ Democracy and Adjustment in Zambia

The case of Zambia provides a marked contrast to that of Senegal and demonstrates how dramatic political change can facilitate adjustment and in particular provide unique opportunities for redirecting resources to the poor.

From independence in 1964 until the October 1991 elections, power in Zambia was controlled by Kenneth Kaunda and his United National Independence Party (UNIP), which imposed a one-party state in 1973. Both the party apparatus and government bureaucracy had entrenched interests in managing the economy and polity according to patronage principles. The system of market distortions and inflated civil service payrolls was supported by copper export revenues during the boom years of the 1960s but became unsustainable with the dramatic deterioration in terms of trade that occurred in the 1970s. Beginning in the late 1970s,[43] a prolonged process of adjustment was launched, in which agreements were made and rescinded shortly thereafter in the face of popular opposition. In the latter part of the 1980s, several programs were introduced to address the social costs of adjustment, such as a food coupon system for maize meal in January 1989 and a social action program in early 1990. Yet, as was often the case in Zambia, these programs were inextricably linked to the party and were used more for political patronage purposes than to reach the poor.[44]

The political context for both adjustment and poverty alleviation changed dramatically when Kaunda and the UNIP party were voted out of power in national elections held on October 31, 1991. The electoral margin by which Frederick Chiluba and the eclectic MMD defeated Kaunda as well as the peaceful manner in which Kaunda turned over power signified a revolution for Zambia and were a surprise to virtually all observers.[45] Chiluba took 76 percent of the votes as well as 125 of 150 parliamentary seats. Nineteen of UNIP's twenty-five seats were concentrated in Eastern Province, where Kaunda had a strong base of support. In the aftermath of the election, the UNIP party virtually collapsed, with thousands of party members resigning or defecting to join the MMD—even in Eastern Province.[46]

Chiluba and the eclectic MMD ran on a pro-adjustment platform and made the elimination of inefficiency and corruption in government a major issue of the campaign and of the new government's initial policies. The government has since embarked on a program of bold economic reform, has implemented major reforms in the health sector, and has made some progress in putting in place programs to protect the poorest and most vulnerable groups in the process.[47] Despite numerous obstacles, the extent and scope of reforms that were implemented by the Chiluba government in its early years was indeed remarkable and signified a turning point after a decade of policy stalemate.

☐ *The Economic Legacy of the UNIP State*

Kenneth Kaunda's vague philosophy of "humanism" dictated that the state would take care of every Zambian. In the early years of independence, when funds were readily available, this resulted in an improvement in living conditions and access to services for a large majority. Later, economic trends and misguided government policy resulted in a dramatic erosion of these improvements. In addition, the politics of the one-party state, which made party membership a prerequisite for virtually all basic services, often resulted in the poorest and most vulnerable being excluded from the benefits.[48] At the same time, the belief that the state should provide all services free of charge led to a general decline in self-help initiative. Donors sanctioned such policies for decades with large assistance flows.[49]

Zambians were considerably worse off at the end of UNIP's term than they were at independence in 1964. Per capita income at that time was $540, among the highest for African nations. Today it is at $390,[50] among the lowest in the world. Although there is a paucity of countrywide data, credible estimates place up to 42 percent of the urban population (52 percent of the population is urban) under the poverty line, with estimates for rural poverty varying between 20 and 80 percent of the total households.[51] Basic social welfare services barely function; hospitals are without beds and medicine and schools without desks and books. Among mothers attending prenatal clinics in urban areas, 25 to 30 percent are HIV positive and there are yearly epidemics of cholera and dysentery.[52]

The precipitous decline of infrastructure and welfare can be attributed in large part to misallocated spending—in particular to the decision to cut recurrent expenditures, such as maintenance of facilities, rather than curbing spiraling personnel costs—and to pervasive corruption.[53] It was also due to a 50 percent decline in terms of trade for copper, which generates 85 to 90 percent of Zambia's foreign exchange, from 1975 to 1986.[54] The delay in curbing boom-year spending practices in the face of the severe decline in the terms of trade proved disastrous, particularly coupled with rapid population growth. Despite a population growth of 3.7 percent per year,[55] formal private sector employment peaked in 1975, with 120,320 positions, and fell to 98,730 in 1979. From 1975 to 1977, government employment continued to grow, from 124,760 to 126,260 government and 116,150 to 128,350 parastatal positions respectively. Even with the economic decline and attempts at adjustment of the 1980s, government employment continued to increase slightly.[56]

□ *The Politics of Adjustment in Zambia*

"Party and government structures that had emerged during the 1976–83 period of the 'command economy' could hardly be expected to support a sharp change in policy orientation aimed at dismantling government controls,"[57] Ravi Gulhati said in 1989. The primary explanation for UNIP's mismanagement of the economy is the pervasiveness of patronage at all levels of government, a phenomenon that is common in Africa. At independence most nations lacked fully developed markets and bureaucracies; thus there was a limit to what politicians could implement through normal administrative channels, and the reliance on patronage to build bases of political support became increasingly prevalent.[58] Finally, as neither participation nor accountability to local structures had been given priority by the colonial administrations, it is no surprise that a great deal of value was not attached to them after independence.[59]

Zambia experienced these problems in a more extreme form than most other countries because its indigenous political and institutional structures were very underdeveloped at the time of independence. Only 4 percent of Zambia's top-level civil service posts were filled by Zambians in 1964, which contrasts sharply with the 60 percent of Ghana's top-level civil service staffed by Ghanaians.[60] Kaunda and his UNIP party had a great deal of national support because they were nationalists, not because they were well equipped to govern. The party built and relied increasingly on an extensive network of patron-client ties, financed by copper revenues and by over $2 billion in reserves left by the colonial administration. Access to the party and the state resources it controlled became the primary means to social advancement in postindependence Zambia.[61]

Kaunda's popularity and UNIP's access to a lucrative pot of state funds eroded as the economy began to decline in the early 1970s. As a result, UNIP began to face more credible opposition, in particular from the United Progressive Party (UPP), which broke off from UNIP in 1971.[62] Kaunda's response was to outlaw all opposition parties and to dissolve parliament in

1972 and to launch the single-party Second Republic in 1973. The UNIP government attempted to impose a centrally planned and controlled economy and tightened party control over all aspects of society. Government structures were matched by party structures at all levels: provincial planning units, district councils, ward development committees, and village productivity committees.[63] The patron-client system was the basis of most transactions, from getting permission for a stall in the local market to conducting business at the highest level. Although a few businesspeople joined the UPP or were active in the opposition in the mid-1970s, most remained in UNIP because it was the only way to get things done.[64]

Less privileged sectors without the resources to buy their way into the patronage system fared less well. One example is UNIP's regulation of access to markets, which resulted in a large increase in illegality and the growth of informal markets in Lusaka.[65] A telling statistic is that Zambia's income distribution is among the worst in the world, and the poorest 25 percent lost the most as trends worsened in the late seventies.[66]

UNIP's increasing monopoly on power also generated opposition,[67] culminating in the formation of the MMD. A key player in the opposition movement and an important interest group that UNIP was never able to fully control was the union movement. One reason for this was the unions' strong position in Zambia prior to the existence of UNIP, particularly among the mineworkers, organized in the Mineworkers' Union of Zambia (MUZ). Strikes among mine workers in the 1930s and 1940s began a tradition of union protest that had a lasting impact on urban politics. Although UNIP received union support in the struggle for independence,[68] it was not able to fully control the unions for its political objectives. The unions had preestablished traditions and organization and placed different criteria on leadership selection than did the patronage-based party. Union members adapted more to company than to party rules, in general rejected political leaders, and believed that the union defended them better than the party.[69] In 1978 the chairman of the Zambian Congress of Trade Unions (ZCTU)—now President Chiluba—stated: "Politicians are all the same. They promise to build a bridge where there is no river. In fact, politics is the conduct of public affairs for private advantage."[70]

UNIP's relationship with the unions reflects a more general trend: the erosion of party support among the more educated and organized sectors of the population by the 1980s. This was ultimately its downfall; these groups formed the basis of the MMD.[71] Perhaps the most notable dynamic is that whereas unions were one of the earliest opponents of adjustment, by the time of the 1991 elections, the MMD, strongly supported by the unions and headed by a former union leader, recognized the dire need for reform and campaigned on a pro-adjustment platform.

☐ *UNIP and Adjustment*

In the early 1980s, the government lacked the political base and even more
the will to sustain an adjustment program. By the time the government
finally became convinced of the need to implement adjustment, the extremity of the economic decline had eroded its support among all key sectors,
including the business community that it had been formerly able to co-opt.

The UNIP government also had a history of troubled relations with the
donor community as early as 1973.[72] The most marked break with donors
took place in December 1986, after a poorly designed attempt to raise the
price of maize meal caused riots and fifteen deaths in several cities. Zambia
broke off relations with the IMF and World Bank in May 1987, reimposed a
regime of price controls and import restrictions, and followed Peru's example of limiting debt payments to 10 percent of export earnings. By late
1988 it became clear that most donors were reluctant to deal with Zambia
unless it reached an agreement with the international financial institutions,
and relations were once again reestablished through a long and arduous
negotiation process.[73] In June of 1990, a new adjustment program was
undertaken, and Kaunda stayed the course although the doubling of the
price of meal was met with more riots and twenty-three deaths as well as
with an attempted military coup.[74] In the 1991 preelection atmosphere,
however, the president abandoned the spending limits of the adjustment
program, both raising salaries for civil servants and increasing subsidies on
maize meal and on housing, and he again broke off relations with the
donors.[75]

There was strong opposition to adjustment within UNIP. Most members had little to gain from a program designed to eliminate a system that
provided them with a host of opportunities for rent seeking. The privileges
granted to nonpoor urban groups through generalized maize meal subsidies,
housing subsidies, high relative levels of civil service wages, and special
prices on items such as maize and beer for the military and some unions
gave several key interest groups a stake in the system, which in theory also
guaranteed universal free health care and education.[76] The perception that
adjustment was being imposed from abroad and lack of understanding of
the measures within UNIP were also responsible for its failure. The riots
against maize price increases, for example, strengthened the hand of the
anti-IMF people in UNIP. This perception may also explain why measures
were often implemented at inopportune times with little research into their
short-term effects. There was little emphasis on communication, and measures appeared in the press as decrees rather than being explained to the
public, which contributed to their political unpalatability.[77] The government's consistent failure to seek public consultation on its policies also led
to considerable uncertainty in the private sector.[78]

The December 1986 maize price increases are a case in point. The subsidy was removed from the more expensive breakfast meal and retained on roller meal, the staple that the poorest buy. But the millers had no confidence that they would be promptly reimbursed for the subsidized meal. They stopped production for roller meal and increased that of the more profitable breakfast meal. So almost overnight, there was no roller meal available, and breakfast meal cost twice as much as before, a situation that was complicated by panic buying and shortages.[79]

Also contributing to the erosion of political and popular will (often called "adjustment fatigue") was insufficient attention to poverty issues or to equitable distribution of the burden of adjustment.[80] The perception that the government is doing something to make the adjustment process less painful can generate important popular support for the government at a critical time; this was not the case in Zambia.[81] Finally, by the end of its tenure the UNIP regime was so discredited that no economic policy it implemented could inspire public confidence. Nothing demonstrates the extent to which UNIP had lost public confidence as much as the 1991 elections.

□ *The 1991 Elections and the Challenges Ahead*

The extent of the opposition's victory, the peaceful manner in which Kaunda transferred power, and the strongly anticorruption and pro–free market bent of the Chiluba government surprised most observers. The opposition began as an eclectic movement of professionals led by a group of economists from the University of Zambia Research Foundation, the private sector, unions, and even disaffected former UNIP leaders. In the aftermath of a 1990 forum on multiparty democracy organized by several members of this movement, the MMD was formed and it soon became the only significant opposition, despite the existence of twelve other minor parties. The MMD coalition was held together primarily by its opposition to UNIP and by the recognition of the need for dramatic reform. UNIP support had not only eroded in the private sector, the unions, and the general population but also in the civil service, at least below the political appointee ranks.[82] The MMD issued a call for change, and its slogan, "the hour has come," captured the popular mood. Zambians were given political choice for the first time in decades. Given the dramatic erosion of living standards in the face of widespread UNIP corruption, it is no surprise that the vote was staunchly anti-UNIP. Increased press freedom and independence on the part of the judiciary in the two years prior to the election also played a major role in the defeat of UNIP.[83]

Kaunda was apparently totally surprised by the results, which demonstrates how out of touch both he and the UNIP were with the popular mood.[84] It is likely that Kaunda, like Augusto Pinochet in Chile, never believed that he could lose and may not have put himself up for election had he thought that events would turn against him. Yet once the process was launched, it was impossible to stop it without resorting to force and widespread bloodshed.[85] The fragile nature of UNIP's support was also demonstrated by the desertion of thousands of UNIP members immediately after the elections.[86]

In its campaign, the MMD warned, albeit in vague terms, that the process of reform would entail substantial popular sacrifice.[87] MMD also called for an investigation of the allegations of massive fraud in the state copper parastatal, Zambia Consolidated Copper Mines (ZCCM) and raised the possibility of privatizing the major public enterprises.[88] UNIP had a different campaign strategy: It warned of the danger of fragmentation, disorder, and chaos if the MMD won, manipulated existing programs for the poor for political purposes, and even wrote into its party manifesto that the price of maize meal had fallen by 20 percent in its last year in office.[89]

Chiluba's statements upon taking power emphasized a new approach: He insisted on being called "Mr. President" rather than "His Excellency," in contrast to Kaunda. He ordered the issuing of a new currency, without Kaunda's portrait but also without his own, in order to play down the personality cult.[90] Chiluba also immediately sought a rapprochement with the international financial community, although he stressed that initiatives and reforms must be internally generated.[91]

There were also some worrisome signs and tensions as some of the former UNIP leaders in the MMD and the cabinet sought to operate the way the UNIP had previously. Michael Sata, minister of local government and a former UNIP leader, made statements such as "at the local level the MMD will operate like a one party state."[92] At the rank-and-file level, overzealous MMD members attacked UNIP party members' property.[93] Given the MMD's electoral margin and Zambia's lack of experience with democratic government, there was a tendency for the MMD to operate like its predecessor.[94] UNIP attempts to generate anti-MMD activity among the military, meanwhile, led to the imposition of a ninety-day state of emergency by Chiluba in March 1993, a measure that eroded public confidence in Chiluba's commitment to full democracy.

Also a challenge for the MMD government were various unrealistic measures passed in the last months of the UNIP government.[95] UNIP gave the 150,000-strong civil service a 100 percent pay raise just prior to the elections, which they accepted only on the condition that they would receive another one in June 1992.[96] The Chiluba government did not have the resources to meet these promises, nor did they fit into a reformist economic strategy. UNIP also spent billions of kwacha during the election campaign, much of which is unaccounted for due to its shredding of vital documents in the days before surrendering power. Finally, the new government had no up-to-date information on the financial situation: The most recent Central Bank report available in 1991 was one issued in December 1987.[97]

Yet there was room for cautious optimism about the MMD's capacity to implement a viable adjustment program. First, the government had a strong political mandate. The experience of several countries indicates that *political* change of a relatively dramatic nature may facilitate the implementation of far-reaching economic changes; the honeymoon period that newly elected governments have is much longer in this case.[98] Second, people were aware of the extremity of the economic crisis, and the government made no false promises in its electoral campaign, which made it easier to implement unpopular measures.[99] Third, Chiluba's labor background guaranteed him a certain amount of union support.[100] Fourth, with UNIP discredited, there was no credible opposition alternative. Fifth, the new government early on received support from the international financial community.[101] Finally, since the UNIP's experiences with food riots, donors were receptive to supporting safety net policies, thus facilitating the implementation of reform. At least in the arena of economic reforms, Chiluba realized that moving quickly while the government had political momentum was essential.

There were also obstacles to reform. First of all, despite his promises to reduce the size of the government, Chiluba appointed at least twenty-one ministers because early on he found himself in need of the support of a variety of provincial and sectoral factions.[102] The MMD was a movement rather than a party, and included several factions, who by the second year, began to erode the cohesion of the new government, most notably evidenced by the removal of Finance Minister Emmanuel Kasonde in early 1993. Kasonde was one of the strongest proponents of adjustment in the government as well as an advocate of safety net policies and was respected in international financial circles. His removal, the result of political infighting, was a blow to the adjustment program as well as to relations with donors. Further cracks in the MMD emerged in the period prior to the 1996 elections, and progress on reform slowed.

Nevertheless, progress was remarkable. Structural reforms, trade liberalization, and privatization all progressed far more quickly than most observers would ever have predicted. The exchange market was freed, price controls and subsidies on most commodities were removed, and the budget for 1992 was balanced. A major reform of the health sector was also implemented, which resulted in the devolution of management responsibility and resources for health care to the local and community levels.[103] In addition, the government was faced with an extremely severe drought in its first few months in office and proved quite successful in administering drought relief aid on a massive scale.[104]

Yet extremely difficult measures remained to be implemented, such as the firing of as many as fifty thousand civil servants, accounting for approximately half the public sector wage bill.[105] And perhaps most worrisome, despite its rhetoric, the government was far less effective at addressing the social costs of its policies. Although Kasonde had placed a great deal of emphasis on targeting the benefits of compensation to the poor and vulnerable rather than the vocal, by the end of 1992 the government had still not appointed anyone to run the social safety net program (discussed later in the chapter).[106] One explanation may be that due to the strong anti-UNIP origin of many MMD members, an antistate sentiment prevailed in many government agencies and ministries.

The *manner* in which measures were presented made a major difference in the popular reaction. In contrast to the Kaunda government, which merely decreed unpopular measures overnight, the Chiluba government placed a great deal of importance on communication. In mid-1992, for example, the dynamic MMD campaign manager, Dipak Patel, was assigned to promote privatization and to "mount a massive publicity campaign, like they did for British Telecom or British Gas, to tell the public the merits and demerits of buying shares."[107]

The change in approach is critical to explaining the lack of protest when the government raised the price of maize two-fold in December 1991. Since then, the price of breakfast meal has been liberalized, resulting in an approximately four-fold increase. The less refined roller meal temporarily remained subsidized, as did large quantities of donated yellow maize. Prior to the price increases, the government also gave millers more incentives to produce the less expensive meal in order to ensure an adequate supply.[108]

The maize meal issue had been the political Achilles' heel of the Kaunda government, which spent almost 17 percent of its total budget on maize subsidies.[109] Eliminating that burden had to be a central objective of any adjustment program, from both an economic and a political point of view, and the Chiluba government's achievements have been impressive. However, much of the urban population spends up to 70 percent of its income on food[110] and cannot afford the increase in the price of meal. Identifying a viable strategy for protecting the truly vulnerable in the face of continued price increases was one of the most immediate—and difficult—challenges facing the Chiluba government.

□ *Safety Net Programs*

The Social Recovery Project (SRP) and Microprojects Unit (MPU), funded by the World Bank and the European Union and run out of the government's National Development Planning Office, are the components of an overall program that reaches the needy rather than the privileged. Initially set up under the Kaunda government in 1990, the program was greatly enhanced by the Chiluba government's commitment to target state spending on the poor and needy and by the end of UNIP's monopoly over local government and virtually all other local initiatives.

The SRP/MPU responds to proposals from community organizations, mostly for renovation of existing infrastructure. Since the introduction of the program in 1989, it has received one thousand requests for projects and it has approved three hundred, with an average project size of $30,000. Over 100 community groups and twenty-one NGOs are currently involved in the program, with approximately 30 percent of the projects implemented by NGOs.[111] The projects require community contributions in cash or in labor. They have been successful in revitalizing the self-help spirit in many communities and in reaching remote areas long neglected by the state and are being expanded substantially under the Chiluba government.

The SRP/MPU has been quite successful in promoting infrastructure rehabilitation based on community contributions, usually in cash in urban areas and in labor in rural ones. The SRP has found that communities are also as likely to mobilize for health as for education projects. After several years of experience, the program also started providing some assistance and training for district- and community-level capacity building while maintaining roughly the same number of projects. SRP also tried to coordinate more closely with the line ministries, particularly at the district levels, to develop their capacity to continue local development activities beyond the duration of the SRP/MPU projects. But the program continues to face constraints in reaching the poorest and most remote communities, which are both the most difficult and expensive to reach and the least likely to present viable project proposals.[112]

Despite the constraints, by giving communities contact with and a stake in a government poverty alleviation program, the SRP/MPU may enhance the political sustainability of economic reform by creating a basis of support among previously marginalized but numerically significant groups. In addition, the demand-based nature of the program inherently encourages such groups to exercise their political voice, something unprecedented in the Zambian context. These changes are likely to have a longevity beyond that of the short-term programs.

Dramatic political change was the necessary catalyst to economic reform and to the introduction of safety net programs focused on the poor. Despite impressive strides on the macroeconomic front, the current context indicates that there are substantial institutional obstacles to sustaining reform. On the other hand, there is no credible political alternative to the MMD at the national level, and the process of democratic opening is ongoing at the local level. While there are limits to what the Chiluba government has achieved, notable progress was made in several critical areas.

Democratic elections were held at national and local levels; major and significant macroeconomic reforms have been introduced and have *not* been reversed as in the past; a major health reform was implemented; some targeted safety net programs for the poor have been introduced; and perhaps most important, although the safety net programs have not been as extensive as they might have, their reliance on participation and community self-help efforts will reinforce individual economic initiative and democratic politics at the local level.

■ Conclusion

It is obviously impossible to draw universal conclusions for the region from two case studies. However, the sharp contrasts between Senegal and Zambia are confirmed by experiences in other countries both in and outside the region. In Bolivia, for example, rapid and dramatic political change allowed the government to divert most compensatory efforts (through the Emergency Social Fund [ESF]) to poor and previously marginalized communities rather than to the traditional beneficiaries of state benefits, the tin miners. The ESF also had important effects on strengthening the local institutions that are essential to poverty alleviation and to democratic government. Since the implementation of economic reform in 1985, two consecutive sets of national elections have been held—for the first time in decades in Bolivia—and proreform candidates took the majority of the vote in both. In contrast, in Venezuela, slow and stalled social sector reform and the virtual breakdown of key public services, among other factors, have resulted in a popular backlash against reform, a rejection of established parties and institutions, and in the election of a populist with no organized political backing in December 1993, a result that did not augur well for either economic reform or democracy. Ghana is a case in which rapid economic reform has led to some gradual political opening, at least at the local level. Nigeria is an example of slow or stalled reform allowing entrenched interests to continue to dominate both economic and political systems.

      The contrasts between Senegal and Zambia suggest that, particularly in Africa, where the record of reform has been poor and opposition is often entrenched in semi-authoritarian political systems, rapid political or economic change may be necessary to implement substantive reform. Once one kind of reform is initiated (economic or political), it tends to reinforce reform in the other arena. The sequence will obviously differ among countries, and there is no evidence of any causal relationship. In addition, the factors that make the launching of reform possible are not necessarily the same as those required to sustain it, as the case of Zambia suggests.

However, rapid reform that undermines entrenched interests in the public sector bureaucracy seems far more likely than incremental change to result in significant structural macro reforms as well as in political opening, both of which are key to poverty alleviation and to democracy in the African context.

■ Notes

1. For a detailed account of the fate of the poor in Peru and Zambia under two regimes that pursued heterodox policies in an attempt to avoid adjustment (Alan Garcia's and Kenneth Kaunda's), see chapters 4 and 6 in C. Graham, *Safety Nets, Politics and the Poor: Transitions to Market Economies* (Washington, D.C.: Brookings Institution, 1994).
2. This trend has been precipitated on the one hand by the extremely poor economic performance of many regimes in the 1980s, and on the other by the collapse of one-party governments in Eastern Europe and the former Soviet Union and by the increased unwillingness of bilateral donors to support "undemocratic" regimes that violate human rights. I discuss this in greater detail in "Zambia's Democratic Transition: The Beginning of the End of the One-Party State in Africa?" *Brookings Review* (spring 1992): 40–41.
3. Steven R. Weissman, "The Lessons from the Experiences of Ghana and Senegal," *World Development* 18, no. 12 (1990): 1010–1018.
4. This is discussed in detail in David E. Sahn, "Structural Adjustment in Africa: Are There Similarities with Latin America?" (paper presented to workshop on Macroeconomic Crises, Policy reforms and the Poor in Latin America, Cali, Colombia, October 1–4, 1991).
5. This term was originally used by Thomas Callaghy in describing adjustment in Nigeria, Ghana, and Zambia in "Lost Between State and Market: The Politics of Economic Adjustment in Ghana, Zambia, and Nigeria," in Joan Nelson, ed., *Economic Crisis and Policy Choice: The Politics of Adjustment in the Third World* (Princeton: Princeton University Press, 1990), pp. 257–319.
6. Particularly in Africa, how the poor fare during adjustment varies among countries, and depends on how urbanized the country is, how dependent the poor are on the market economy, in urban areas the extent to which prices for products that the poor consume were subsidized prior to adjustment, and in rural areas the extent to which inputs such as fertilizer were subsidized prior to adjustment.
7. Sahn, in "Structural Adjustment in Africa," notes that the slower the pace of reform, the longer the lag in poverty alleviation.
8. I am grateful to Habib Fettini of the World Bank for introducing this point.
9. The cases of Ghana in the early 1980s and Zambia in 1991 are examples of crises precipitating economic (Ghana) or political (Zambia) change that leads to significant attempts at adjustment. Gradual change alone is not enough to undermine existing governments in Africa. Either external pressure, war, or extreme economic crises have preceded most political openings. As many governments in the region have survived for decades with questionable bases of legitimacy, lack of legitimacy alone is not enough to precipitate political openings. (This point was raised by Achille Mbembe in a seminar on Political Transformation in Africa, Brookings Institution, Washington, D.C., February 27, 1992.)

10. The two case studies presented here are based on field work by the author in October-November 1991 and on the longer versions of the cases that resulted. They appear as chapters 5 and 6 in C. Graham, *Safety Nets.*

11. Larry Diamond, "Roots of Failure, Seeds of Hope," in Larry Diamond, Juan Linz, and Seymour Martin Lipset, eds., *Democracy in Developing Countries: Volume II—Africa* (Boulder, Colo.: Lynne Rienner Publishers, 1988). Diamond notes that the "semi-democracy" of Senegal is the best example of the liberalization of a one-party state in Africa. For a detailed description of differences between one-party regimes in Africa, see Ruth Berins Collier, *Regimes in Tropical Africa: Changing Forms of Supremacy 1945–1975* (Berkeley: University of California Press, 1982).

12. Interview with Robert Nichols, Regional Representative for West Africa, OXFAM, Dakar, October 29, 1991.

13. Lucy E. Creevey, "Muslim Brotherhoods and Politics in Senegal in 1985," *The Journal of Modern African Studies* 23, no. 4 (1985): 715–721; and Christian Coulon, "Senegal: The Development and Fragility of Semi-Democracy," in Diamond, Linz, and Lipset, *Democracy in Developing Countries.*

14. After the February 1988 elections one Dakar resident was quoted as saying that he rather liked the opposition candidate but that he would vote for incumbent President Diouf because, after all, "that's what the marabout ordered" (Franziska Oppmann, "Senegal: The Myth of Democracy?" *Africa Report* no. 3 [May-June 1988]: 23–26). Creevey ("Muslim Brotherhoods") and Coulon ("Senegal") agree with the role of the marabouts in determining voter behavior. The influence of the marabouts was also confirmed by the author's interviews with three groups of women (approximately fifteen each) in two poor urban areas in Dakar and one rural village approximately one hour outside Dakar, on October 26 and November 2, 1991.

15. The largest union, the Confédération Nationale des Travailleurs du Sénégal (CNTS), is affiliated with the PS, which has a limited degree of control over the union. In return the CNTS is guaranteed four seats in the National Assembly and now holds the vice presidency. This guarantees it a certain amount of influence but also links its fate to that of the governing party. (U.S. Embassy, "Senegalese Unions and Political Influence," unpublished paper, Political Section, Dakar.)

16. Samba Ka and Nicolas van de Walle, "Senegal: Stalled Reform in a Dominant Party System," in Stephan Haggard and Steven B. Webb, eds., *Voting for Reform: Democracy, Liberalization, and Economic Adjustment* (New York: Oxford University Press, 1994).

17. Georges Salem, "Crise Urbaine et Contrôle Social à Pikine: Bornes-Fontaines et Clientelisme," *Politique Africaine* 45 (March 1992): 21–38.

18. Ka and van de Walle, "Senegal."

19. This raises the question of whether it is better to lift the largest possible number of people at the margin of the poverty line above it, using a straight head count measure of poverty, or to focus efforts on improving the lot of the poorest, even if the number of people below the poverty line remains the same. The Sen index, for example, combines the head count ration with the average income shortfall and the measure of inequality among them to determine the severity in addition to the incidence of poverty.

20. Ka and van de Walle, "Senegal."

21. Ibid. Other countries, such as Poland and Costa Rica, have used similar tactics to avoid rapidly increasing unemployment. The drawback of such a strategy,

in addition to the wage bill, is that it generates a negative incentives system in the public sector.

22. Interview with Nicholas Roffe, Director, Agence de Crédit Pour L'Enterprise Privée, Dakar, October 24, 1991. Roffe, who runs one of the few credit agencies in Senegal with an impeccable repayment record, refuses to lend to religious leaders and cites their responsibility for "destroying the Banking system."

The negative effects of clientelism on loan practices is also well demonstrated by the record of the DIRE, which is discussed in detail later in the chapter.

23. It is estimated that for every salaried Senegalese worker there are up to ten dependents. This condition was noted by a variety of people interviewed, including Roffe and Jacques R. Delons, International Labour Organisation Adviser to the DIRE, whom I interviewed in Dakar on October 22, 1991. For a detailed account, see Carolyn M. Somerville, "The Impact of Reforms on the Urban Population: How the Dakarois View the Crisis," in Christopher Delgado and Sidi Jammeh, eds., *The Political Economy of Senegal Under Structural Adjustment* (New York: Praeger, 1991). This phenomenon is not unique to Senegal. For a detailed account of its effects regionwide, see Mamadou Dia, "Indigenous Management Practices: Lessons for Africa's Management in the 90's" (World Bank, February 1992, mimeographed).

24. This conclusion is also based on the author's interviews with over forty politicians, NGO representatives, and independent observers, as well as approximately forty-five urban and rural poor women in Dakar and its environs, October-November 1991.

25. Interview with Abdoulaye Bathily, Secrétaire Générale du Ligue Démocratique/Mouvement Pour le Parti du Travail, Dakar, October 28, 1991. The LD/MPT was one of the main parties—along with the PDS and the PIT—that formed the Alliance Sopi in 1988. LD/MPT and Jef/Mouvement Revolutionnaire pour la Démocratie Nouvelle (AJ/MRDN) were the two opposition parties outside the government with the largest following after May 1990. Both were Marxist in theory but rather eclectic and pragmatic in practice.

26. The author interviewed approximately forty-five women, two-thirds in group interviews in poor urban areas of Dakar (poor areas of Medina and Niarry Tally), and one group of fifteen in a rural *peulh* village (Tivaouane Kaay Baax) one hour outside Dakar. Most of the women did not even know of or understand the changes at the center. Those that did said that even with the changes, nothing had changed, that the poor remained in the same situation, that the politicians were only interested in the middle class, and that "the price of rice was still going up." The rural women remarked that even at the local level political changes meant little to them, as they had little access to political manipulation, which was done by the men.

These conclusions about the political views of the disaffected were confirmed by the author's interviews with several NGOs who work primarily with the poorest and most marginalized groups. These include Mazid Ndiaye, Director, RADI, Dakar, October 28, 1991; Fatime Ndiaye, Director, CONGAD, October 25, 1991; and Daouda Diop, Director, ABACED, Dakar, October 23 and November 1, 1991.

27. Eliot Berg, "Adjustment Postponed: Economic Policy Reform in Senegal in the 1980s" (report prepared for U.S. AID/Dakar, Development Alternatives International, Bethesda, Md., October 1990); Ka and van de Walle, "Senegal." At $100 per capita per year, Senegal receives four times as much donor aid per capita than the average for African nations.

28. Ka and van de Walle, "Senegal."

29. Ka and van de Walle, "Senegal"; and Katherine Marshall discussing the Ka and van de Walle chapter at a conference on Voting for Reform: The Political Economy of Adjustment in New Democracies, World Bank, Washington, D.C., May 4, 1992.

30. Somerville, "Impact of Reforms."

31. "Enquête Emploi, Sous Emploi, Chomage en Milieu Urbain" (Rapport Préliminaire, République du Sénégal: Ministère de l'Economie, des Finances, et du Plan; Direction de la Prévision et de la Statistique; Primature; Commissariat Général à l'Emploi; Projet PNUD/BIT, April–May 1991). Approximately one-quarter of the population of seven million lived in Dakar in 1987. The service sector makes up 52 percent of GDP, most of which is government, whereas industry makes up 27 percent and agriculture 10 percent. ("Introduction," Delgado and Jammeh, eds., *The Political Economy of Senegal.*)

32. An increase in unemployment usually results in more workers entering the informal sector. This, coupled with a decrease in formal sector demand, places a downward pressure on informal sector wages.

33. Franziska Oppmann, "Senegal: The Myth of Democracy?"

34. "Extrait des Minutes du Greffe de la Cour Suprême: Elections Législatives du Fevrier 1988," *Le Soleil,* March 4, 1988.

35. Author's interview with Abdoulaye Wade, Minister of State, Dakar, October 24, 1991; and Oppmann, "Senegal: The Myth of Democracy?"

36. This entails a number of changes, including giving 18-year-olds the vote and instituting a system of proportional representation for the 50 percent of the vote that is not taken by the majority. (Interview with Edward Malchik, Political Officer, U.S. Embassy, Dakar, October 25, 1991.)

37. Author's interview with Abdoulaye Wade.

38. Ka and van de Walle, "Senegal."

39. "Commission Announces Parliamentary Election Results," *Foreign Broadcast Information Service-Africa* 93-093, May 17, 1993.

40. Interview with Tyjan Sylla, General Secretary to the President, Dakar, November 5, 1991.

41. The DIRE gave loans of $11,000 and $50,000 to recent university graduates with no accountability mechanisms and no provision for training or repayment support, for example. Most of the loans were not used to start viable businesses and were never repaid. For details, see C. Graham, *Safety Nets,* chapter 5.

42. For details on the extent and nature of poverty in Senegal, see Graham, *Safety Nets,* chapter 5.

43. The first attempted agreement with the IMF was as early as 1973, but the reform program was stopped in the face of opposition from the Mineworkers' Union in 1974.

44. One notable exception is the Microprojects Unit (MPU), which is under the auspices of the National Commission for Development Planning but is funded and supervised by the European Community and, since 1991, the World Bank. Although the MPU is not a program designed to protect the poor or to exclusively reach the poorest groups, its role in stimulating community participation in the improvement and maintenance of social welfare infrastructure is an extremely valuable one, and an experience that should be incorporated into ongoing efforts at poverty alleviation in Zambia. The MPU will be discussed in detail in a later section.

45. This also had important implications regionwide. Detailed accounts can be found in Michael Bratton, "Zambia Starts Over," *Journal of Democracy* 3, no. 2 (April 1992): 81–94; and Carol Graham, "Zambia's Democratic Transition," 40–41.

46. Ridgeway Liwena, "Mtonga Quits UNIP," *Times of Zambia* November 13, 1991; "2000 Desert UNIP in Chipata," *Zambia Daily Mail,* November 12, 1991; and "UNIP Chiefs Split," *Zambia Daily Mail,* November 15, 1991.

47. This conclusion is based on the author's following the media and the press in Zambia in the immediate postelectoral period, as well as conversations with a variety of government officials and nongovernment observers, including the new finance minister, Emmanuel Kasonde, on November 15, 1991.

48. Ian Scott documents this phenomenon in the rural cooperatives, for example, in "Ideology and the Cooperative Movement in Zambia," *Journal of Administration Overseas* 19, no. 4 (October 1980). It is also well demonstrated by the current food coupon scheme, as documented in Richard Pearce, "Food Consumption and Adjustment in Zambia," Food Studies Group, Queen Elizabeth House, University of Oxford, Working Paper no. 2, December 1990; and the Prices and Incomes Commission, "A Preliminary Report of the Effectiveness of the Food Coupon System," Lusaka, August 1990; as well as by the author's interviews with government officials and nongovernmental organizations in Lusaka focusing on this issue in November 1991. Zambia is not unique in this phenomenon, meanwhile; the one-party system in neighboring Zaire has produced similar results.

49. One donor noted that when criticizing Zambia's poor economic management, it was important to recognize the extent to which it was sanctioned by large flows of international aid. (Interview with Dag Aarnes, Senior Programme Officer, Norwegian Agency for Development Cooperation, Lusaka, November 11, 1991.) Of the six other southern African countries rated as very poor in the Southern African Development Coordination Conference (SADCC), for example, Zambia was the highest recipient of IDA funds for 1991, receiving nearly $300 million by the end of the fiscal year (June 30). ("Zambia Tops IDA Loanees," *Zambia Daily Mail,* November 15, 1991.)

50. Some estimates are as low as $290.

51. Pearce, "Food Consumption and Adjustment in Zambia;" and *UNICEF Annual Report on Zambia, 1991.* Pearce uses Prices and Incomes Commission data to measure urban poverty. The 20 percent figure for rural poverty is based on Prices and Incomes Commission data, and the 80 percent figure is based on a 1980 ILO study. Rural poverty is much harder to measure due to the importance of nonmonetary income in rural households.

52. *UNICEF Annual Report 1991;* and "Hospital Labs Shut Down," *Zambia Daily Mail,* November 13, 1991.

53. Examples of such corruption are detailed in the next section. It is relevant to note here, however, the extent to which UNIP plundered the public coffers in its last few months in power. The Chiluba government reported that over 50 billion kwacha (100 KW = U.S.$1) were absconded from the public budget in UNIP's final year (a figure that is too high to be realistic) and that it was in the process of allocating itself KW19 billion more when the November 1 transfer of power took place. In addition, many billions more remain unaccounted for and probably always will, because there was a massive shredding of government documents by UNIP officials prior to vacating government offices. ("UNIP Abused State Funds," *Sunday Times of Zambia,* November 17, 1991; and author's coverage of the press and other news media in Lusaka during the two weeks following the elections.)

54. Zambia's percentage decline in terms of trade over 1974 (terms trade index 1974 = 100) was 45.8 from 1975–1979 and 63.8 from 1980–1986. (Ravi Gulhati, "Impasse in Zambia: The Economics and Politics of Reform," Economic Development Institute (EDI) Development Policy Case Series, Analytical Case Studies no. 2, World Bank, Washington, D.C., 1989.)

55. *World Development Report* (Washington, D.C.: World Bank, 1990).

56. Morris Szeftel, "Political Graft and the Spoils System in Zambia: The State as a Resource in Itself," *Review of African Political Economy* 24 (May-August 1982); and Zambia Prices and Incomes Commission, *Social Economic Bulletin* 1, No. 1 (April 1991).

57. Gulhati, "Impasse in Zambia."

58. Policy decisions were often determined by "non-economic factors that affect economic decisions [and] impose social obligations on individuals that limit their interest and capacity to support public concerns outside the community." (Goran Hyden, *No Shortcuts to Progress: African Development Management in Perspective* [Berkeley: University of California Press, 1983], p. 241.)

59. Hyden, *No Shortcuts.*

60. Gulhati, "Impasse in Zambia."

61. This process is discussed in detail in Szeftel, "Political Graft," and Scott, "Ideology."

62. Cherry Gertzel, ed., *The Dynamics of the One-Party State in Zambia* (Oxford: Manchester University Press, 1984).

63. A similar "decentralization" process occurred in Ghana under the Limann and the PNDC governments. For a comprehensive account of the decentralization process in the seventies, see Michael Bratton, *The Local Politics of Rural Development: The Peasant and the One Party State in Zambia* (Hanover: University Press of New England, 1980).

64. See Tina West, "The Politics of the Implementation of Structural Adjustment in Zambia," in *The Politics of Economic Reform in Sub-Saharan Africa* (unpublished report prepared for U.S. AID, Center for Strategic and International Studies, Washington, D.C., November 1991).

65. For an account of UNIP control of market stalls, see Earl P. Scott, "Lusaka's Informal Sector in National Economic Development," *Journal of Developing Areas* 20 (October 1985). For an account of the private sector's relations with the UNIP, see Andrew A. Beveridge and Anthony R. Oberschall, *African Businessmen and Development in Zambia* (Princeton: Princeton University Press, 1979), chapters 1 and 7.

66. The extent of wealth that the political elite derived from illegal exports—principally gemstones, ivory, and subsidized commodities—is still not fully known. (See West, "Structural Adjustment in Zambia"; and Venkatesh Seshamani, "Towards Structural Transformation with a Human Focus: The Economic Programmes and Policies of Zambia in the 1980's," *Innocenti Occasional Papers* no. 7 [Florence: Spedale degli Innocenti, 1990].)

67. One example that reflects this is that voter turnouts were higher in the 1978 elections than in 1973. While Kaunda ran unopposed in both elections, in 1978 the opposition decided that a stance of "active rejection" was preferable to boycotting the elections as they had in 1973. Voter turnouts were also higher because there were more concerted attempts at voter education, six hundred new polls were opened, and there was a heightened political atmosphere due to Zambia's role in Zimbabwe's struggle for independence. (Gertzel, *One-Party State in Zambia,* chapter 2.)

68. Gertzel, *One-Party State in Zambia;* and Gulhati, "Impasse in Zambia." Both UNIP and the MUZ supported equal pay scales for black and white workers.

69. Robert Bates, *Unions, Parties, and Political Development: Copperworkers in Zambia* (New Haven: Yale University Press, 1971), chapter 7.

70. Szeftel, "Political Graft."

71. In the 1973 elections, for example, the no vote was much higher in mining constituencies and in urban areas where the UPP was able to undermine UNIP support. The no vote was 11.2 percent in 1973 and 19.3 percent in 1978. Voter turnout was also low in 1978: 39.8 percent (versus a still low 45 percent for the 1990 elections). For details, see Bratton, "Zambia Starts Over."

72. Report of the Social Action Program (SAP), Lusaka, 1991; and Callaghy, "Between State and Market." The rescinded 1973 agreement called for consumer subsidy removal, wage freezes, and export diversification. The 1978 agreement called for the elimination of arrears on external credit, a 10 percent devaluation of the kwacha, a halt to the expansion of domestic credit, a wage freeze, higher agricultural producer prices, and rationalized copper production. In 1980, a three-year Extended Fund Facility for SDR 800 million was signed with the IMF with the objective of comprehensive structural adjustment, including expenditure restraint, reform of monetary and fiscal policy, redirection of government spending from urban subsidies to agriculture, revamping of copper production, a review of exchange rate policy, and the elimination of debt arrears. The following series of agreements culminated in Kaunda's ill-fated May 1987 decision.

73. Author's interview with Emmanuel Kasonde, Former Permanent Secretary for Economics, 1964–1972, and Current Finance Minister, MMD Government, Lusaka, December 15, 1991.

74. "Death Toll Rises to 23 in Zambia," *Washington Post,* June 28, 1990.

75. Interviews with Aarnes, and Torsten Wetterblad, Senior Economist, Swedish Development Cooperation Office, Lusaka, November 18, 1991.

76. Cadman Atta Mills, "Structural Adjustment in Sub-Saharan Africa," EDI Policy Seminar Report no. 18, World Bank, Washington, D.C., 1989, p. 8.

77. Interview with Kasonde. One could argue that in other countries public understanding of measures and careful explanation for them has done a great deal to make them palatable. In Peru, the August 1990 shock program, in which food prices went up by 500 percent and gasoline by 3,000 percent overnight, was carefully explained to the public in a two-hour address by the Prime/Finance Minister. Not only were there no riots, but in the trimester after the shock, Prime Minister Juan Carlos Hurtado Miller was the most popular man in the country! (For a detailed account, see C. Graham, *Peru's APRA: Parties, Politics, and the Elusive Quest for Democracy* [Boulder: Lynne Rienner Publishers, 1992].)

78. Seshamani, "Towards Structural Transformation."

79. The maize meal issue is discussed in detail in the next section. A detailed account of the decisionmaking process that preceded the implementation of the measures appears in West, "Structural Adjustment in Zambia," pp. 92–95. Not only did the government not research consumption patterns well—only the poorest of the poor were consuming roller meal, as the price differential prior to December 1986 was not that great and the quality difference was, but the government also failed to properly explain a rather complex new pricing system to either the millers or to the public. In the millers' case, the into-mill price was raised on December 4, and only on December 9, the last day of the riots, did the government send a memo to the millers explaining the subsidy system and enclosing forms for registration. The registration process could hardly have been completed in less than a week, and the millers faced a minimum of a two-week delay if they produced and sold subsidized roller meal. (West, "Structural Adjustment in Zambia.")

80. Gulhati, "Impasse in Zambia."

81. I would like to thank Joan Nelson for introducing me to this concept in a series of discussions. For details in specific countries, see C. Graham, "The Politics

of Pro-Poor Measures During Adjustment: Bolivia's Emergency Social Fund," *World Development* 20, no. 9 (September 1992); and C. Graham, "From Emergency Employment to Social Investment: Alleviating Poverty in Chile," *Brookings Occasional Papers* (The Brookings Institution, Washington, D.C., November 1991).

82. Interview with Robin Hinson-Jones, Political Officer, U.S. Embassy, Lusaka, November 14, 1991. Hinson-Jones points out that one reason that the MMD was able to succeed was that so many civil servants helped them in terms of organization and access to information. UNIP's strategy of threatening to fire MMD supporters was, if anything, counterproductive.

83. John Battersby, "Zambia's Gutsy Independent Press Had Key Role in Election," *Christian Science Monitor,* November 8, 1991. Several observers interviewed noted the increase in freedom in the two years before the election. Blatantly antigovernment newspapers such as the *Weekly Post* began to operate freely, and the highly public trial and sentencing to death for murder of Kaunda's son, for example, demonstrated the extent to which the judiciary had established its independence. Kaunda deserves credit for allowing this process to continue.

84. Interview with Hinson-Jones.

85. For a brief account of the Chilean transition, see C. Graham, "Chile's Return to Democracy," *Brookings Review* (spring 1990). In Zambia, the important role of Jimmy Carter's team in guaranteeing free elections was cited by many observers and the press throughout the author's interviews. For example, Maffat Muza, MMD Member, November 7, 1991; Chisasa Mulenga, Election Observer and MPU Staff Member, November 15, 1991; and P. Henriot, Election Observer, November 19, 1991.

86. "UNIP Seeks to Oust Kaunda," *Weekly Post,* November 15–21, 1991; "UNIP Chiefs Split," *Zambia Daily Mail,* November 15, 1991; and "2000 Desert UNIP in Chipata," *Zambia Daily Mail,* November 12, 1991.

87. MMD Political Manifesto, Lusaka, 1991.

88. Mike Hall, "Kaunda Officials Accused of Big Copper Fraud," *Financial Times,* September 25, 1991.

89. *UNIP: The Critical Choice* (Lusaka: Party Manifesto, 1991). For detail on the Kaunda government's manipulation of safety net programs, see Graham, *Safety Nets.*

90. Such an approach was echoed by key members of his team, such as the finance minister, who stressed that "the people voted you into power, they are the bosses, they have a right to be consulted." (Interview with Kasonde.)

91. *Weekly Post,* November 8–14, 1991; "UNIP Abused State Funds," *Sunday Times of Zambia,* November 17, 1991; "Work Hard, Cabinet Told," *Times of Zambia,* November 12, 1991; and author's following of press and television coverage in the two-week period following the election in Lusaka. At the time of reinitiating trade, Chiluba stated: "Zambia may not be the centre of the universe, but it is the centre of our universe."

92. "Get Back Coop Markets," *Times of Zambia,* November 14, 1991.

93. "UNIP Homes Stoned," *Times of Zambia,* November 11, 1991; and "Evict UNIP Officials," *Times of Zambia,* November 11, 1991.

94. "UNIP Crumbles," *Weekly Post,* November 15–21, 1991. Not only were there mass-scale UNIP defections, even in Eastern province, but there was an immediate move to attempt to oust Kaunda from power. It is difficult to imagine UNIP as any kind of coherent political force any time in the near future.

95. This is frighteningly reminiscent of the last few months of the APRA government in Peru, in which all kinds of unrealistic promises were made to labor

unions, and at the same time, state sector workers were not paid for the last two months, leaving an enormous debt for an already indebted new government. (For details see C. Graham, *Peru's APRA.*)

96. Interview with Lester Gordon, Harvard Institute for International Development adviser to the Finance Ministry, Lusaka, December 16, 1991.

97. "Bank of Zambia Fails to Cope with Its Accounts," *Weekly Post,* November 8–14, 1991.

98. This is demonstrated by the contrasting cases of Peru, Zambia, and several Eastern European countries on the one hand, and Senegal on the other. In Peru, for example, the strong mandate given to Alberto Fujimori in 1990 because he was from outside the established political system gave him a great deal of room to maneuver and allowed him to implement a draconian stabilization program (which he had actually campaigned against!) with virtually no popular protest. The Chiluba government's liberalizing of the maize price without popular protest is also indicative. In both cases, people voted for political change and an end to prolonged processes of economic decline and were willing to bear some sacrifices to attain those objectives. In Senegal, in contrast, political competition remains limited to debate among a small elite and is dominated by the governing Parti Socialiste. Popular unrest in the face of adjustment measures is as often a protest against the political system as against the measures themselves, as the February 1988 riots indicated. For detail, see chapter 7 of Graham, *Peru's APRA.*

99. Even some high-level UNIP officials agreed on the need to move forward quickly in implementing a free market strategy! (Interview with John Liswaniso, Permanent Secretary, National Commission for Development Planning, Lusaka, November 13, 1991.)

100. There were even criticisms that Chiluba had "co-opted" unions into supporting his adjustment program. (Melinda Ham, "Zambia: One Year On," *Africa Report* (January-February 1993.)

101. Britain forgave 60 percent of Zambia's debt following the election, while the United States made the forgiveness of $110 million in debt conditional on an agreement with the multilaterals, which followed shortly thereafter. In January 1992, the government worked out a deal with bilateral donors to pay the $50 million to the World Bank that had left it suspended from Bank operations. The deal allowed the Bank to resume Zambia's disbursements and to plan a new lending program. "Late Arrears Deal Precedes Preston's Zambia Trip," *The World Bank Watch,* February 17, 1992; "UK to Cancel Zambia's Debt," *Zambia Daily Mail,* November 9, 1991; and "US to Scrap $270 Million Debt," *Times of Zambia,* November 18, 1991.

102. Chris Chitanda, "Loyalists Grab Key Cabinet Portfolios," *Weekly Post,* November 8–14, 1991; and *Sunday Times of Zambia,* November 10, 1991. Five different factions were identified in the Chiluba cabinet. The first was the "Group of Seven" and included Defense Minister Benjamin Mwila and Foreign Affairs Minister Vernon Mwaanga. This group's influence stemmed from their financial strength and connections to the private sector. The second faction was the "unionists," led by Home Affairs Minister Newstead Zimba. Chiluba owed a great deal to Zimba and the labor movement, where he developed his leadership skills, and which gave him a platform from which to launch his political career. The third faction was the "Young Turks," led by Higher Education Minister Akashambatwa Mbikusita-Lewanika. This group has its origins in the Zambia Research Foundation, a University of Zambia–based pressure group that was key in the promoting the formation of the MMD. Mbikusita-Lewanika and Derrick Chitala of this

group were the organizers of the 1990 Garden House symposium on multiparty democracy that resulted in the founding of the MMD. Within the cabinet, this group claimed the most of the ministerial and deputy ministerial posts filled by educated young professionals. The fourth group was the "Veterans' Group," which was led by Finance Minister Kasonde. It was a Bembe-speaking group whose regional strength lay in the north. Prior to the announcement of the ministerial posts, this group served as a kitchen cabinet and had been strongly opposed to the appointment of Levy Mwanawasa, a technocrat and outsider, as vice president. The fifth and least influential faction was the "party men," which included Minister Without Portfolio Godfrey Miyanda, the de facto number three in government; Dipak Patel, the MMD campaign manager; Guy Scott, the Agricultural Minister; Stan Kristofar, the Information Minister; and others with no strong interest group representation who had joined the MMD to fight for democracy.

103. Although there have been some negative effects of the health reforms, in particular due to new user fees, the reforms are credited with revitalizing a sector that was virtually dysfunctional. For detail, see C. Graham, "Macroeconomic and Sectoral Reforms in Zambia: A Stakeholders' Approach?" (Brookings Institution, June 1995, mimeographed).

104. Ham, "Zambia: One Year On."

105. Tony Hawkins, "Now Zambia Points Way to Fiscal Rectitude in Adversity," *Financial Times,* February 10, 1993.

106. Interview with Kasonde.

107. Melinda Ham, "Zambia: Luring Investment," *Africa Report* (September/October 1992).

108. "Zambia's Goal: Both Austerity and More Social Spending," *The World Bank Watch,* February 24, 1992.

109. "A Preliminary Report of the Effectiveness of the Coupon System," Prices and Incomes Commission, Lusaka, August 1990. Maize-related subsidies as a share of the government budget reached their highest level in 1988 at 16.9 percent.

110. Prices and Incomes Commission, Household Survey, Lusaka, August 1991.

111. World Bank, Human Resources Division for Southern Africa; and the author's visits to the Lusaka program offices as well as to several community projects in November 1991.

112. Interview with Clare Barkworth, Technical Adviser to the Social Recovery Project, Lusaka, April 24, 1995, and presentation by the SRP Management Team, World Bank, Washington, D.C., May 12, 1995. The SRP's activities and funding profile is 94 percent spent on community initiatives; 3 percent spent on poverty monitoring; and 3 percent spent on poverty analysis.

6

Highjacking Change: Zaire's "Transition" in Comparative Perspective

Michael G. Schatzberg

Since the late 1980s the world has witnessed the decline and, in many cases, the seeming demise of various forms of authoritarian rule. Besieged everywhere by the forces of change, long-ruling autocrats of both the left and the right have pursued a range of strategies and tactics to remain in power. Few have gracefully ceded their coveted positions as heads of a state-party without resistance; fewer still have openly and sincerely embraced the new crosscurrents of political change. The vast majority of them have waged a fierce and occasionally violent political struggle to retain both their positions and their power. Zaire's president, Mobutu Sese Seko, is no exception.

Even when autocrats have either departed or been removed from the scene, however, we should not assume that the political struggle is over, because they often leave behind them political forces and erstwhile allies who continue to fight to preserve or restore the old order that nurtured them. The Nigerian military is a case in point, as Peter Lewis explains in Chapter 7. Although the precise tactics such politicians pursue in hijacking the processes of political change may vary because of specific contextual differences, certain strategic commonalities have nevertheless begun to emerge from the welter of information surrounding particular cases.

This chapter is about the "hijacking," or the co-optation and subversion, of political movements directed either against autocrats who have long been part of the political landscape or against the repressive and antidemocratic forms of political order that have survived their departure. Except indirectly, this chapter does not discuss "democratization"—a term of distinctly limited applicability in the present political moment. Although it is certain that we are witnessing an increasingly clamorous retreat from autocracy, to label this historically open-ended autocratic recessional as democratization is to confuse a normatively desired goal with a complex series of political processes whose outcome is far from predetermined.

Simple logic would dictate that our analyses should not conflate the substance of democracy with the process that might eventually lead there. Democratization, in other words, is a term best used retroactively, after certain democratic thresholds have been crossed. Unfortunately, in most of Africa this has simply not yet occurred, so discussions of democratization in various African states are premature. Furthermore, similar discussions of democratization are equally premature, and for the same reason, when they occur in reference to Russia, Eastern Europe, Central Asia, and other portions of the globe.[1]

How have authoritarian rulers and the political forces they represent thus far subverted the political movements directed against them? In the first section of this chapter I will focus mostly on Zaire, a country that Basil Davidson correctly sees as paradigmatic.[2] Because a paradigmatic case is never unique, in the second section I shall also discuss similar processes in Kenya and Cameroon, where presidents Daniel arap Moi and Paul Biya have tried to channel the forces of political change so as not to threaten their regimes.[3] This section will also provide a more focused attempt at explanation through a series of analytic explorations centered on the themes of international influence, institutional control, and political legitimacy. All three of these cases show arresting variations on a similar theme; all are instructive as we explore the hijacking of political change in Africa.

■ Mobutu's Third Republic, 1990 to the Present

□ The Background

By the end of the 1980s, trends and events both outside and inside Zaire had combined to create an explosive situation. Internally, both the economic and political situations had continued to deteriorate. In April 1990, U.S.$1.00 equalled Zaires (Z) 530. In June 1993, on the parallel currency market in Kinshasa, U.S.$1.00 = Z 4,000,000. As the salaries of the army and civil service became more sporadic and less able to ensure survival, the second economy mushroomed.[4] As it grew, the state's ability to provide its citizens with even the most rudimentary social services declined to almost nothing. In many locales, the army degenerated into groups of warriors for hire. The Catholic Church, moreover, began to speak openly and explicitly of the country's crisis of political legitimacy. Zairians now perceived Mobutu, his extended political family, and the barons of the state-party—the Mouvement Populaire de la Révolution (MPR)—as voracious bandits who gave little thought to the needs of the society as a whole.[5]

Externally, the end of the Cold War had left Mobutu vulnerable in sev-

eral regards. First, the revolutions of 1989 in Eastern Europe and the resulting downfall of several long-ruling Communist leaders had a marked effect
on Zairian politics. Zairians particularly noted the political fall and brutal
execution of Romania's dictator, Nicolae Ceauşescu, because Mobutu and
Ceauşescu had long maintained a cordial and mutually flattering relationship. In addition, both had operated state-parties based on the exploitation
and repression of their citizens; both had increasingly come to rely on their
security forces and political police to remain in power; both had become
fabulously wealthy by using the resources of the state as their own; and
both had salted the key institutions of the state with relatives and loyal
friends, however incompetent they might have been.[6]

Second, the end of the Cold War also meant that the West's major reason for supporting the Mobutu regime had disappeared. No longer could
French, Belgian, or especially U.S. administrations justify their political
support of Mobutu's regime to increasingly skeptical domestic constituencies as a necessary evil in the great game of Cold War geopolitics. The
facile formula that had long shaped U.S. foreign policy toward Zaire,
"Mobutu or chaos," with its corollary that chaos would shortly be followed
by communism, could no longer withstand even the friendliest critical
scrutiny.[7] In addition, as the Cold War wound down in the late 1980s, it had
also become apparent that Mobutu could no longer be seen as a credible
arbiter in the Angolan crisis.

Lastly, these extraordinary events had already had an effect on politics
in other African states. Beginning with Benin in 1989, the cry went up from
long-suppressed opposition groups and politicians throughout the continent
for the convocation of national conferences grouping all of society's politically active and aware forces. Students, workers, women, and other groups
demanded political change. Civil society, at least in its urban, associational
form, emerged from a lengthy hibernation. The desired national conferences would be sovereign and would have the power to decide basic political questions pertaining to the new constitutional order, for example, the
type of government, the number of political parties, the frequency of elections, and the enshrinement of basic civil and political liberties such as a
free press.

In 1990, President Mobutu decided to hold a series of public meetings
to discuss the country's problems and to solicit suggestions, via written
memoranda, on how to solve them. This was both a clever ploy to forestall
potentially more extreme forms of protest against the regime and an effort
to channel popular discontent into forms which the regime's security apparatus could handle easily. Mobutu's intent seems to have been to provide a
safety valve for a carefully controlled venting of popular discontent while
insuring that these "slight" manifestations of unhappiness did not develop
into anything more substantial that could potentially threaten either his

position of supreme power or the sanctity of his state-party regime. That Mobutu intended this operation to contain rather than to promote change is demonstrated clearly in his choice of Mokolo wa Mpombo, former head of the political police, to become the director of the Office of National Consultation.[8] The outcome of the exercise surprised the regime. Thousands of people and groups seized the opening to voice their extreme displeasure. Many memoranda called for Mobutu's resignation, the dismantling of the MPR, and the installation of a multiparty democracy. Others demanded an end to the abuses of the state's security services. The level of tension in Kinshasa was acute.

☐ *The Speech, the Clarification, the Massacre*

On April 24, 1990, Mobutu delivered a speech that sounded the death knell of the Second Republic. In ushering in the Third Republic, Mobutu authorized the formation of three political parties, resigned as head of the MPR, neatly separated party and state, and insisted that in his capacity of head of state (a role he did not relinquish) he would be an arbiter above the play of partisan politics. He was to be the last resort—*l'ultime recours*.[9] He also stated that a prime minister would be designated to form a government that would manage the political transition. In formally divorcing party and state, the president was also insisting on the depoliticization of the civil service and the armed forces, a point that he made explicitly. But it was clear that the coercive arms of the state (the army, the gendarmerie, the political police) would remain under Mobutu's direct control.

    Reactions were not long in coming. Concerned about its future, the MPR's hard-line faction pressured Mobutu to modify his position. The president probably listened, for on May 3, 1990, another speech reassured his cronies that because political parties did not yet exist in Zaire, they therefore could not hold marches, meetings, or demonstrations. The president agreed, however, that future leaders could organize informal consultations in their living rooms "around a cup of tea, a glass of lemonade or any other drink, but preferably nonalcoholic, to permit them, calmly and reflectively, to put down the bases of their future political parties."[10] In other words, these changes in the political configuration of the state were both quite formalistic and introduced from the summit without consulting the populace or its recognized representatives. According to the *Mobutiste* scheme, democracy was to be a top-down affair.[11]

    But the genie was already out of the bottle. In the aftermath of the April 24 speech, a lively and relatively unfettered press appeared almost overnight. No longer did the regime enjoy a monopoly on the means of mass communication, and this marked a major departure from the political contours of the Second Republic. In addition, regardless of the restricted number that might have been legally authorized, a profusion of new political parties wrought a second major transformation in Zairian politics. Suddenly, Etienne Tshisekedi's Union pour la Démocratie et le Progrès Social (UDPS), founded in 1982, was no longer the only political organization in opposition. The regime persecuted Tshisekedi and other leaders of the illegal UDPS, throughout the 1980s. By the end of the decade, Tshisekedi's political stature was considerable. But now there were also entirely new political parties that were often attached to erstwhile barons of the regime, such as Joseph Ileo or Nguza Karl-I-Bond, who had hastily left the MPR. These groupings seemed to display some independent existence and were often closely associated with one of these new press outlets. Still other parties, however, had no independent existence outside their name, letterhead, and an occasional speech by their founder. Observers believed that many of them were under President Mobutu's political and financial control.

But while Mobutu experimented with certain formalistic and institutional changes, he seemed unwilling to change his regime's abusive behavior toward the population. On the night of May 11–12, 1990, the regime slaughtered university students in Lubumbashi. When politically active, anti-Mobutu students moved against the regime's network of campus informers, drawn mostly from the president's Ngbandi ethnic group, commandos surrounded the campus and massacred students who had been active in antiregime politics. Although the precise number of dead remains disputed, it is safe to say that approximately sixty students were murdered.[12]

☐ *Spiraling Violence and Political Deadlock*

A striking political evolution occurred in Kinshasa during the remainder of 1990 and 1991. For one thing, there was an explosion of organizational life as civil society was reborn. And for another, the regime's "authorization" of an unfettered multipartyism belatedly recognized in statute what had already occurred in fact. Several of the more important and visible of these new parties made tentative and halting attempts at unity through an umbrella front called the Sacred Union (Union Sacrée), which in July 1991 counted 115 members. Nonetheless, Mobutu was able to irrigate the seeds of discord among the opposition with the customary offers of public office and the usual array of financial blandishments. One veteran of the First Republic, Thomas Kanza, reflecting generally on the state of politics, wrote: "Are we manipulated and remote-controlled by money? Certainly. It seems to me that it is money which leads the political dance in Zaire. . . . Ideological oppositions are almost nonexistent. The political oppositions due to differences in political programs are only theoretical. Everything, or almost everything, is a function of money."[13] Long adept at the co-optation of his political enemies, Mobutu excelled at this game.

Much of this period witnessed a political minuet between the regime and the various factions of the opposition as they struggled over whether a national conference à la Benin was to occur. Precisely who would be represented and in what proportions? Would this conference be a "sovereign" constitutional convention? Would it have the writ to call *everything* into question? Could it establish the contours of a new and presumably post-Mobutu political order? The political atmosphere in Kinshasa was tense, a barely repressed violence in the air, when the National Conference formally opened at the end of July 1991.

On September 20, 1991, approximately three thousand members of the 31st Parachute Brigade, usually considered an elite and disciplined force loyal to the president, mutinied. Ostensibly at issue was their meager pay packet. The preceding month their officers had promised them a raise after they had threatened to take matters into their own hands if something were not done to ameliorate their paltry salaries and atrocious living conditions. When their salary boost did not materialize at the end of September, they ignited a bout of pillaging that lasted for days and that all but destroyed Kinshasa's commercial and industrial infrastructure. Perhaps equally upsetting to them was the fact that the soldiers could only angrily compare their own derisory monthly salaries of Z 200,000, just about enough to buy one sack of manioc, with the per diem of Z 750,000 bestowed on delegates to the National Conference.

Although this must remain speculative, Mobutu was probably aware of the situation prevailing in one of the most critical units in his army. It is thus at least conceivable that he simply permitted matters to run their course as his troops rioted, attempting in this way to gain foreign support for his regime by demonstrating to his friends abroad that the alternative to his ironfisted rule was, indeed, chaos. It is also at least conceivable, and these are not mutually exclusive propositions, that the regime tried to channel and direct this mutiny. In this regard it is significant that the first wave of military looters systematically spared the goods, property, and wealth of President Mobutu and his closest collaborators. Ironically, however, later waves of both civilian and military looters deliberately avoided the property of prominent members of the opposition while putting to the torch the houses and stores of those still in the MPR. They also attacked the property of the "dinosaurs" who were implicated in the excesses of the Second Republic, even if they had subsequently left the MPR to form other political parties. Others targeted in this wave were foreign nationals whose governments had supported the Mobutu regime. Parenthetically, Mobutu did get the attention of his allies, and the Belgians and French sent paratroopers to evacuate their citizens from Kinshasa. But these interventions, unlike those of Shaba I and Shaba II in the late 1970s, were in fact limited to the rescue of European civilians from the increasing disorder. In the end, more than 100 people were killed and more than fifteen hundred were wounded.[14]

One result of this episode was that Mobutu, for the first time since he had seized the state in 1965, agreed to share power with members of the opposition. The outcome was an uneasy coalition with Tshisekedi as prime minister and Mobutu as president and head of state. This *cohabitation* of sworn enemies lasted only a month before Mobutu decided to revoke Tshisekedi's mandate and remove him from office, perhaps because the latter was making a serious attempt to gain control of the armed forces— something Mobutu simply would not tolerate. The removal was a typically subtle Mobutiste maneuver: The president dispatched troops who locked Tshisekedi and his team out of their government offices. The political stalemate contributed to the frustration of Kinshasa's citizens who found themselves in the streets facing troops loyal to Mobutu throughout the month of October as Tshisekedi refused to relinquish his position as head of government.[15] In November, the ever-ambitious Nguza Karl-I-Bond broke ranks with the opposition to declare that he would be available to serve as prime minister in a new government, an offer which was soon forthcoming from the presidential palace.

During the last months of 1991 and most of 1992 Mobutu and the opposition tussled continuously over the shape of the government. While these political scenes were played out, the economy continued to decline and the level of endemic violence in Kinshasa continued to rise. The powder keg exploded anew in February 1992 when troops loyal to Mobutu opened fire on a peaceful rally led by Catholic priests. Billed as a "March of Hope," the event was convened to protest Mobutu's continued leadership as well as to demand the resumption of the National Conference, which had been suspended in January. Published in the local press, the formal appeal and invitation emphasized that

> Zairians are constantly victims of a society expressly organized with the sole goal of assuring a profit and maintaining the powers of a minority through the limitation of rights and the exploitation of the largest number. . . . This disaster requires efficacious and urgent solutions. The people have understood that they must not remain powerless when faced with pillage, corruption, extortion, the inversion of values where illicit enrichment, magic, maraboutage, fetishism predominate. . . . We invite you to a march of hope . . . to demand the immediate reopening without conditions of the works of the Sovereign National Conference.[16]

According to eyewitness accounts, soldiers loyal to the regime launched tear gas grenades and then fired on marchers in several parts of the city.

Despite the low number of casualties cited in the Western press, other sources indicate that forty-nine marchers were killed and 106 were wounded when the troops opened fire.[17]

Two months later, in April 1992, the Conference resumed after much wrangling between Mobutu and the opposition and declared itself to be "sovereign." Under the presidency of a compromise candidate, Laurent Monsengwo Pasinya, the Archbishop of Kisangani, the conference concerned itself not only with the shape of the future but also with the shape of the past. Committees were formed to look into the political assassination of numerous Zairian leaders as well as to determine who benefited economically from the theft of the nation's wealth and resources under Mobutu's rule. In these instances the purpose of these committees and their final reports was to attribute responsibility and blame where that was possible and to educate Zairians about the making of their own history. One result was a steady stream of publicity and press commentary placing Mobutu and the MPR regime in a less than flattering light.[18]

In August 1992 the conference appointed Tshisekedi as prime minister, thus replacing Nguza, who was seen as collaborating with Mobutu in an attempt to gain supreme power for himself. The strain between Nguza and Tshisekedi was no doubt augmented by reports of violence between their respective ethnic groups (Lunda and Luba) in Shaba Province. Tensions steadily escalated between Mobutu and Tshisekedi until the end of the year. In December the conference adjourned with a declaration that its work would be continued by a transitional legislature, the High Council of the Republic, which Mobutu promptly suspended.

Throughout this period Zaire's economic straits had become ever more desperate. In late January 1993 the crisis intensified when Tshisekedi instructed Kinshasa shopkeepers not to accept Mobutu's new Z 5,000,000 banknotes (then worth less than $2.00) as legal tender. Unfortunately, Mobutu had paid his troops using the new currency and when they discovered that the new money was no good, they again vented their anger and frustration in a destructive fit of pillage and plunder. The French ambassador was murdered, and French troops again entered Zaire to protect their nationals. Of course, Mobutu responded to all of this by, once again, dismissing Tshisekedi while the troops surrounded the High Council of the Republic and held legislators hostage.[19]

By March 1993 Mobutu controlled the forces of coercion and the treasury, while Tshisekedi controlled the High Council. Mobutu had also reconvened the old national assembly to act as "his" legislature. The "transition," in other words, seemed locked in a permanent stalemate. Mobutu then successfully lured Faustin Birindwa, formerly of the UDPS, from the ranks of the opposition and named him prime minister. The High Council of the Republic rejected the nomination, once again declaring its support of

Tshisekedi. Tshisekedi, of course, simply refused to recognize the legitimacy of the Birindwa government. An already confused situation thus became
even more complex as three would-be poles of power competed for control,
instead of the two that had dominated the political arena for the previous
eighteen months.[20]
    In the countryside the violence continued. Reports throughout much of
1993 indicated that ethnic strife was on the upswing in Shaba and Kivu
provinces, as thousands became both internal and external refugees. In July
the situation became even more acute in those troubled regions as accounts
surfaced of "ethnic cleansing" wrought against Kasaians living in Shaba, as
well as against Zairians of ethnic Rwandan origin living in Kivu. Even
worse, there were clear indications that the Mobutu regime had knowingly
fomented and encouraged the ethnic hatred and violence in both Kivu and
Shaba. In December 1993 Shaba declared its "autonomy" under Nguza.[21]
    In late September 1993 Mobutu and the opposition finally arrived at a
formula to break the deadlock and end the anomaly of dual, or even triple,
government. The agreement called for a Transition Parliament to replace
the High Council of the Republic. But this deal, like others between
Mobutu and the opposition, was short-lived. In January 1994, after further
economic, social, and political turmoil exacerbated by the chaotic and
badly implemented introduction of a new currency (the New Zaire),
Mobutu announced that he was dismissing both his own Birindwa government and opposition Tshisekedi government. As part of the package,
Mobutu also declared "his" parliament dissolved and proclaimed that he
would appoint a new government. Tshisekedi, of course, rejected the initiative, claiming that Mobutu had no authority to dismiss his government.
Later in the month Mobutu tried to merge his national assembly with the
High Council, in a move one opposition politician described as an "institutional coup." In February 1994 the World Bank declared Zaire "insolvent,"
closing its office in Kinshasa and canceling all of the country's outstanding
lines of credit.[22]
    Since then, the crisis has continued and, in some ways, worsened. The
genocide in Rwanda that began in mid-1994 and the resulting flood of
refugees into eastern Zaire has created further strains on an already devas-
tated economy.[23] Moreover, a state that once aspired to control most
aspects of daily life throughout the country now scarcely exists outside
Kinshasa and a few other urban areas. Since Léon Kengo wa Dondo
became prime minister in June 1994, Mobutu's political tangles have been
as much with him as they are with Tshisekedi and the rest of the Sacred
Union. Kengo, despite his reputation as one of the most rapacious of
Mobutu's former henchmen, has enjoyed some support from the West
because he has tried to introduce some needed economic reforms over
Mobutu's objections. National elections, currently scheduled for 1997,

have been repeatedly postponed, and, ironically, Mobutu is one of the very few politicians who now wants them to occur. He is no doubt confident that he will be able to hijack them.

■ Explanatory Factors

This portion of the chapter will explore why anti-authoritarian political change is susceptible to hijacking. In doing so, it compares the experiences of Zaire with those of Kenya and Cameroon along three dimensions. First, the section on the international dimension advances the notion that although the changes that have occurred in the international system since the end of the Cold War generally favor democratic rule, some of the messages emanating from various international sources are nevertheless quite ambiguous. Not all international influence flows in an anti-authoritarian direction, and external support for various political opposition movements is rarely unqualified. The second section deals with institutional control. It notes that long-serving autocrats continue to maintain control over key state institutions that facilitate their attempts to hijack political change. Finally, the third section discusses political legitimacy, arguing that political change is likely to be a slow process and that regimes will be in continuous danger of hijacking as long as these new political orders lack legitimacy.

☐ The International Dimension

Addressing a predominantly Kenyan audience in late 1993, Chief Emeka Anyaoku, the Secretary General of the Commonwealth, offered an appreciation of the role of the international system in the current phase of political change. "It says everything," he argued, "about the political sea change which has taken place in Africa today, [that] there are few plausible African politicians who would seriously argue that the balance of political virtue is to be found on the side of the one-party system."[24] Anyaoku is correct. The international political climate today is far different from what it had been during the Cold War. African state-parties no longer have a ready-made source of international approval and legitimacy in the Eastern bloc states and, at least for the moment, there would appear to be no coherent contender to rival the dominance of democracy as a source of international political legitimacy. With the dissolution of the Soviet empire in the late 1980s and early 1990s and the growing intellectual and political disrepute of the socialist model of the welfare state, liberal democracy in its multiparty and capitalist guises is the only game in town.[25]

The meaning of this enormous change remains unclear. During the

Cold War the West often paid no more than lip service to the principles of democracy. The promotion of democratic ideals and regimes often had to cede pride of place to the globalist policy of containing the Soviet Union and its allies, which was the primary political struggle for most Western policymakers. More than occasionally in various parts of the Third World, antidemocratic tyrants could receive support from the West if they simply recited the anti-Soviet mantra. Mobutu was a classic example. He and his tyrannical regime were warmly supported by every U.S. president from John Kennedy to George Bush.[26] Kenya, unlike Zaire, maintained under both Jomo Kenyatta and Daniel arap Moi an occasionally lively tradition of parliamentary debate and electoral rotation. As in Zaire, however, there had always been an ominous tradition of political assassination, which cost Pio Gama Pinto, Tom Mboya, J. M. Kariuki, and Robert Ouko their lives.[27]

During the Cold War Mobutu knew that if his regime were seriously imperiled, his friends in the West would react because Zaire was strategically important for its mineral wealth, its military bases, its window on Angola and southern Africa, and its borders with nine neighboring states. This was certainly what occurred in the late 1970s during Shaba I and Shaba II. But the European military interventions of 1991 and 1993 were quite different—and quite limited to the protection of their citizens at risk. Kenya, however, never became a major battlefield in the Cold War. But it, too, had some strategic importance in the eyes of the West given its proximity to the Indian Ocean, the Horn of Africa, and the Persian Gulf. For some years Kenya granted the U.S. Navy access to port and refueling facilities at Mombasa. Cameroon had much less importance in the Cold War than even Kenya, but the repressive regimes of Ahmadou Ahidjo and Paul Biya were firmly under France's African umbrella and, therefore, not a source of concern or preoccupation.[28]

By the 1990s, however, strategic importance had become a much less vital factor. The West thus became more active in promoting democracy, good governance, and aid for nongovernmental organizations in civil society. In many instances a simple focus on the formal, institutional aspects of democracy was easier to advance than an approach seeking to encourage the more complex political and cultural substance of the phenomenon. The number of political parties thus became crucial; "free and fair" elections became a must. In Zaire, for example, from 1990 to 1993 the United States probably facilitated Mobutu's attempts to hijack political change by maintaining that Mobutu, as president of the republic, was a legitimate part of the transition process that would lead to free and fair elections, rather than a serious impediment to it. In Kenya President Moi came under enormous pressure to "open" the Kenyan political arena in 1990 and 1991. The international financial institutions and the donor community brought their economic power to bear and turned off the financial tap. The pressure was

effective, and Moi yielded to Western desires in this matter. His regime
authorized opposition political parties, and multiparty elections were held
in late 1992. To absolutely no one's surprise, the opposition fragmented and
Moi's Kenya African National Union (KANU), long the ruling state-party,
won the election and retained control of the government.

The report of the Commonwealth Observer Group on the December
1992 Kenyan elections, a masterpiece of confusion and contradiction, illustrates nicely the bizarre mental gyrations that this emphasis on institutional
form over political and cultural substance can produce. It is worth citing at
some length.

> It was evident to us from the start that some aspects of the elections were
> not fair . . . problems include a lack of adequate training of registration
> officers, registration of young persons of doubtful age qualification, the
> failure of the proper authorities to issue identity cards to the many citizens
> . . . the incidence of multiple registration. . . . The nomination proceedings
> for parliamentary and civic elections were marred by the physical preven-
> tion of a substantial number of prospective candidates from handing in
> their nomination papers. . . . The campaign was marred in the Rift Valley
> and neighbouring provinces by widespread tribal disturbances, threats and
> harassment of party supporters, in particular supporters of the opposition
> parties . . . widespread bribery by political parties, particularly the ruling
> party. Some of our members witnessed the passing of money in significant
> amounts to party supporters. . . . [As far as] de-linking the activities and
> resources of government from those of the ruling party [is concerned.] . . .
> The Kenyan experience has shown that the failure to implement a timely
> de-linking programme spells trouble for the process of transition.
>
> These elections were an important turning point in Kenya's history
> and for Kenya's future. Despite the fact that the whole process cannot be
> given an unqualified rating as free and fair, the evolution of the process to
> polling day and the subsequent count was increasingly positive to a
> degree that we believe that the results in many instances directly reflect,
> however imperfectly, the expression of the will of the people. It consti-
> tutes a giant step on the road to multiparty democracy.[29]

The bottom line is that even though the elections were seriously flawed,
elections are still elections and these results "in many instances" reflected
"the will of the people." One close observer of the situation argued that the
government had never intended to put on more than a minimally acceptable
election and that "most observers gave the government and its Electoral
Commission failing or near-failing grades on each of the many steps leading up to the casting of ballots, but accorded them relatively high marks on
election day itself. In the final analysis, the government achieved its objective of conducting a 'C-minus' election."[30] Appearance had trumped
essence.

The role of the international system in promoting anti-authoritarian
political movements and in preventing or discouraging the hijacking of

political change may thus be less positive and more ambiguous than is commonly realized. On the one hand external financial pressure opened the Kenyan system, while, on the other hand, at least one international electoral watchdog accepted the validity of an election that had glaring problems.

The October 1992 presidential election in Cameroon is another case that demonstrates the ambiguity of international signals. The Cameroon Supreme Court declared President Paul Biya the victor with 39.9 percent of the vote. The candidate of the Social Democratic Front, John Fru Ndi, came in a close second with 35.9 percent, while the standard-bearer of the National Union for Democracy and Progress, Bello Bouba Maigari, polled 19.2 percent of the vote. But these were the official, state-announced, results. Virtually all observers of this election, both internal and external, agreed that these results were seriously flawed. The National Democratic Institute for International Affairs filed a report that found "serious fault" with the election and noted that its delegation could not "determine the rightful winner of the election." In addition, "widespread irregularities during the preelection period, on election day and in the tabulation of results seriously call into question, for any fair observer, the validity of the outcome . . . the overwhelming weight of responsibility for this failed process lies with the government of Cameroon and President Paul Biya."[31]

In the wake of this election the United States announced that it would suspend the U.S. Agency for International Development's economic assistance program in Cameroon, citing a failure to achieve political and constitutional reforms as well as continuing abuses of authority and disrespect for human rights by the state's coercive arms.[32] The message of the French government was equally clear, however: business as usual and no interruption of economic assistance. Although the Cold War may be over, realpolitik is not. It is thus unrealistic to expect the international system to speak with a single voice on issues of governmental or electoral reform, especially when long-standing political and economic interests are at stake. The anti-authoritarian position French president François Mitterrand enunciated at the La Baule summit in 1990 has to be understood as only one current in French policy—and almost certainly not the most important one. Autocratic rulers can thus use these contradictory and ambiguous messages to provide themselves with breathing space and room to maneuver as they seek to hijack political change in a more congenial direction.

☐ *Institutional Control*

To explain how autocrats such as Mobutu Sese Seko, Daniel arap Moi, and Paul Biya hijack the processes of political change we must also consider the role of state institutions. Although their absolute power has surely been diminished by the recent changes in their respective political systems, these rulers remain relatively powerful because they have not yet relinquished the levers of state command. In many cases they remain, and by far, the most powerful individuals in the polity. The intelligence services, key parts of the military establishment, and crucial sectors of the state's financial apparatus all remain under their direct control or extensive influence. To be sure, these three cases are not identical. Disintegration of the state has proceeded much farther and much faster in Zaire than it has in Kenya, with Cameroon occupying an intermediate position on the continuum. In consequence, the way Mobutu attempts to exercise political control in Zaire looks much more extreme and much less stable than Moi's efforts in Kenya. Moi seduces opposition members of parliament (MPs) with promises of cooperation on development issues in their electoral constituencies, administrative districts, and ethnic bailiwicks. Mobutu purchases his support outright. Biya again falls somewhere between the two.

Although the various opposition parties did win significant numbers of seats in parliament in the 1992 elections, Moi has since then used the considerable powers of his office to lure lost sheep back into the fold. It can be most difficult to resist the financial and political advantages of "making nice" with the president. For example, in November 1993 one FORD-Asili MP from Western Kenya displeased his party's leadership by saying that he was all in favor of cooperation with KANU for the sake of economic development in his area and that he would certainly invite the president to visit his constituency in the future. He added that his people "want to enjoy the fruits of independence and we can only achieve this if we accept and recognise President Moi, who is the head of state." Unsurprisingly, this MP defected to KANU less than one month later after Moi and some of his ministers had circulated substantial sums of money through *harambee* (self-help) development gatherings in the MP's area. President Moi also announced his support for the idea that the new convert to the cause would be KANU's only candidate for the parliamentary seat in the upcoming by-election (which the KANU newcomer won). Even the leader of the official opposition, Oginga Odinga, seemed to be engaged in a rapprochement with the president shortly before his death. In the context of a plea for the resumption of international donor assistance, Odinga said that God had seen to it that President Moi had had a change of heart about matters such as transparency and accountability. One Kenyan publication noted that Odinga sounded more like a KANU bureaucrat than the leader of the official opposition when "he described leadership as God-given and told the opposition to work towards ensuring good governance rather than confronting the government."[33]

It should be noted in passing that parliamentary carpet crossing in response to the government's control over the state's resources is one of the major reasons the Westminster model failed in most West African countries during the early years of independence. W. Arthur Lewis noted the phe-nomenon and sketched the relevant incentives thirty years ago: "The idea that the quality of democracy is to be tested . . . by the extent to which the rights of the minority are respected is novel. Elections are a zero-sum game. Those who vote the wrong way are penalized; the roads in that area are left to deteriorate."[34] This remains a problem even today.

This presidential dominance of key institutions in Zaire, Cameroon, and Kenya coupled with a legacy of twenty or thirty years of deference to presidential authority perhaps helps us to understand why the process of political change was initiated from the top. The autocrats—Moi, Biya, and Mobutu—"granted" "democracy" to the population. In none of these cases did the population well and truly seize the anti-authoritarian initiative. Although in Kenya there were the *saba-saba* disturbances of July 1990— when an estimated twenty-eight prodemocracy demonstrators were shot dead—and the continuing periodic demonstrations in Nairobi after that, there is little reason to assume that these would have been successful at forcing Moi's hand in the absence of sustained pressure for multiparty elec-tions from the international financial institutions and the rest of Kenya's donors. In the final analysis, it was still Moi who bestowed the political opening even though he was under considerable external pressure to do so.

The Zairian experience has been similar. In a remarkable tract analyz-ing Zaire's recent political trajectory, José Mpundu, a Kinshasa-based parish curé active in one of the church's consciousness-raising groups, noted well the fact that it was Mobutu who had bestowed the political opening on the masses in April 1990. He wrote:

> The initiative of consultations with the people was taken by the President of the Republic. In this manner, he wanted to remain the master of the game. It was he who asked the people to tell him what they thought of the country's political institutions and their operation. It was he who went through the results of these consultations with the people. It was again he who presented the conclusions of them in his speech of political orienta-tion on 24 April 1990.
> A rereading of this speech clearly shows that the President of the Republic never had the intention of placing the country on the road of true democracy but rather of a democratization or a "humanization" of the dic-tatorship. . . . Speaking of himself [Mobutu] said, . . . "The Zairian people have clearly spoken about my own person and have asked that I continue to preside over the destinies of our country." This means, in clear terms, that the dictator continues but is going to clothe himself in the skin of a democrat.[35]

Thus it was Mobutu who decided to preempt the threat to his regime by opting for a highly managed transition to a humanized dictatorship with only three authorized political parties and with his own role as supreme and "neutral" arbiter still intact in the transition. Only when this formula proved unworkable did Mobutu set out to manage things by buying up as many of the new parties as he possibly could.[36]

Cameroon's path closely resembled Zaire's. In June 1990 Biya also sought to preempt both the internal and external forces of political change by announcing that he was about to usher in a new political epoch in Cameroon's history. He introduced a series of reforms that eventually led to the revival of freedom of the press and anticipated the advent of a multiparty system in December 1990.[37] Biya wanted to control the process of change, not to accede to its requirements. The repression of popular movements, electoral fraud, and the continuing violation of human rights have all played their part in keeping Biya in power.

If there is a lesson here, it is that anti-authoritarian movements are more vulnerable to hijackings if they are not initiated, or at least sustained, from below in the form of popular agitation led by legitimate representatives of the various organized branches of civil society. Outside actors might well be instrumental in facilitating these transitions, but unless an angry, tired, or frustrated populace actually seizes the moment and demands a hearing, they are unlikely to endure. They are also unlikely to last if the same public cannot maintain its sway long enough to impose changes in both the state's institutional structures and in its critical personnel. Even if political openings are imposed from abroad, local populations must struggle to make them work.

Long-ruling autocrats such as Mobutu, Moi, and Biya have made sure that they have retained control of the key coercive arms of the state and have not hesitated to use coercion, violence, and terror to maintain their dominance. Since such weapons served them well when their regimes were not threatened, it is certainly logical to assume that they would not hesitate to employ these weapons when their political existence is at stake. Once again, the Zairian case is the most extreme. As we have seen, Mobutu has had no qualms about using the levers of coercion against his own people. The massacre of students in Lubumbashi, his cynical manipulation of the armed forces resulting in the September 1991 riots in Kinshasa, and the continuing atmosphere of violence and physical intimidation directed against Tshisekedi and the rest of the political opposition are all examples of the ends to which he will go to remain in power. Because the ever-present reality of violence makes his subsequent attempts to co-opt, subvert, and suborn the members of the opposition seem all the more "reasonable," these violent tactics contribute mightily to the hijacking of political change. In such an atmosphere it seems apparent that genuine anti-authoritarian institutions cannot hope to survive.

As a somber afterthought, it should also be noted that state-driven ethnic cleansing has appeared as a tool of "statecraft" with alarming regularity.

The violence directed against the Luba in Shaba Province is little more than a thinly veiled message from Mobutu to Tshisekedi. Such ethnic violence is also part of Kenya's political scene. Kalenjin "warriors" attacking Gikuyu farmers in Rift Valley Province is but one example. Agents of the state have mobilized these "warriors" to send a two-fold political message to the Gikuyu community. The first part is that President Moi (himself a Tugen, one of the smaller Kalenjin groups) will not relinquish office without a fight; the second part is that the land in the Rift Valley, long a source of heated disputes, belongs to the Kalenjin. Both Moi and Mobutu have long been adept at playing on fears of ethnic exclusion. The reemergence of electoral politics or anti-authoritarian political movements simply provide these masters of manipulation with new arenas in which to ply their trade. They are both very skilled politicians.

☐ *Political Legitimacy*

As I have argued elsewhere, political legitimacy is a necessary, although far from sufficient, condition for the emergence of secure democratic rule.[38] Hijacking political change certainly does not contribute to the construction of a legitimate political order. Political legitimacy should not in any way be assumed to be characteristic of anti-authoritarian movements. Such legitimacy must ultimately derive from popular understandings of, and consensual agreement on, the forms of political behavior that are acceptable in any society. Cultural factors, in other words, may ultimately be of greater importance than any particular institutional arrangement in establishing a politically legitimate order. For example, Johannes Fabian argues that in Zaire it is widely recognized that, according to the cultural axiom, "power is eaten whole" (*le pouvoir se mange entier*).[39] If power in much of sub-Saharan Africa has to be "eaten whole" and is thus indivisible, then the political movements directed against the old and less than democratic political orders will have an uphill struggle because many of those in political opposition are not really democrats interested in sharing power through the elaboration of new institutional arrangements. Instead, they should be seen as those who have been long deprived and are now clamoring to occupy the single place available at the dining room table.

It is thus of great significance that many of these anti-authoritarian movements have remained fragmented. The experiences of both Zaire and Kenya are apposite in this regard. In Zaire much of the opposition is composed of "dinosaurs" who were seriously implicated in the excesses of the Second Republic. Even Etienne Tshisekedi, certainly the most serious of the lot, served in high-ranking positions and was quite close to Mobutu in the early days of the regime. At least Tshisekedi's years of ferocious opposition and single-minded sacrifice have made him a reasonably credible figure. But it is difficult to see the likes of Nguza, Ileo, Kengo, and the others as anything other than opportunists intent on "eating." These men were responsible for some of the worst excesses of the ancien régime. In Kenya, one of the major reasons the opposition was unable to achieve unity prior to the elections in 1992 was because the new parties were all dominated by politicians who cared for little but achieving supreme power. They fought the election over neither ideology nor policy. What mattered to Oginga Odinga, Kenneth Matiba, Mwai Kibacki, and Daniel arap Moi was who got to occupy the one chair at the table, and who got to eat.

For this reason opposition movements have not been able to persuade many of their compatriots that they are politically legitimate alternatives to the long-serving autocrats. Those who are not caught up in the immediacy of urban political life often remain skeptical that the members of the political opposition are harbingers of a new, legitimate, political order. Their policies and stands rarely go beyond the necessity of removing the tyrant. And although many can certainly agree on the necessity of that, opposition leaders have yet to demonstrate their own longer-term relevance to the vast majority of the population. People have long memories and may thus quite realistically view the conversion of many of these politicians to the side of democracy with some well-founded suspicion. The opposition movements, in other words, no more than the autocrats they would replace, have not yet convinced many of their fellow citizens that they will improve matters. People know that such politicians have eaten too well in the past and have yet to be persuaded that this will change if these individuals come to power.

■ Conclusion

Political struggles over the expansion of human rights and governmental accountability are never-ending. The processes we are now witnessing in Africa, although perhaps in their early stages, do not differ fundamentally from the same processes elsewhere in the world. Because these processes are always and everywhere the result of a political struggle, they are never unilinear and their outcome is never preordained. Hijackings and other reversals are quite common and should not surprise us. What remains a bit more certain and what the cases of Zaire, Kenya, and Cameroon demonstrate is that if the probabilities of political hijackings are to be lessened, the international system needs to exert consistent pressure on autocrats while sending them unambiguous signals. In addition, both domestic and international forces need to cooperate in breaking the institutional hold of autocrats on the critical levers of the state's coercive power. Finally, Zairians, Kenyans, and Cameroonians will have to forge new political and institutional arrangements that are not at odds with their societies' culturally derived notions of legitimate political authority.

■ Notes

An earlier version of this chapter was presented at a conference on democratization at the Paul H. Nitze School of Advanced International Studies, Washington, D.C., April 15–16, 1994. This research is part of a larger project entitled "Contested Terrain: Political Thought, Language, and Legitimacy in Africa" and was begun while I was a fellow at the Woodrow Wilson International Center for Scholars during 1990–1991. More recent work on this project was facilitated by a Vilas Associates Award from the University of Wisconsin–Madison. I am most grateful to both of these institutions for their generous support, but neither bears any responsibility for the contents of this chapter. Equally absolved are Edward Friedman, Marina Ottaway, Crawford Young, and William Zartman, who were good enough to offer critical comments on earlier drafts.

1. For a more detailed version of this argument, see Michael G. Schatzberg, "Power, Legitimacy and 'Democratisation' in Africa," *Africa* 63, no. 4 (December 1993): 445–461. But for an interesting argument that Benin might have already crossed these democratic thresholds, see Bruce A. Magnusson, "The Domestic and International Politics of Democratic Regime Legitimation in Benin: Institutions, Social Policy Reform, and the Public Sphere" (Ph.D. diss., University of Wisconsin–Madison, 1997).

2. Basil Davidson, *The Black Man's Burden: Africa and the Curse of the Nation-State* (New York: Times Books, 1992).

3. For an explicit comparison of Kenya and Zaire, see Jennifer A. Widner, *The Rise of a Party-State in Kenya: From "Harambee!" to "Nyayo!"* (Berkeley: University of California Press, 1992).

4. Frédéric Fritscher, "Le Zaire à la dérive," *Le Monde* (Paris), July 21, 1993, p. 5. On the informal economy, see Janet MacGaffey et al., *The Real Economy of Zaire: The Contribution of Smuggling and Other Unofficial Activities to National Wealth* (Philadelphia: University of Pennsylvania Press, 1991).

5. For two revealing Zairian commentaries on the 1980s, see Emmanuel Dungia, *Mobutu et l'argent du Zaire: Les révélations d'un diplomate ex-agent des services secrets* (Paris: L'Harmattan, 1993); and Thassinda uba Thassinda H., *Zaire: Les princes de l'invisible—L'Afrique noire bâillonnée par le parti unique* (Caen: Editions C'est à dire, 1992).

6. On Ceauşescu's style of Communist rule, as well as for details on Romania and its revolution, see Andrei Codrescu, *The Hole in the Flag: A Romanian Exile's Story of Return and Revolution* (New York: Avon Books, 1990); Martyn Rady, *Romania in Turmoil: A Contemporary History* (London: IB Taurus, 1992); and Mark Almond, *The Rise and Fall of Nicolae and Elena Ceausescu* (London: Chapmans, 1992). For a treatment of the Ceauşescu regime's ideology see Katherine Verdery, *National Ideology Under Socialism: Identity and Cultural Politics in Ceausescu's Romania* (Berkeley: University of California Press, 1991).

For studies of the Mobutu regime and Zaire's Second Republic, see Crawford Young and Thomas Turner, *The Rise and Decline of the Zairian State* (Madison: University of Wisconsin Press, 1985); Thomas M. Callaghy, *The State-Society Struggle: Zaire in Comparative Perspective* (New York: Columbia University Press, 1984); Michael G. Schatzberg, *The Dialectics of Oppression in Zaire* (Bloomington: Indiana University Press, 1988); Colette Braeckman, *Le dinosaure: Le Zaire de Mobutu* (Paris: Fayard, 1992); and Jean-Claude Willame, *L'automne d'un despotisme: Pouvoir, argent et obéissance dans le Zaire des années quatre-vingt* (Paris: Karthala, 1992).

7. Stephen R. Weissman, *American Foreign Policy in the Congo 1960–1964*

(Ithaca: Cornell University Press, 1974); and Michael G. Schatzberg, *Mobutu or Chaos? The United States and Zaire, 1960–1990* (Lanham and Philadelphia: University Press of America and Foreign Policy Research Institute, 1991).

8. On this point, and indeed for much of the narrative of events during this period, see the excellent account by Jean-Claude Willame, "Zaire, Années 90 (Vers la Troisième République), vol. 1: De la démocratie 'octroyée' à la démocratie enrayée (24 avril 1990–22 septembre 1991)," *Les Cahiers du CEDAF* 5–6 (1991): 34-35. (Hereafter Willame, "De la démocratie.")

9. Mobutu Sese Seko, "Discours du 24 avril du Président de la République au Palais de la N'Sele (Extraits)," cited in Willame, "De la démocratie," 82–89. There are some indications that Mobutu never really intended to resign as head of the MPR during this speech and that he had fully expected that his announcement would have been drowned out by cries of protest from the party's *animateurs* to which he would then graciously accede. This never happened. See Braeckman, *Le Dinosaure*, p. 345.

10. Mobutu Sese Seko, "Discours du 3 mai 1990 prononcé par le Président de la République à l'occasion de la journée parlementaire (Extraits)," cited in Willame, "De la démocratie," 97.

11. Willame, "De la démocratie," 132.

12. The report of the Sovereign National Conference on Political Assassinations published a list of sixty-three students who were unaccounted for after the massacre. They are missing and presumed dead. See République du Zaire, Conférence Nationale Souveraine, Commission des Assassinats et des Violations des Droits de l'Homme, "Rapport," Kabamba Mbwebwe, rapporteur et Kasusula Djuma Lokali, président. Kinshasa, 1992, vol. 2: 178–179. Consulted at CEDAF, Brussels, Dossiers 2527 III and 2528 III. Also see Braeckman, *Le Dinosaure,* pp. 345, 13–27; and Ligue Zairoise des Droits de l'Homme, *Rapport sur l'état des libertés au Zaire (octobre-novembre-décembre 1990)* (n.p. [Kinshasa]: n.d. [1991]), 28–32. CEDAF, Dossier 2228 III.

13. Thomas Kanza, "Le zairois serait-il maudit, inconscient?" *Elima* (Kinshasa), September 19, 1991, p. 8. CEDAF, Dossier 04.03.01. VI. 1991.

14. The preceding paragraphs are drawn from a range of sources. See the accounts of these events in *Le Soir* (Brussels), September 24, 1991, p. 7; Catherine Simon, "Et si les pillages avaient été orchestré par le régime," *Le Monde,* September 28, 1991; Colette Braeckman, "Zaire: Sans espoir de retour?" *Le Soir,* September 30, 1991, p. 7; Wadambe N'gini, "Le M.P.R. liquidé par La FAZ," *La Reférence Plus* (Kinshasa) 8 (October 2, 1991), p. 5; and Colette Braeckman, "Les émeutes de septembre étaient une manipulation: Les Services de sécurité au coeur du système zairois," *Le Soir,* November 5, 1991. CEDAF, Dossier 04.03.01. VI. 1991.

15. "Prime Minister Kicked Out," *Weekly Review* (Nairobi), October 25, 1991, p. 35.

16. "Appel à la marche d'espoir du 16 février 1992," *Le Phare* (Kinshasa) 108, s.d., p. 3.

17. See a note placed in CEDAF, Dossier 2358 III, 1992 for these figures. Reports in the U.S. press indicated that there were substantially fewer casualties. See, for example, "Soldiers Open Fire in Zaire, Killing 13," *New York Times,* February 17, 1992, p. A3. Eyewitness accounts and testimony are reproduced in Mission des ONG Belges au Zaire, "Rapport de synthèse," Kinshasa, February 14–21, 1992, typescript, pp. 22-23. CEDAF, Dossier 2390 III.

18. République du Zaire, "Rapport"; and Lambert Mende Omalanga (rappor-

teur) et Tshilengi wa Kabamba (président), "Rapport de la Commission des Biens Mal Acquis," September 1992. République du Zaire. Conférence Nationale Souveraine. Commission des Biens Mal Acquis. Palais du Peuple. CEDAF, Dossier 2492 III.

19. "A Fairly Moderate Course," *Weekly Review,* September 4, 1992, p. 45; "Zaire Troops Briefly Occupy Offices of the Prime Minister," *New York Times,* December 13, 1992; "Farce," *Economist* (London), December 12, 1992, pp. 53–54; Kenneth B. Noble, "Zaire Opposition Pleads for Foreign Military Aid," *New York Times,* February 5, 1993, p. A5; and also the reports in the *Times* on February 2, 1993, and January 30, 1993.

20. *Economist,* "A Three-Headed Monster," April 17, 1993, p. 42.

21. Kenneth B. Noble, "Tens of Thousands Flee Ethnic Violence in Zaire," *New York Times,* March 21, 1993, p. A3; "Last Chance to Resolve Crisis," *Weekly Review,* March 26, 1993, pp. 39–40; Colette Braeckman, "Luttes ethniques au Shaba et au Kivu: Le Zaire implose," *Le Soir,* July 16, 1993, p. 1; C.B., "Troubles du Kivu: Kinshasa admet," *Le Soir,* July 19, 1993, p. 5; and *West Africa* (London), December 27, 1993–January 9, 1994, p. 2357.

22. *West Africa,* October 11–17, 1993, p. 1833; Kenneth B. Noble, "Zairians Strike over Leader's Decision to Dissolve Parliament," *New York Times,* January 20, 1994, p. A5; *West Africa,* January 24–30, 1994, p. 132; and *West Africa,* February 14–20, 1994, p. 275.

23. For a local-level perspective on Rwanda, see the recent work of Timothy P. Longman, "Christianity and Crisis in Rwanda: Religion, Civil Society, Democratization and Decline" (Ph.D. diss., University of Wisconsin–Madison, 1995). Also see the collection of articles on Rwanda in *Issue* 23, no. 2 (1995).

24. Chief Emeka Anyaoku, "The Challenge of Political Pluralism," *Weekly Review,* November 19, 1993, p. 22–28. Citation, p. 24.

25. For lack of space I shall not consider here the potential competition that various forms of religious fundamentalism offer.

26. Sean Kelly, *America's Tyrant: The CIA and Mobutu of Zaire—How the United States Put Mobutu in Power, Protected Him from His Enemies, Helped Him Become One of the Richest Men in the World, and Lived to Regret It* (Washington, D.C.: American University Press, 1993).

27. See E.S. Atieno-Odhiambo, "Democracy and the Ideology of Order in Kenya," in Michael G. Schatzberg, ed., *The Political Economy of Kenya* (New York: Praeger, 1987), pp. 177–201; and David Goldsworthy, *Tom Mboya: The Man Kenya Wanted to Forget* (London: Heinemann, 1982).

28. For an overview, see Michael G. Schatzberg and I. William Zartman, eds., *The Political Economy of Cameroon* (New York: Praeger, 1986).

29. "Moi's Election Scrutinised" (excerpts from the Report of the Commonwealth Observer Group), *West Africa,* February 1–7, 1993, p. 142.

30. Joel Barkan, "Kenya: Lessons from a Flawed Election," *Journal of Democracy* 4, no. 3 (1993): 95.

31. National Democratic Institute for International Affairs (NDI), *An Assessment of the October 11, 1992 Election in Cameroon* (n.p. [Washington, D.C.]: NDI, 1993), pp. vi, vii.

32. U.S. Agency for International Development (USAID), "Congressional Presentation (Sustainable Development Program), Cameroon FY 1995," Internet, USAID Gopher, 1994.

33. "Shikuku's Dilemma," *Weekly Review,* November 19, 1993, p. 7; "KANU Lures Another One," *Weekly Review,* December 10, 1993, pp. 12–14; and, for

the citation, "Odinga Appeals for Donor Aid," *Weekly Review,* October 22, 1993, p. 14.

34. W. Arthur Lewis, *Politics in West Africa* (Toronto: Oxford University Press, 1965), p. 76.

35. José Mpundu, "Le Zaire en marche vers la démocratie," February 23, 1992, mimeographed, pp. 5, 8. CEDAF, Dossier 2358 III, 1992.

36. See Willame, "De la démocratie," to which I am indebted for this analysis.

37. NDI, *An Assessment of the October 11, 1992 Election in Cameroon,* p. 13.

38. Schatzberg, "Power, Legitimacy and 'Democratisation' in Africa."

39. Johannes Fabian, *Power and Performance: Ethnographic Explorations Through Proverbial Wisdom and Theater in Shaba, Zaire* (Madison: University of Wisconsin Press, 1990). See, too, the elaboration of this theme in Michael G. Schatzberg, "Power in Africa: A Cultural and Literary Perspective" (paper delivered at the 35th Annual Meeting of the African Studies Association, Seattle, Washington, November 20–23, 1992).

7

Civil Society, Political Society, and Democratic Failure in Nigeria

Peter M. Lewis

In seeking explanations for the differential success of political transitions in Africa, many observers have focused on regime-centered variables: the character of personal rulership, the institutional dynamics of the old regime, and the structure of clientalism and state authority.[1] The nature of opposition to authoritarian rule has been less systematically considered. Moreover, studies of political opposition in Africa have converged chiefly on the role of civil society, or the arena of independent associations and societal groups.[2] In this chapter, I focus on a pivotal yet often neglected relationship in democratic transitions: the relation of *civil society* and *political society*. Civil society is considered here as an organized realm of society operating within a public sphere; political society refers to the civilian political class and the party system.

Among the myriad factors contributing to successful democratic transitions, the conjunction of political elites and civic actors appears strategically important. The relative strength of democratic movements is linked to the emergence of a preeminent party, or an effective multiparty alliance, among the political opposition. Resistance to an authoritarian regime is also bolstered by alliances between the emergent political class and influential elements of civil society. In circumstances where these coalitions have not emerged, incumbents have been relatively successful at preempting or obstructing democratic pressures.

Beginning in June 1993, Nigeria entered an extended political crisis that threatened the stability and potentially the cohesion of the federation. After defaulting on a promised transition to democratic rule, Nigeria's military elite reasserted political dominance, spurning popular aspirations for electoral pluralism, disenfranchising millions of voters, and alienating southern regions of the country. The political imbroglio prompted intermittent civil violence, rising ethnic and regional tensions, and rapid economic decline. Observers compared the situation to the turbulent period of 1966–

1967, which preceded Nigeria's devastating civil war. Domestic opposition to the military regime attained unprecedented momentum during the summer months of 1994, and the protests were paralleled by international isolation and diplomatic censure.

However, General Sani Abacha prevailed over the disparate opposition to his rule and after September 1994 he markedly strengthened his control. In the face of military factionalism, societal opposition, and international condemnation, Abacha and his predatory military clique pursued an increasingly authoritarian course. The deterioration of civic morale and the specter of political collapse added urgency to the crisis, though such hazards provided scant motives for accommodation. A weak and scattered international response had little impact on the military's autocratic designs.

The abrogation of the planned political transition and the assertion of personal dictatorship highlight basic dilemmas in the conditions for democratic change in Nigeria. Aspirations for constitutional rule and competitive politics are seemingly deep-seated in Nigerian society, yet the democratic movement has been diffident and feeble. The facility of Abacha's dictatorship is somewhat puzzling in light of Nigeria's profound social fissures and the comparatively high levels of civic organization in the country. Among the factors hindering constitutional governance, trends within the state, including the predilections of military leaders, the imperatives of ethnic hegemony, and evolving patterns of clientalist politics, are most consequential. Yet the inability or reluctance of popular forces to advance the democratic process and the diffidence of aspirant politicians have blunted the potential strength of anti-authoritarian elements. Nigeria's crisis has revealed a paucity of countervailing pressures to authoritarian rule.

Two features of social and political organization in Nigeria provide some insight into the anemic challenges to authoritarianism. The first is the inherent weakness of civil society. Civic organizations, impaired by social fragmentation, scarce resources, and state repression, have furnished irregular resistance to the Abacha regime. In addition, communal and factional divisions among the civilian political class have undermined the possibility of an effective opposition block. Political society in Nigeria has largely receded from the public arena, and substantial segments of the fragmented civilian elite have been co-opted by the government. Perhaps most important, little evidence exists of durable affiliation between politicians and societal groups. In consequence, a splintered, localized civil society has engaged in piecemeal opposition to a resolute dictatorship.

The following section briefly outlines the concepts of civil and political society and their application to transitions in sub-Saharan Africa. An overview of Nigeria's transition crisis follows. The character of civil society in Nigeria and the political role of the associational realm is then discussed, followed by consideration of the party system and the political class.

■ Civil Society and Political Society

The recent resurgence of democratic pressure in Africa has drawn attention to the character of associational life throughout the region. Discussions of civil society in Africa have generally made use of inclusive or restrictive definitions.[3] Inclusive treatments define civil society as a diverse intermediate realm of organizations, occupying the domain between family and state. Consequently, a broad array of local, ethnic, cultural, and economic associations are covered in the concept. From this vantage, most social networks, economic coping mechanisms (such as informal markets), and parochial groups may constitute elements of civil society.

Restrictive approaches to civil society, in line with the stance taken in this chapter, insist that civil society constitutes part of a civic realm or public sphere in which state and society interact over issues of common concern.[4] Civil society, in this view, constitutes the domain of associations that are engaged with the state (in cooperative or adversarial relations) over nominally public issues.[5] Civil society extends beyond nonparty political opposition, yet it is demarcated by the civic orientations of its constituents. Purely parochial or private activities do not enter the civil domain; indeed they may often serve to impede the formation of a common political community. In this context, we may assess the relative development of civil society, or even its absence, in diverse settings.

The notion of political society is of more recent genesis and carries more specific meaning. Departing from Antonio Gramsci, who treated "political society" as synonymous with the state, Alfred Stepan has distinguished political society from the state on the one hand and from civil society on the other.[6] Political society, in his usage, denotes the stratum of party organizations, politicians, and political professionals. It is not an integral part of the state and is evidently distinct from the particular and diverse interests within civil society. Political society may serve crucial functions in bridging disparate societal concerns and the prerogatives of government. As many analysts of democracy have observed, party systems and politicians are essential for interest aggregation, mediation, and representation.

The evolution of political and civil society and the relationship between these strata constitute an important nexus in the democratic movement. While stressing nonregime sources of democratic change, I do not argue that these elements are the only relevant factors in a given transition. Intrastate dynamics are often decisive in determining the outcome of transitional struggles. However, the quality and character of political opposition evidently plays an instrumental role in regime change.

Robert Dahl has portrayed the democratic contest as a struggle between the repressive capabilities of authoritarian incumbents and the vigor of political challengers.[7] He predicts the emergence of democratic rule when dissidence and popular participation exceed the stamina of a restrictive state. This is infrequently a contest of pure power—witness the former Soviet Union and Eastern Europe—but more typically one of will and organization. Consequently, the capabilities of societal groups and the presence of unified leadership with an institutional identity appear as crucial elements of the democratic equation. Guillermo O'Donnell and Philippe Schmitter have similarly emphasized the coincidence of a cohesive political elite and concerted popular mobilization as a key dimension of successful transitions.[8]

Independent associations and professional politicians play distinct roles in the process of democratic change. The recent global challenges to authoritarian governments have emerged mainly from elements within civil society, whether small circles of intellectual dissidents, broad alliances of organized labor, or militant organizations of students. It is often true that prior liberalization by the regime provides the chance for civic action, yet incumbent rulers have frequently lost the initiative after opening the political arena. As the authoritarian elite is eclipsed by growing democratic momentum, attempts to curb opposition forces are often ineffectual.[9]

However, action by unaffiliated societal groups will rarely bring about a full transition. Coherent democratic leadership and an organizational vehicle for change provide necessary complements for advancing the democratic agenda. Consequently, politicians and parties form an integral correlate in many successful democratic coalitions. Sometimes, as in Poland or Zambia, political leaders emerge from civic organizations. In much of Latin America, southern Europe, Asia, and Africa, resurgent parties or politicians, suppressed under the old regime, have returned to guide popular movements. In other instances a generational shift has occurred, with a renaissance of party structure bringing forth a new group of leaders.

The disparity and uncertainty of African transitions render generalization difficult, yet some patterns have emerged from the region's diverse political changes. In countries such as Zambia, South Africa, and Benin, political opposition converged around a single party or an effective multiparty coalition. These groups brought forward identifiable leaders with significant popular legitimacy. Moreover, the emergent democratic political organizations had strong linkages with strategic elements of civil society. Aspirant politicians could mobilize and ally with popular sectors in the campaign for regime change. A coherent set of political demands, backed by a recognizable institutional vehicle, provided the catalyst for democratization. In countries such as Kenya, Cameroon, and Nigeria, division or fragmentation among the political class and a more diffuse relation with the associational realm have weakened democratic advocates vis-à-vis their authoritarian adversaries.

The failed democratic transition in Nigeria illustrates the importance of strategic linkages among civil and political societies and the liabilities where such linkages are absent. The following sections offer a broad overview of the context of the transition, events leading to the collapse of the military's democratization program, and the respective roles of civil and political society in the developing crisis.

■ From Transition to Crisis

Since independence from Britain in 1960, Nigeria has been ruled by the military for a total of twenty-five years. Following the overthrow of the First Republic in 1966, there has been only one civilian interregnum, the short-lived Second Republic of 1979–1983. Throughout Nigeria's civil-military cycles, nearly all military rulers have sought to legitimize their rule by promising transition to a constitutional order. In addition, military regimes have often permitted wide latitude for associational activity, media independence, and even political debate.[10]

Shortly after ousting the military regime of Muhammadu Buhari in August 1985, Major-General Ibrahim Babangida promised a rapid reinstatement of democracy. The story of Babangida's transition program has been elaborated elsewhere, and the following account covers only the salient highlights.[11] In 1987, Babangida elaborated a complex democratization schedule, with provisions for constitutional change, political party registration, a national census, and an extended sequence of local and national elections. The transition framework also established a nominally independent electoral commission and a network of civic education.

The military regime exerted tight control over the pace and substance of the transition process. The Constituent Assembly of 1988–1989, charged with revising the constitution, received repeated admonitions from the president over the boundaries of acceptable reform. In late 1989, only months after the ratification of party activity, the government vetoed all independent political organizations and created two government-sanctioned parties. The center-left Social Democratic Party (SDP) and the center-right National Republican Convention (NRC) were bestowed with official manifestos and organizational charters. During the next three and a half years, these parties provided the framework for competitive politics in local, state, and national elections.[12] Previous civilian politicians were initially prohibited from participation and then provisionally admitted in 1991.

The rancorous nature of civilian political competition and the inevitable administrative glitches of the transition agenda offered ready opportunity for the military to delay the democratization program. Babangida repeatedly cited factional squabbling, legal wrangling among candidates, or logistical problems as pretexts for rescheduling elections. The political transfer date was postponed three times before finally being slated for August 1993. In an effort to allay rising public criticism that he harbored a "hidden agenda" to retain power, Babangida appointed a civilian Transitional Council in January 1993.[13] Headed by a prominent business-man, Chief Ernest Shonekan, the council was to function as a shadow cabi-net through the final months of the transition.

The penultimate stage in the transition schedule was the presidential election set for June 12. Two candidates emerged from the nomination process with the implicit sanction of the regime. Alhaji Bashir Tofa and Chief M. K. O. Abiola were both wealthy Muslim business figures, and each had close personal and business linkages with the military. Tofa, the NRC candidate, hailed from the northern Hausa-Fulani section of the coun-try, and the SDP's Abiola was from the ethnically Yoruba southwest. The obscure Tofa was eclipsed by Abiola's prominence as a media baron and philanthropist.

An uncharacteristically civil campaign preceded the election, reflecting both public apathy and a desire by the politicians to avoid giving pretext for revoking the transition. The June 12 elections were held amid widespread confusion because a series of legal challenges threatened injunctions against the polling and then against the release of results. The suits were brought by the Association for a Better Nigeria (ABN), whose leader, Arthur Nzeribe, was a crony of the generals and widely regarded as a proxy for their designs. Despite the legal limbo surrounding the poll, the June 12 exercise was generally viewed as credible and fair, with almost none of the violence and fraud characteristic of previous elections.[14] Unofficial results, leaked in the days after the election, indicated a solid 58 percent margin for Abiola. The voting patterns were noteworthy for their ethnic and regional breadth.[15]

Within ten days, the regime annulled the election, a measure Babangida later justified with references to the administrative and legal dis-array accompanying the poll. The invalidation of the June 12 results pro-voked intense ethnic, regional, and populist antipathy, mainly in the Yoruba region. Civil violence in the southwestern states had been instrumental in the breakdown of Nigeria's previous democratic republics, and the repudia-tion of Abiola's victory threatened a major ethnoregional cleavage.[16] Popular apprehension in the weeks after the election prompted economic paralysis and urban-rural flight, as southerners trickled from the cities to the security of their home villages.

For two months following the elections, Babangida parried challenges from domestic opponents and the international community. The democratic cause was pursued by a loose array of human rights activists, professionals, students and academics, elements of the labor movement, and a residual faction of the SDP. An ad hoc campaign of protests and demonstrations urged Babangida to recognize Abiola's mandate. As tensions mounted, Abiola fled the country for several weeks in an effort to mobilize foreign support. Although external admonitions called for the regime to abdicate, they were not supported by specific demands or compelling sanctions. Ultimately, however, the combination of popular pressure, military ambivalence, and foreign urgings prompted Babangida to leave. The general resigned the presidency and his commission at the end of August and hastily installed Shonekan's council as an Interim National Government (ING). He appointed his chief of staff, General Sani Abacha, as defense minister.

The civilian caretakers lasted less than three months. Lacking a popular mandate or a clear program, Shonekan's group floundered in a political wilderness. In mid-November 1993, an attempt to improve relations with foreign creditors by raising domestic fuel prices proved fatal for the ING. The national labor confederation staged a general strike, and within days General Abacha forced Shonekan's resignation. Abacha, who had moved quickly after Babangida's exit to secure his own power base within the military, easily consolidated his hold on the state. The new military rulers counseled patience from Abiola's camp, who hoped for a rapid civilian restoration. They also enlisted the cooperation of numerous politicians through lucrative positions in the new cabinet and a regime-sponsored Constitutional Conference.

Throughout the first half of 1994, Abacha's reign was facilitated by a divided opposition, popular ambivalence toward the politicians, and a deepening economic depression that distracted attentions from the political drama. Abiola's political capital was depleted after he lost his party organization and electoral base outside the southwestern districts of the country. Despite his populist image, Abiola's elitism and detachment alienated important elements of a potential democratic coalition, including northern progressives, organized labor, and many political factions. The presidential hopeful was hampered by his apparent preference for backroom deals with the military rather than building a wider coalition. Divisions widened within the democratic movement among advocates of Abiola's "June 12 mandate" as the basis for political transition and a growing segment who were amenable to compromise, including new elections. Abacha exploited these fissures and dispersed abundant favors in order to gain the acquiescence of the civilian political class.[17]

However, democratic demands attained new momentum in the weeks before the first anniversary of the June 12 election. Backed by the newly formed National Democratic Coalition (NADECO), in late May 1994 Abiola launched a campaign to claim his mandate. NADECO, a multiethnic group of former politicians, notables, and retired military officers, provided Abiola's loyalist camp with a revitalized organizational presence.[18] Fortified by this base and assisted by his media outlets, Abiola publicly challenged the military to abdicate. The government quickly proscribed NADECO, and Abiola himself became a fugitive when he declared himself president at a political rally on the eve of the election anniversary. After briefly eluding the police, Abiola allowed himself to be arrested, where-upon he was charged with treason, potentially a capital offense.

Almost simultaneously, regime and opposition intensified their con-frontation. The emergent vanguard of the democratic movement came from an unexpected quarter, the previously quiescent labor movement. In July, the oil workers' union, the National Union of Petroleum and Natural Gas Workers (NUPENG), initiated a strike to demand Abiola's release and recognition of the June 12 mandate. Shortly thereafter, the peak labor con-federation, the Nigerian Labour Congress (NLC), threatened a general strike in support of the NUPENG demands, while the blue-collar oil work-ers were joined by the Petroleum and Natural Gas Senior Staff Association (PENGASSAN), the union of senior petroleum employees. The petroleum unions were soon accompanied by disgruntled bank employees and prodemocracy academics, as spontaneous protests and sporadic rioting erupted in several southwestern cities.

For nine weeks, the petroleum workers' actions paralyzed the nation. The strikes depressed exports and crippled the domestic economy, as driv-ers and refinery workers choked off fuel supplies.[19] The NLC, whose lead-ership had generally complied with the military's political program, briefly joined the strikes but quickly retreated in response to assurances from the regime. Nonetheless, the loose coalition of organized labor, professional groupings, and civic and political organizations constituted the most mili-tant public opposition to military rule in Nigerian experience.

Abacha's resolve proved equally surprising. The regime quelled the opposition through legal manipulations, selective coercion, and widespread inducements. In mid-August, Abacha moved to end the standoff by decapi-tating the labor organizations and consolidating authoritarian control. Following a summary dismissal of petroleum union executives, the offices of the unions were sealed and their leaders arrested. The government closed three prominent independent media groups and promulgated a decree exempting itself from the jurisdiction of the courts.[20] A preventive deten-tion order facilitated the arrest of democratic activists, and anonymous attackers staged assaults on the homes of several prominent dissidents.[21] More than 120 street protesters were killed as security forces put down dis-turbances in major cities.

By early September, the crackdown had taken effect. As the strikes flagged, petroleum flows were restored and economic activity resumed. Leading opponents of military rule, including Chief Abiola, remained in detention. Over the next few months, Abacha pursued the classic tactics of authoritarian consolidation. Civilians were purged from the ruling council, the cabinet was dissolved, and suspect military personnel were sidelined or detained.[22] The Constitutional Conference ambled along, first recommending that Abacha transfer power to civilians by the end of the year, then withdrawing its motion and adjourning in June 1995 with no firm endorsement of a handover date. In October, the general announced another protracted transition program, which would supposedly culminate in 1998. Few observers gave credence to the purported transition.

Meanwhile, in March 1995 the regime announced it had frustrated an attempted coup. As many as four hundred officers and civilians were arrested or detained, including Brigadier Lawan Gwadabe, the purported coup leader; retired General Shehu Musa Yar'Adua, an aspiring presidential candidate; and General Olusegun Obasanjo, the former head of state and outspoken critic of recent military regimes. The veracity of the plot was questioned, prompting suspicion that Abacha had contrived the incident as an excuse for preempting domestic opposition.[23] A secret military tribunal was convened, and in July the panel convicted more than forty people of complicity in the alleged conspiracy. Although the harsh sentences were later commuted, the trial had a chilling effect on public debate and political activity. The pall deepened with the hasty November executions of Ken Saro-Wiwa and eight other Ogoni activists following a flawed and largely opaque murder trial. Viewed in tandem with the continued detention of Chief Abiola, unremitting suppression of the media, and harassment of democratic activists, Abacha's government reflected the most repressive rule in Nigerian history. The beleaguered elements of the democratic movement provided a feeble counterweight to a determined authoritarian regime.

■ Civil Society in Nigeria

Throughout the political turmoil surrounding the June 12 crisis, segments of Nigeria's civil society have offered the most consistent and vital source of democratic pressure. To the extent that there is a democratic constituency within Nigeria, it is expressed in the realm of independent associations—notably labor, the professions, and the universities—rather than the aspiring political elite or nascent party organizations. The democratic elements of civil society have tentatively and often expediently allied with elements of a fledgling political society.

Nigeria has engendered a more fully realized civil society than many

other African countries. This is reflected in a wide array and scope of associations, some with extensive popular foundations, significant resources,
and long organizational experience.[24] Nigeria's civil society spans a range
of activities and interests, from community and professional associations to
political organizations and formal interest groups. A number of associations
operate on a nationwide scale and are engaged in issues of broad public
concern. In the early 1980s, many associations and groups were preoccu-
pied with the consequences of fiscal austerity and economic decline, but
more recently a collection of civic groups have converged around the
preservation of human rights, the defense of political participation, and
opposition to military rule.[25]

Within the current political context, several elements of civil society
can be distinguished, each with a different relationship to the ongoing crisis
and the question of democratization. The first segment incorporates numerous groups engaged directly in the democratic movement and self-con-
sciously oriented toward the transitional agenda associated with June 12.
Many of these are intermingled with elements of political society, and a
number of politicians and party organizers are involved. At the forefront of
this circle are the organizations supporting Chief Abiola. Since May 1994
NADECO has been a vanguard of democratic influence both internally and
abroad. NADECO mainly comprises Abiola loyalists, although it reflects a
multiethnic leadership and includes members with military and civilian
backgrounds. A coalition of forty-two activist organizations, the Campaign
for Democracy (CD), represents a somewhat less partisan segment of the
democratic movement, although they have protested the June 12 annulment
and have urged Chief Abiola's release from prison. The CD organized
under the Babangida regime to press for democratic rights and to promote a
political transition.

The petroleum unions, who played the pivotal role in 1994's protests,
emerged recently and briefly as a crucial force in the democratic camp.
They have a regionally diverse membership, including many from the
southeastern states. Their fervent support for Abiola's mandate significantly weakened the regime's contention that the June 12 movement was
chiefly an ethnic Yoruba cause. Within the universities, both the National
Association of Nigerian Students (NANS) and the Academic Staff Union of
Universities have been democratic stalwarts. NANS members have suffered some of the most intense harassment and the greatest number of casualties among the various organizations working for democratic change.[26]
Several traditional rulers, notably in the southwestern states, have openly
supported NADECO's program.

A second group of organizations, not always exclusive of the first,
have been engaged in ongoing struggles for civil liberties, democratic

rights, the rule of law, and political representation. These organizations fight principally to defend political and social rights, and they broadly support an early transition to civilian rule. However, they have not been linked with partisan demands for a particular candidate. Many constituent organizations of the Campaign for Democracy are included in this group, along with the leading civil rights organizations: the Civil Liberties Organization, the Campaign for the Defense of Human Rights, and the Constitutional Rights Project.

These groups have frequently been joined by an array of professional associations. The Nigerian Union of Journalists has been a vocal defender of press rights and an advocate for detained journalists. The Nigerian Bar Association has fought an essentially rearguard struggle to maintain the rule of law and judicial integrity. The Nigerian Medical Association has sought to preserve minimal health-delivery standards while also moving their protests in an explicitly political direction. Even air traffic controllers and bank employees, whose relationship to the political crisis is largely tangential, have staged job actions in sympathy with political detainees or professional cohorts. And, despite the generally accommodating stance of their senior leadership, other constituent unions within the Nigerian Labour Congress have supported democratic demands.

As noted above, the NANS and the Nigerian Women's Association have long been active across a range of social and political issues. At critical moments during the political crisis, elements of the Anglican and Catholic hierarchies in Nigeria have called for the respect of human rights and the recognition of democratic aspirations. The Movement for the Survival of Ogoni People (MOSOP) of the southeastern oil-producing region, formerly led by the late journalist and activist Ken Saro-Wiwa, has agitated in recent years against regional exploitation and military repression.[27] And finally, it is noteworthy that a northern organization, the Movement for Unity and Progress, led by the progressive politician Balarabe Musa, has conspicuously allied with southern democrats.

A number of organizations and networks have been peripheral to the current struggle, often deliberately so. Some groups, notably the NLC and the religious community, are clearly divided over the political agenda. The business community has been split between acquiescence and activism. Many of the peak business associations have confined their involvement to narrow economic concerns and have been distant from the democratic movement. The Manufacturers' Association and most chambers of commerce fall into this category, along with the emerging Nigerian Economic Summit, whose political utterances have been understated and oblique. The leaders of the Nigerian Association of Chambers of Commerce, Industry, Mines, and Agriculture (NACCIMA) (the peak association of chambers of commerce) and the more assertive Concerned Professionals (many of whose members come from the business community) have urged a return to democracy.

The Nigerian Labour Congress has traced a peculiarly ambivalent path between co-optation and opposition. Since the late 1980s, the NLC has experienced recurrent political intervention in its leadership and organizational affairs. The NLC's strike following the November 1993 fuel price increases helped to pave the way for Abacha's coup, and the labor confederation subsequently played a diffident role in the democratic opposition. During the 1994 petroleum strikes, the NLC made a brief, halfhearted attempt to call a general strike, but the leadership relented almost immediately in the face of military admonitions, and the union was soon enfeebled by decree.

Many important civic figures and institutions have simply stood apart from the political fray, whereas some have actively cooperated with the regime. Most of Nigeria's leading religious authorities, especially Islamic leaders, have been conspicuously absent from the public discourse over democracy. Some have openly supported the government's position and issued critical comments about prodemocracy forces, often with regional and ethnic overtones. The wide array of ethnic and local associations along with many traditional rulers outside the southwest have also stood at arm's length from the political impasse. Other societal groups have remained aloof from the current political contention, mainly local associations with ethnic, community, social, or cultural orientations. In sum, civil society in Nigeria reflects a disparate set of organizations and interests, with political roles ranging from democratic partisanship to open cooperation with the military regime.

■ Democratic Struggles and the Dilemma of Civil Society

Despite the breadth and apparent leverage of the groups arrayed against the military government, popular pressure failed to dislodge the military oligarchy. The train of events since June 1993 reveals limits to the scope of mobilization and the reach of associational activity in Nigeria. The democratic elements of civil society have been unable to constitute a viable counterweight to authoritarian rule. A number of structural and strategic traits have impeded the political efficacy of Nigeria's civic realm.

First among these is the segmentation within civil society. The democratic movement has been spearheaded by a modest group of middle-class professionals, mainly from the southwestern and southeastern portions of the country. Class divisions and ethnic parochialism have served to limit the reach and capacity of the democratic organizations. Organized labor has been virtually neutralized as a source of militant opposition, and business interests see little incentive for engaging in politics. Other important segments of society have become alienated from the democratic cause for ethnic or factional reasons. Rightly or wrongly, many areas of the country have come to see Abiola's claims as a "Yoruba" issue. Such divisions make it difficult to mobilize broad segments of popular action against authoritarian rule.

A second, obvious impediment to civic action is state repression. Beginning with Babangida's rule and continuing under Abacha, the military oligarchy has considerably hampered popular activity. Indeed, Abacha has gone further than any previous Nigerian ruler in abrogating basic civil liberties and political rights. The current regime has detained hundreds of activists while passing decrees suppressing the press and voiding judicial authority over the government. It has also used extensive harassment and selective state terror against opponents and has given security forces carte blanche in suppressing popular protest. The severity of the secret military tribunals and the judicial killings of the Ogoni activists have had a chilling effect on public opposition and private debate, effectively intimidating most of the challengers to Abacha's continued tenure. Blunt repression has been balanced by the co-optation of key groups, including labor, politicians, business elites, and traditional rulers. The lack of durable alliances with elements of the civilian political elite, which is elaborated in the following section, constitutes another strategic weakness in the political role of civic groups.

■ **Political Society: The Expectant Elite**

Civilian politicians in Nigeria are commonly regarded as a "political class," denoting the fusion of political influence and personal accumulation characteristic of this elite.[28] During Nigeria's First and Second Republics, the political class reflected significant continuity, mirrored in the structure of the party system. The emergent system at independence centered on three regionally based parties, reflecting different ideological orientations but relying primarily on ethnic and personal appeals. Both civilian republics evolved rapidly toward dominant-party rule. The hegemonic control of northern elites was bolstered through expedient pacts with eastern parties, alliances with local notables in minority areas, and encouragement of restive factions in the western states.[29]

The aspiring parties during Babangida's transition partially reflected these historical factions and alliances. However, a combination of constitutional rules and executive manipulation created incipient changes in the structure of political competition. The mandatory two-party structure imposed certain crosscutting alliances on the political elite, somewhat accentuating the role of ideological coalitions. In addition, the temporary proscription of veteran politicians created a generational shift, if only by default. Senior politicians, while reigning as "kingmakers," unavoidably yielded ground to an emergent new breed of younger claimants.[30] Yet the contrived quality of politics under military tutelage rendered these shifts more speculative than real. The currents and eddies of Nigeria's political class were essentially moot in the absence of autonomous, institutionally defined political competition.

Throughout the recent political crisis, several factors have enervated the democratic potential of the civilian political class. These tendencies reflect latent aspects of political contention evident since the late colonial era. The first is an orientation toward personal rather than programmatic allegiances, fomenting chronic organizational weakness. The factional and individual nature of political loyalties has undermined the durability of political blocks while encouraging expedient defections by politicians.

The unstable nature of partisanship is fostered by the tenuous linkages between party organizations and societal groups. Political parties have displayed an ability to erect formidable patronage networks during intervals of democratic rule, yet they command scant allegiance once robbed of their resources and formal status. Apart from uneven ethnic mobilization, the party system has not engendered an identifiable constituent base. Consequently politicians have little accountability to blocks of voters, and organized interests lack representation in party hierarchies. Party organizations have been shaped by contention among elite networks with few enduring linkages to broader grassroots constituencies.

Organizational weakness and modes of political change have engendered passivity among the civilian political class. With no heritage of struggle for political power, scant history of wielding substantive authority, and few institutional foundations, Nigerian politicians have little penchant for actively promoting democratic rule. The civilian political elite has historically awaited the bestowal of power from authoritarian rulers, whether the colonial state or an indigenous military government. Since the coups of 1966, there has been a tacit agreement by the military that a circulation of elites would occur and that officers would ultimately cede power to civilians. The transition to the Second Republic bolstered the credibility of this understanding, and a dozen years of authoritarian rule have only gradually betrayed the vacuousness of the military's promises. For the aspirant political class, such assurances have not lost their allure, as evidenced by civilian participation in Abacha's Constitutional Conference and a flurry of activity following the June 1995 restoration of party politics.

These characteristics of the civilian political elite are readily exploited by a dexterous authoritarian regime. The military has relied upon the atomization of the deposed politicians and their susceptibility to a range of inducements for cooperation.[31] The absence of any durable popular identification with individual politicians or recognized organizational blocks has essentially divorced the civilian political class from its central source of potential leverage. The negation of democratic rule has been easily relegated to the orbit of intra-elite politics, with little sustained response from mass constituencies.

The rift between civil society and the aspirant political class constitutes a basic flaw in the democratic movement. In the absence of a clear avenue for political transition or a credible group of aspirants for office, democratic initiatives within civil society lack focus. In short, Nigeria exhibits a weak civil society because there is no corresponding "political society" with which to form a strategic coalition. The result has been a thin, fragmented stratum of activist organizations, unable to advance a coherent agenda or to repudiate the program of the authoritarian regime.

■ Conclusion

Despite widespread, earnest opposition to military rule, in mid-1995 the array of forces could not effect a transition to constitutional government. Abacha's leadership group hardened its position against the democratic opposition while cynically announcing its own transition program to undermine the demands of independent dissidents. The military oligarchy amply demonstrated the effectiveness of strong-arm tactics to maintain control. Modest repression and intimidation were readily bolstered by co-optation and patronage made possible by the military's deep pockets. The democratic movement, deficient in resources and popular support, was subdued and isolated. A few dozen arrests, legal proscriptions, and targeted killings sufficed to keep these groups at bay.

In consequence, no countervailing power existed to challenge authoritarian rule. The petroleum unions were uniquely situated to impose economic distress, and their suppression removed the opposition's most significant leverage. Perhaps most discouraging was the ambiguous disposition of the political elite.[32] Former politicians and party leaders did little to champion the democratic cause and proved broadly responsive to the blandishments of the regime. Few of the participants in the Constitutional Conference registered a popular following, while the characteristic opportunism and corruption of the civilian political class alienated the public. In short, democratic partisans had few allies in whom to place their confidence for advancing a transitional agenda.

It is likely that elements of Nigerian civil society will continue to provide the engine for the democratic movement. The associational realm clearly offers the strongest avenue for effective pressure against the military oligarchy. However, the Abacha regime has been resolute and effective in fending off these pressures, at least in the near term. In the absence of greater cohesion among key democratic groups, a stronger popular base for oppositional action, and a strategic alliance with party organizations and political professionals who can press a transitional agenda, Nigeria's democratic aspirations are likely to remain unrealized.

Having elaborated the particularities of Nigerian political experience, it is useful to summarize the comparative lessons of Nigeria's failed transition. Discussions of political opposition and regime change in Africa have focused on two dimensions of political life: the state and civil society. While arguing for a delimited treatment of civil society in Africa, I also include political society as an important variable in explaining the outcome of political transitions in Africa. The relative cohesion of political society and the establishment of effective linkages with key popular associations form two strategic underpinnings of successful transitions. These attributes of democratic opposition have been lacking in Nigeria, as in countries such as Cameroon, Kenya, and Zaire where democratic challenges have been blocked by authoritarian incumbents. Alternatively, we have witnessed democratic successes in Zambia, South Africa, and Benin, where these structural requisites were arguably in evidence. Although a more detailed discussion is beyond the scope of this chapter, I will suggest that these dynamics might also be consequential for the consolidation of democratic regimes as well as the course of political transition.

■ Notes

1. The outstanding analysis in this vein is Michael Bratton and Nicolas van de Walle, "Neopatrimonial Regimes and Political Transitions in Africa," *World Politics* 46, no. 4 (July 1994). Elsewhere, Bratton and van de Walle have analyzed the dynamics of political opposition; see "Popular Protest and Political Reform in Africa," *Comparative Politics* 24, no. 4 (1992).

2. See, for example, John Harbeson, Donald Rothchild, and Naomi Chazan, eds., *Civil Society and the State in Africa* (Boulder, Colo.: Lynne Rienner Publishers, 1995); Naomi Chazan, "Africa's Democratic Challenge: Strengthening Civil Society and the State," *World Policy Journal* (spring 1992); and Peter M. Lewis, "Political Transition and the Dilemma of Civil Society in Africa, *Journal of International Affairs* 46, no. 2 (summer 1992).

3. On definitional issues see Lewis, "Political Transition and the Dilemma of Civil Society." Several fine essays in Harbeson et al., *Civil Society and the State in Africa,* elucidate these issues, including Crawford Young, "In Search of Civil Society"; Michael Bratton, "Civil Society and Political Transitions in Africa"; and Thomas Callaghy, "Civil Society, Democracy and Economic Change in Africa: A Dissenting Opinion About Resurgent Societies." For a broader theoretical treatment, see John Keane, ed., *Civil Society and the State* (London: Verso, 1988).

4. The notion of a public sphere has been advanced by Jürgen Habermas, *The Structural Transformation of the Public Sphere* (Cambridge, Mass.: MIT Press, 1989).

5. Callaghy, "Civil Society, Democracy and Economic Change in Africa," p. 235.

6. Alfred Stepan, *Rethinking Military Politics* (Princeton: Princeton University Press, 1988). Michael Bratton elaborates Gramsci's discussion in "Civil Society and Political Transitions in Africa," p. 55.

7. Robert Dahl, *Polyarchy: Participation and Opposition* (New Haven: Yale University Press, 1971).

8. Guillermo O'Donnell and Philippe Schmitter, *Transitions from Authoritarian Rule: Tentative Conclusions About Uncertain Democracies* (Baltimore: Johns Hopkins University Press, 1986).

9. Ibid. See also Bratton and van de Walle, "Popular Protest and Political Reform in Africa"; and Samuel Huntington, *The Third Wave: Democratization in the Late Twentieth Century* (Norman: University of Oklahoma Press, 1991).

10. This section draws upon my earlier article, "Endgame in Nigeria? The Politics of a Failed Democratic Transition," *African Affairs* 93 (July 1994).

11. See, for example, Larry Diamond, "Nigeria: The Uncivic Society and the Descent into Praetorianism," in Larry Diamond, J. Linz, and S. M. Lipset, eds., *Politics in Developing Countries: Comparing Experiences With Democracy,* 2d ed. (Boulder, Colo.: Lynne Rienner Publishers, 1995).

12. The early stages of the transition program have been detailed by Larry Diamond in "Nigeria's Search for a New Political Order," *Journal of Democracy* 2, no. 2 (spring 1991). See also Peter Koehn, "Competitive Transition to Civilian Rule: Nigeria's First and Second Experiments," *The Journal of Modern African Studies* 27, no. 3, 1989.

13. See Lewis, "Endgame in Nigeria?" 324–325, and Tom Forrest, *Politics and Economic Development in Nigeria,* 2d ed. (Boulder, Colo.: Westview Press, 1995), p. 235.

14. Diamond, "Nigeria: The Uncivic Society," p. 457.

15. The election tabulation was published in most major newspapers and periodicals. See *Newswatch* (Lagos), June 28, 1993, p. 10.

16. The breakdown of the Second Republic is chronicled by Richard Joseph in *Democracy and Prebendal Politics in Nigeria* (Cambridge: Cambridge University Press, 1987). On the dynamics of both previous democratic regimes, see Diamond, "Nigeria: The Uncivic Society."

17. See Paul Adams, "The Deepening Stalemate," *Africa Report* (July-August 1994): 62–64.

18. These developments are detailed by Nats Agbo, "Sign-Post for Democracy," *Newswatch,* January 9, 1995, p. 10.

19. Ironically, there is considerable evidence that senior military officers and their civilian cronies, with heavy involvement in oil lifting, garnered a windfall from the crisis. See "Military Machismo," *Africa Confidential* 35, no. 18.

20. These developments are documented in "Nigeria: The Dawn of a New Dark Age," *Africa Watch* 6, no. 8 (October, 1994).

21. Utibe Ukim, "The New Offensive," *Newswatch,* September 12, 1994, pp. 8–13.

22. Paul Adams, "Reign of the Generals," *Africa Report* (November-December 1994), pp. 27-29.

23. Howard French, "In Nigeria, A Strongman Tightens the Vise," *New York Times,* March 31, 1995, p. A3.

24. See, for example, Attahiru Jega, "Professional Associations and Structural Adjustment," and Yusuf Bangura and Bjorn Beckman, "African Workers and Structural Adjustment: A Nigerian Case Study," both in Adebayo Olukoshi, ed., *The Politics of Structural Adjustment in Nigeria* (London: James Currey, 1993).

25. On the evolution of civil society in the 1980s, see Adebayo Olukoshi, "Associational Life During the Nigerian Transition to Civilian Rule" (paper presented at the conference on Democratic Transition and Structural Adjustment in Nigeria, Stanford University, August, 1990).

26. The Civil Liberties Organization has regularly chronicled the repressive measures against civic associations in Nigeria. See the CLO, *Annual Report on Human Rights in Nigeria,* Lagos, various years.

27. The activities of MOSOP and the military campaign in Ogoniland are detailed in Human Rights Watch: Africa, "The Ogoni Crisis: A Case Study of Military Repression in Southeastern Nigeria," Washington, D.C., July, 1994.

28. See Richard Sklar, *Nigerian Political Parties* (Princeton: Princeton University Press, 1963). Sklar's seminal study has entrenched the use of the term "political class" to refer to the stratum of civilian politicians in Nigeria. The military, while undeniably part of a broader political elite in the country, is usually treated separately from this designation. Despite the presence of military rule for twenty-five years, and an unquestionable melding of political power with economic interests among the officer corps, conventional usage has continued to refer to the political class as a civilian group.

29. These dynamics are reviewed by Billy Dudley, *An Introduction to Nigerian Government and Politics* (Bloomington: University of Indiana Press, 1982).

30. William Reno, "Old Brigades, Money Bags, New Breeds and the Ironies of Reform in Nigeria," *Canadian Journal of African Studies* 27, no. 1 (1993): 66–87.

31. Peter da Costa, "The Politics of 'Settlement'," *Africa Report* (November-December 1993), 53–57.

32. The inducements for members of the Constitutional Conference are detailed by Nats Agbo, "When Will Abacha Go?" *Newswatch,* January 23, 1995, p. 12. See also Mike Akpan, "The Joker," *Newswatch,* February 20, 1995, pp. 13–18.

8

On Promoting
Democracy in Africa:
The International Dimension

David F. Gordon

The absence of democracy in Africa is not a simple matter of poor constitutions and power-hungry elites, easily curable by outside pressure and technical support to democrats. The most serious and intractable obstacles to democratic transitions and to the consolidation of democracy in Africa are structural, rooted in the underlying socioeconomic conditions and characteristics of most African states and societies.

There is no doubt that specific African leaders have been, and remain, major obstacles to any real effort at political reform in their countries. For example, the chances of holding free and fair elections in Zaire are virtually nil as long as Mobutu Sese Seko remains in power. He has amply demonstrated his enormous capacity for manipulation, co-option, and corruption of the opposition. Similarly, the chances for free and fair elections under General Sani Abacha's tutelage in Nigeria are dim. However, even if both Mobutu and Abacha could somehow be removed from the scene, the transition to democracy would remain a long and arduous journey in both countries. The Mobutus and the Abachas are not simply intransigent individuals standing in the way of change but are the products of a particular context and reflect the difficult circumstances that democracy faces in Africa.

The chapters in this book have highlighted some of the major social, economic, and political linkages that make democratic transformation in Africa so complicated and challenging at this point in history. In many ways, the existing economic, social, and political conditions are all unfavorable for the nurturing of democracy. This provides a special challenge for those in the international community who are working to promote democracy in Africa. As one of Africa's most astute observers, Ali Mazrui, noted in recent testimony before the U.S. House of Representatives Subcommittee on Africa, "The U.S. must recognize the paradox of a strong African desire for democracy combined with a fragile African capability for it."[1]

The good news is that in many African countries conditions are changing for the better in terms of the prospects for democracy. The bad news is that the social and economic changes that in the long run will support democratization do not necessarily provide a short-term impetus forward. The linkages among the various processes of change are complex and defy simple generalizations.

If this is the situation, what can be done to promote democracy in Africa? This is not a purely academic question. Democracy promotion has become, in the 1990s, an important consideration in the Africa policies of most of the major foreign powers in Africa, including the United States. In addition, the international financial institutions, whose role in Africa is perhaps even more important than that of any individual foreign government, have been pushed by their major shareholders toward a more explicitly political stance, under the broad rubric of "governance." As a result, political conditionality has joined economic conditionality in international aid negotiations, and foreign-funded democracy promotion projects are becoming a part of the African landscape. Originally limited to assisting elections, such programs are becoming increasingly sophisticated in their approach and ambitious in their scope.

But can foreign donors help? The experience of the United States and other countries to date suggests that although democracy promotion programs can have some positive effects and are an appropriate tool for donor countries, expectations should be kept modest. For a wide range of reasons, the ability of the United States or any other external power to facilitate democracy in Africa is and will remain limited. We should not have unrealistic expectations about the prospects for rapid democratization in Africa. Nor should we conclude that, if democratic outcomes in a particular country are not achieved, it is primarily because the international community did not take promotion of democracy seriously enough.

These conclusions are based on the experience of the United States but are relevant to other countries as well. For all of the major foreign powers in Africa, it will be impossible for democracy promotion to become the central organizing theme of Africa policy, because both the range of interests at stake and the situation on the ground will make it unavoidable that other themes or problems take precedence at times. But although expectations should be downsized, democracy promotion programs can have positive impacts. From this experience we derive suggestions on how democracy promotion in Africa can be made more successful.

■ Crisis Proliferation and Democratization

In the post–Cold War era, the three themes of conflict resolution, economic reform and sustainable development, and democracy have dominated the

rhetoric and thinking of the major external powers in Africa. But the proliferation of conflicts and crises in Africa in the past several years has made it
much more difficult for policymakers to focus either their attention or
diplomatic and financial resources on the democratization goal. The quest
for political order seems to be eclipsing both democratization and market
reform as the underlying concern of the international community in Africa.

This has occurred in a couple of different ways. First, responding to
crises and the associated need to prevent the spread of various crises
crowds out democratization issues on the agendas of both policymakers in
London, Washington, or Paris and of their representatives on the ground.
Second, the proliferation of crises has led, in practice, to a lessened willingness by foreign governments to undertake proactive democracy promotion
programs. Such programs have the tendency to become controversial and
can involve officials placing themselves in a confrontational relationship to
host governments because they seek to alter the existing political balance
and rules. There appears to be a growing fear in the international community that such programs entail great risks and that in many circumstances in
Africa they are likely to lead to disorder and crisis rather than to democratic
change.

This new hesitancy is seen clearly in international policy toward
Kenya, where, between 1990 and 1992, increased pressure was placed on
President Daniel arap Moi to legalize opposition parties and engage in multiparty elections. In the past three years, despite a sharp deterioration in
Kenya's democratic processes, the international response has been much
more muted. A major reason for the change was the fact that the descent
into anarchy in Somalia and the civil war and genocide in Rwanda now
weigh heavily on the mind of policymakers in the West who are fearful of
making a bad situation worse and are less optimistic about the possibility of
a democratic outcome.

■ Opposing Autocracy Versus Building Democracy

Recent evidence from Africa, much of it reviewed by the participants in
this book, strongly suggests that it is much easier, particularly in the short
term, to exert pressure successfully against nondemocratic governments
than it is to influence the positive evolution of political openings into
democratic directions. To return to the example of Kenya, international
efforts were largely responsible for the introduction of the multiparty system in Kenya in 1992, but political practice in Kenya today is not what
Westerners associate with democracy. Lacking clear targets, such as holding elections or allowing multiparty competition, how the international
community should support democracy in Kenya today is less obvious than

it was in 1991. The basis for coordinated international action, which existed in the early 1990s, will be difficult to recreate.

Similarly, in central Africa, international efforts played a major role in creating the conditions for the recent and successful multiparty elections in both Malawi and Zambia. But in Malawi those elections begat an ethnically and regionally divided polity. Malawi is still in the early phases of the democratic transition, and the ability of foreign powers to help the process in the aftermath of the elections is less certain. In Zambia, continuing problems of corruption and political manipulation threaten the legitimacy of President Frederick Chiluba's government. In response, the international community, led by the UK, imposed a partial cutoff of aid to Zambia. But corruption and political manipulation are much less amenable to external pressures than are changing a constitution or holding an election. It will be very difficult for external actors to address these deeply rooted elements of Zambia's political economy and political culture.

The distinction between the relative ease of exerting pressure against authoritarianism and the difficulty of positively influencing democracy is the foreign policy counterpart to Michael Bratton's important distinction between political liberalization, which is widespread in contemporary Africa, and democratization, progress toward which is much more tenuous. Political liberalization involves essentially getting rid of barriers to political participation. This is generally amenable to external efforts. Democratization involves creating institutions, values, and patterns of behavior conducive to respect for human rights, acknowledgment of the rule of law, enhanced transparency and accountability of government, and a vibrant civil society. The increasingly acknowledged hard fact is that consolidating democracy in Africa will take a long time to achieve. Positively affecting this consolidation is more difficult for external actors than was helping to initiate democratization.

In practice, if not always in rhetoric, the international community recognizes how difficult it is to build democracy in the African context and has sought intermediate solutions with more immediate benefits. Especially in situations of severe conflict in Africa, international diplomacy appears to be aiming at "mutual accommodation" as an intermediate goal on the road to democracy. The political pacts that the international community has facilitated and supported in Angola, Namibia, Mozambique, and even in South Africa have in common limiting the winner-take-all mentality that has marked African politics and encouraging an inclusive approach to governance. They are less concerned with the formal trappings of democracy. I believe that this is an appropriate approach.

The genius of the South African transition was not the purely democratic nature of the 1994 election. Indeed, thoughtful South Africans such as Lawrence Schlemmer have emphasized that future South African elections need to pay more attention to the formal attributes of "free and fair" elections and that the first free election does not provide a good operational model for the future. Rather, the South African elections marked the culmination of a long process of political accommodation and bargaining between the country's main political forces—the African National Congress and the National Party and, to a lesser extent, the Inkatha Freedom Party and the white right wing. What we have witnessed so far in South Africa is the successful transition from confrontation to accommodation. Although this provides a strong impetus toward democracy, South Africa's current political situation can best be described as "pre-democratic." In South Africa, as elsewhere, one election does not a democracy make.

The practical goal of mutual accommodation extends beyond southern Africa. The evolution of U.S. policy toward Uganda and Ethiopia reflects this emphasis. In recent years, the United States has supported President Yoweri Museveni in Uganda despite his lack of commitment to multiparty democracy. Museveni gained U.S. support largely because he has tried to create a broad-based regime. In 1995 and 1996, when the political breadth of Museveni's regime began to contract substantially, the United States expressed public concern about the political direction in which Uganda was heading. A similar concern exists in U.S. policy toward Ethiopia. The United States remains somewhat concerned about the course that Prime Minister Meles Zenawi has taken in Ethiopia, not because he has rejected formal democracy (which he hasn't), but because he appears to eschew inclusiveness in favor of narrow majoritarianism. The United States fears that such majoritarianism facilitates the zero-sum winner-take-all mentality.

■ Constraints on Democracy Promotion

International efforts to promote democracy in Africa face three sets of difficult constraints: (1) conditions on the ground, (2) conflicting foreign policy pressures, and (3) limited interests and resources.

The ability to promote democracy in Africa is constrained by the fact that Africa lacks many of the social concomitants for democratization. Social structures in most African countries are dominated by a diffused peasantry, a mostly "outsider" or "crony capitalist" commercial class, and a substantial government bureaucracy—hardly the ideal social context for the flowering of democracy. Africa's long-standing, severe economic crisis further weakens the prospects for democracy. Although failed economic performance is one of the main sources of the collapse of authoritarian regimes in Africa, the context of economic collapse is not conducive to sustaining democracy. This infertile social and economic environment is reinforced by the lack of democratic institutions and the pervasive patrimonialism that marks both the structure of society and the political culture of most African societies. Thus, it is not surprising that the crisis of authoritarianism has not necessarily led to a flowering of democracy in Africa.

In the last several years, the impact of the less than favorable environment for democracy has been felt in a number of ways that have not been amenable to effective external influence. First, there is the political resurgence of the autocrats in a number of key countries, including Zaire, Nigeria, and Kenya. As Michael Schatzberg points out in Chapter 6, autocrats who sustained themselves through the initial crisis of authoritarianism have learned how to manipulate the politics of democratic transitions. Indeed, it seems as if the "permanent transition" has become the (so far successful) strategy for maintaining autocratic rule by Mobutu in Zaire and by the Nigerian military dictatorship. Second, there has been the overthrow of democratic regimes by disgruntled militaries in a number of countries, including Niger and The Gambia. In none of these situations have the actions of external actors countered these setbacks to democracy.

The ability of foreign powers to promote democracy in Africa is also constrained by the existence of other foreign policy interests and pressures that draw policymakers' attention away from democracy. During the Cold War, this was the overwhelming source of the very obvious disjuncture between ostensible U.S. support for democracy and the reality that the United States was aiding and abetting dictators and other nondemocratic forces all over the continent. Thus the United States supported Jonas Savimbi in Angola because the Angolan regime was aligned with Moscow; the United States backed Mohammed Siad Barre in Somalia as a counter to the communists in Ethiopia; and Mobutu was the U.S. bulwark against communism in central Africa. For other Western powers, the competing interests have often been economic or commercial. For France, an entire web of relations culminating in the Franc Zone linked French commercial and financial networks to the incumbent regimes in Africa.

Today, the Cold War is over, but competing foreign policy pressures still exist. For France, its self-image as a major power continues to be closely linked to its influence in its former African colonies. Although France did not step in to support incumbent regimes during the spate of "national conferences" in the early 1990s, its actions more recently have been less supportive of democracy. Paris did nothing to block the overthrow of the democratically elected government in Niger and has facilitated the legitimacy of its military-based successor. Although Britain's international role is less at stake in Africa, British economic interests and the position of large numbers of UK passport holders in many of their former colonies has complicated UK efforts to facilitate democracy.

For the United States, the competing interests are not generally economic. Rather, the need to cooperate on global and regional issues, especially conflict resolution and peacekeeping, has tended to put democracy issues further back on the agenda in several countries. Certainly in Kenya, the need to cooperate with the Kenyan government on regional conflict issues in Somalia and the Sudan and on responding to the threat of famine in the greater Horn of Africa has drawn U.S. attention away from the focus on democracy that dominated U.S. policy between 1990 and 1992.

The capacity of foreign actors to promote democracy in Africa is also constrained by limited political interests and financial resources. Most of the major donors to Africa are facing a reduction in resources, the result of some combination of budget pressure and aid fatigue. Although the organized groups in the United States, Canada, the UK, and other countries who try to influence Africa are broadly supportive of democracy, most focus their attention on other themes such as child survival, environmental protection, poverty reduction, or population. For example, in the United States, the nongovernmental organizations (NGOs) that heavily influence foreign assistance policy and practice have been generally skeptical about the use of foreign aid funds to promote democracy.

Moreover, within many of the official foreign assistance agencies, the organizational culture has traditionally been antipolitical. In the United States, one of the main themes of the Development Fund for Africa, when it was created in 1987, was to "fence off" African assistance programs from political pressure from the State Department. Although this did help the fund to escape the political imperatives of the Cold War, it generated a strong feeling among career officers that AID (U.S. Agency for International Development) should focus on development issues, not politics. Similar views were obtained in several of the other agencies.

■ **Policy Instruments for Promoting Democracy**

The policy instruments available to external actors to promote democracy in Africa essentially fall into four categories: (1) policy "sticks" such as aid reductions, diplomatic isolation, public condemnation, visa restrictions, and others; (2) policy "carrots" such as increases in foreign aid, enhanced military cooperation, and trade and investment missions; (3) the instruments of traditional diplomacy—persuasion, consultation, and the provision of good offices; and (4) democracy promotion programs, which can be divided into short-term electoral support activities and longer-term institution-building efforts. Each of these instruments has difficulties attached to it.

The use of sticks can be very effective in the early phases of democratization, and indeed in the early 1990s the success of external actors in promoting democratization in Africa was the result of the willingness to use such disincentives, most importantly the withdrawal of government-to-government assistance. Within the international community, it was U.S. leadership that put these instruments on the agenda in Africa. But, for complex reasons, over time there has been less of a willingness on the part of the United States to use sticks in pursuit of democracy in Africa. As a result, they have had a diminishing role in efforts by the international community to promote democracy in Africa.

A major problem with sticks is that they demand a multilateral approach to be effective. But sustaining multilateral commitment to promoting democracy in Africa has proven difficult if not impossible. The international community has failed to develop multilateral consensus on the application of even modest economic sanctions against the Nigerian military regime, despite the widespread agreement about its ruthless and autocratic character.

Sticks work best when directed against specific and visible restrictive political practices. They are simply far less useful in dealing with the deeper constraints facing democratization such as corruption, the political culture of patrimonialism, and the need for improved economic performance, and they do not address the pressing need for institution building. Finally, sticks become weak reeds unless they are accompanied by substantial carrots.

The distinction between helping to open up an undemocratic political system and facilitating the consolidation of democracy, which was discussed earlier, leads to the conclusion that "political conditionality" (i.e., the conditioning of foreign aid on progress toward democracy) is viable as a tool for promoting democracy only in the very early stages of the process. The era of "political conditionality" in Africa, except in very exceptional circumstances, has probably ended.

Unfortunately, the carrots available to foreign actors for promoting democratization in Africa are also limited and difficult to wield. The main carrots available are foreign aid of one form or another and trade and investment incentives. Both have their inherent problems.

The foreign aid carrot is of limited practical use because of the difficulties in shifting resources rapidly from one country to another and the unwillingness of most donors to substantially shift aid resources in response to short-term political trends. Assistance programs in Africa generally take the form of multiyear activities for which long "pipelines" accrue. In the United States, moreover, strong opposition has emerged in Congress to the types of aid that are most amenable for use as carrots, that is, economic support funds transfers, quick-disbursing "nonproject" assistance, and military assistance. The types of foreign aid that retain strong congressional support—population and child-survival programs, microenterprise development, and NGO support activities—are quite simply not so attractive to recipient governments to carry much weight.

Trade and investment carrots also have inherent difficulties. First, the interest groups within the Western powers that are promoting increased trade and investment tend to be different from those that have pushed democracy promotion. These business and financial interests tend to oppose linking trade and investment promotion with democracy promotion. Second, the effectiveness of trade and investment as a carrot depends upon the actions of commercial actors, who have a very different set of calculations from those of governments. Third, the low level of integration of African countries into the international economy minimizes the availability of these types of carrots.

The inherent weakness of the instruments involved in "carrots and sticks" diplomacy to promote democratization in Africa has led most foreign powers to focus their efforts on traditional, less coercive diplomacy and democracy support programs. Indeed, these efforts have been given too little credit in explaining recent successful efforts by the international community to forward the democratic process in Africa. In South Africa, a steady diplomatic posture by the United States and the UK helped to ensure that the Nelson Mandela–F. W. de Klerk negotiation process remained on track and was crucial in bringing Chief Gatsha Buthelezi into the final agreement. In Mozambique, international diplomatic efforts were crucial in keeping Mozambique National Resistant Movement's (RENAMO) leader, Afonso Dhlakama, on board with the peace process. Even in Kenya, although the freezing of international assistance to the Kenya government was given credit for the introduction of multiparty democracy, the role played by the consistent and public reiteration of support for democracy, especially by the United States, Germany, Canada, and the Nordic states, was often overlooked.

The final set of policy instruments are democracy support programs. But democracy support programs face difficult strategic and organizational issues. Donor governments have faced a difficult debate about the extent to which such programs should focus on short-term objectives of facilitating multiparty elections or on longer-term objectives of institution building. In the early 1990s, democracy support programs in Africa were heavily focused on short-term electoral support. As Joel Barkan argues, there are strong arguments motivating a concentration on short-term electoral support. First, donors believed that one-party regimes were inherently undemocratic and that multiparty electoral competition was the defining characteristic of democracy. Second, multiparty elections were considered essential in recent transitions to democracy outside of Africa, in countries such as the Philippines, Nicaragua, and Argentina. Third, both incumbents and challengers sought support for multiparty elections. Fourth, institutions such as the International Fund for Electoral Support could provide assistance. Finally, electoral support was attractive because it was time-bound. It involved minimal entanglement in the political life of the recipient country.

But over time the limitations of short-term electoral support came to dominate thinking about democracy promotion efforts. Recently, democracy support programs have been increasingly integrated into the larger development agendas of many of the leading donor nations. These programs increasingly focus on longer-term efforts to strengthen key public sector institutions such as legislatures, the judiciary, and local government and to support civil society.

However, some inherent difficulties have emerged from this integrated approach. First, due to the U.S. Agency for International Development's (USAID) bureaucratic requirements, it has been difficult to maintain the flexibility needed to respond to fluid political environments that demand a timely response to new opportunities and needs. Second, it has been difficult to reconcile the need for a long-term perspective and risk taking in democracy support programs with the new emphases in U.S. foreign assistance on results and dollar-by-dollar accountability. Finally, democracy support programs are not "model activities" that can then be replicated in a wide range of circumstances. To the contrary, democracy programs need to be designed to fit specific political and institutional circumstances that vary widely by country.

■ Enhancing Democracy Promotion Efforts

How might foreign powers be more effective in supporting democratization in Africa? First, foreign powers can articulate more consistently, especially in nondemocratic settings, their support for democracy and engage more extensively with local protagonists. For instance, U.S. policy has been most successful where the U.S. embassy has combined consistent and explicit support for democratic principles with a willingness to engage and accommodate the widest range of political actors.

Second, the international community should focus debt relief on countries in the forefront of efforts in both democratization and economic reform. Current international debt policy is based on modest debt relief for a broad range of countries eligible under Paris Club criteria. Given that resources for debt relief are limited, a more effective approach would be to provide more substantial relief to a smaller set of countries, those taking the lead in the dual transition to both democracy and a market economy.

Third, the major foreign powers should promote a much more participatory approach by the World Bank in its economic reform efforts. Just as political conditionality is of marginal use, the existing top-down World Bank model of economic policy conditionality has probably outlived its utility. The major powers need to encourage the World Bank to develop approaches to economic reform that encourage responsibility and account-ability by African governments.

Fourth, foreign aid resources should be more focused on democratic states. The major donors have cut most aid resources to African autocrats, but aid is still spread too thinly in Africa. Progress in democracy should become a more important determinant of the allocation of aid resources. Many donor nations claim to be doing this, but they could still reduce aid programs in nondemocratic countries.

Finally, countries should not allow domestic popular sentiment against governments in Africa to prevent assistance programs from strengthening the capacity of African states. In the United States, enthusiasm for the pri-vate sector among conservatives and for NGOs among liberals threatens to undermine U.S. support for democratic governments in Africa. One of the best ways that the international community can help both the private sector and NGOs in Africa's new democracies is to improve the quality of gover-nance in areas such as the legal system, the regulatory framework, and poli-cy implementation. This involves helping Africa's new democracies to carry out the basic functions of government.

In sum, international efforts to promote democracy in Africa can mat-ter in two ways. First, in the early stages of democratization, international efforts can help move recalcitrant autocrats and can facilitate processes of mutual accommodation among long-time political foes. In the longer run, international efforts need to be more subtle; they can serve as a catalyst for democratic consolidation but cannot drive these efforts. Although these efforts are less visible than confrontations over constitutional change and aid conditionality, they offer the key to addressing the deep structural con-straints against which African democracy has to contend.

■ Note

1. "Africa: The Democratic Balance Sheet," testimony presented to the House Subcommittee on Africa of the Committee on Foreign Affairs, Hearings on "Africa: Potential and Promises," September 27, 1994, Washington, D.C.

Afterword:
The Best Hope for Now

Daniel Simpson

T he subject of this book is African democratization. Inevitably, it is also a wiser U.S. foreign policy toward Africa.

Independent African countries have been ruled from the late 1950s to the present by a wide range of government types animated by a wide range of philosophies. The structures have ranged from monarchy and empire to military dictatorships and even to what—in Uganda and the Central African Empire—could be characterized only as cruel, institutionalized buffoonery. There have been fashions in African government, a kind of "flavor of the time." Most countries came to independence with a form of government similar to that of the colonizing state, elected within a multiparty system. These elected governments were replaced in many cases by military ones. The next round was the single-party state, which sometimes claimed to be multitendency, proclaiming itself "participatory" within the single-party state. Then came the "national conference" in the French-speaking states, the mode of the early nineties. And—in some countries—then came democracy.

In the 1990s, the United States concluded that democracy might be a benign vehicle to prevent or cure what so manifestly ailed African countries—the names of Somalia, Liberia, Angola, Burundi, Rwanda, Zaire, Nigeria, and the Sudan signal clearly that the problem of governance has not yet been resolved in Africa. To some degree at least, the United States pulled in its train a skeptical or cynical France, UK, and other still-interested powers who were unable or unwilling to profess themselves opposed to the concept of democracy.

U.S. advocacy of democracy as the key to a turnaround in Africa has prompted the usual range of headshaking. Arguments have ranged from "What right do we have?" to the European version, "They aren't ready for it," to the minimalist statement, "The United States shouldn't try to do anything in Africa because it can't sustain a policy given the current low priority it is attaching to foreign affairs in general and Africa in particular."

The case for advocacy of democratization is simple. If people have a legitimate and peaceful means of changing their governors, theoretically those governors—wishing not to be turned out of office—have reasons not to steal, not to install their relatives and ethnic kin exclusively at the trough, and not to abuse human and civil rights or otherwise torment the governed. Instead, the governors will rule wisely and will pursue constructive long-term economic policies. Simple and beautiful in principle, very complex in practice. And if democratization doesn't work, then what?

What happens if multipartyism produces political parties based on ethnicity, making the electoral process into a slightly more genteel form of ethnic warfare, stimulating centrifugal forces, and turning the governing process into a broader-based form of the same old zero-sum approach to managing the country's resources? Structure can help. The imposition of an obligatory two-party system is one approach, tried by Nigeria but marred by fraud. The building of multiethnic alliances is another. In general, it is probably right to suggest that the fewer political parties the better (as long as there are more than one)—this will force coalition building and cooperation.

What happens if an important sector of society—whether it be the military or a strong, significant ethnic or social group—simply won't play, won't accept the outcome of democratic elections? There is Nigeria. There is Algeria. Sadly, there are Rwanda and Burundi. And there are no easy solutions.

What happens if a country has democratic elections and a reasonably representative, honest, and enlightened government still finds itself face-to-face with unspeakable economic problems? With elections scheduled a few years down the road, the newly elected government is faced with a range of all bad choices. One thinks of Zambia, Benin, and the Central African Republic. The world expects fiscal responsibility of the new government, even imposes it as a condition of aid, but the population expects development—that is why they got rid of the old bunch. If the newly elected group doesn't put some points on the board fairly quickly, a new round of "turn out the rascals" will soon occur. International donors must help here. These new democratic governments have the right to ask donors to help demonstrate to their peoples that democracy can bring a better life.

What happens when, no matter what anyone does, the problems of a country are so severe that even democracy cannot bring change in the form of a rising standard of living? Benin probably poses such a problem. The answer there, I would suggest, is just to keep trying. The road is still right. None of this is done quickly.

What happens if fundamentally undemocratic forces reach power in democratic elections? The case of Algeria presents us with the dilemma of conflict between democratic form and democratic content. So does Zaire, where everyone wants elections, but of course Mobutu Sese Seko must not win. To the degree that there is general international agreement that the

Islamic fundamentalists couldn't be allowed to take over in Algeria and that the purpose of democratic elections in Zaire is to get rid of Mobutu, we have to ask ourselves what the real basis of our attachment to democratic elections is.

The coming years will provide many indications of the success and failure of democracy in Africa. One is capital flows. If African political leaders and entrepreneurs continue to send abroad every nickel they can put their hands on, there will be no progress. Democracy and development are really about the confidence of the people in the future of their country and their acceptance of responsibility for it. It is domestic confidence, not the confidence of international donors and financial institutions, that will make a difference.

Another indicator of the progress of democracy is the fate of successive elections. Will those who turned out the rascals the first time play the game according to the rules when their position is at stake?

A third element to watch closely is the military. Some governments elected in the 1990s have already succumbed to military intervention. The Zairian armed forces loom menacingly over that country's elections, promised for 1997. And one must watch with suspicion even such a hitherto stable democracy as Botswana, where the military is building up its strength despite the absence of obvious external enemies.

Not all countries will overcome the obstacles to democratic transformation. Some, saddled with the enormously unhelpful lines the colonial powers drew on the map, are collapsing or will collapse and may eventually rebuild sustainable political systems in new ways. The international community may have to learn to live with the absence of national government in a country as drawn on the map, and the subsequent emergence of sustainable government from the mixing bowl of each situation. The ultimate form of self-determination on the part of a people may be the collective decision to have no central, national government. If we profess respect for people's rights to self-determination and for democratic choice, we need to learn to stay calm when presented with this "no national government" phenomenon and accept it as part of the transformation of the authoritarian African states. The argument for tolerance of no government is not advocacy of a back-to-nature approach to African nations. The problems created for Africa and the world by a proliferating number of no-go zones are formidable, disheartening, and, perhaps in the end, intolerable in the overall global order. People in collapsed states are isolated and at a serious disadvantage, no longer part of the world economic-commercial-financial scene. Such territories cannot be included in global environmental policies. They have a tendency to become centers of narco-trafficking, terrorism, and other activities that flourish in the absence of organized government.

Nonetheless, it is essential that Africa be allowed to work seriously with possible alternatives to the structure of the postcolonial nation-states. Democracy is worth a very serious shot by viable states. But failed states should be allowed to seek to reconstitute themselves from a precolonial base.

About the Contributors

David F. Gordon is director of the U.S. Policy Program at the Overseas Development Council (ODC). He has taught at the College of William and Mary, the University of Michigan, the University of Nairobi, Boston University, and Michigan State University. He is the author of several books and numerous articles on international relations and economic development issues, primarily on Africa.

Carol Graham is a visiting fellow in the Foreign Policy Studies Program at the Brookings Institution and professorial lecturer in Latin American Studies at the Johns Hopkins University School of Advanced International Studies. She is the author of *Safety Nets, Politics and the Poor: Transitions to Market Economies* (1994) and *Peru's APRA: Parties, Politics and the Elusive Quest for Democracy* (1992). She is also the author of several articles on the political economy of reform.

Eboe Hutchful was born in Ghana in 1946 and received his Ph.D. from the University of Toronto in 1973. He is presently a professor in the Department of Africana Studies at Wayne State University in Detroit, Michigan. He has researched and written on African and Third World military politics, debt and structural adjustment, and environmental issues. His publications include *The IMF and Ghana* (1987), an edited volume with Abdoulaye Bathily, *The Military and Militarization in Africa* (forthcoming), and a forthcoming book on structural adjustment in Ghana.

Peter M. Lewis is assistant professor at the School of International Service, American University, Washington, D.C. His work centers on economic reform and political liberalization in developing countries, with a focus on sub-Saharan Africa. He has written extensively on Nigerian political economy as well as on broader regional issues of participation, democratic transition, and economic adjustment in Africa.

Marina Ottaway is a professorial lecturer in African Studies at the Johns Hopkins University School of Advanced International Studies. She has lived in Africa and taught at African universities for many years, following the successive political transitions on the continent from nationalism to African socialism, Afrocommunism, and now democracy. Among her many books are *South Africa: The Struggle for a New Order* (1992) and *Democratization and Ethnic Nationalism: African and Eastern European Experiences* (1994).

Michael G. Schatzberg is professor of Political Science at the University of Wisconsin–Madison. He is the author of *The Dialectics of Oppression in Zaire* (1988) and *Mobutu or Chaos?: The United States and Zaire, 1960–1990* (1991).

Daniel Simpson, a career foreign service officer, is presently U.S. ambassador to Zaire. Earlier, he served in Somalia during the U.S. intervention there, was Deputy Commandant at the U.S. Army War College, and was ambassador to the Central African Republic.

Nicolas van de Walle is an associate professor of Political Science at Michigan State University and currently a visiting fellow at the Overseas Development Council in Washington, D.C. He is the author of numerous articles on African economic and political issues and coauthor of *Democratic Experiments in Africa: Regime Transitions in Comparative Perspective* (forthcoming).

Jennifer A. Widner is associate professor in the Department of Political Science at the University of Michigan and policy scientist at the Institute for Policy Research. She is the author of several books and articles on political liberalization, agricultural policy, and institutional performance in Africa.

Index

About the Book

Five years of multiparty elections and democratization in Africa have yielded uncertain results and a wealth of experience about the difficulties involved in the transition from authoritarianism. This volume brings a broad perspective to the process of transformation, challenging facile assumptions and pointing to the issues that need to be addressed by African leaders, political parties, and elements of civil society—as well as by aid donors—before democracy can become a reality in Africa.

Marina Ottaway teaches in the African Studies Program at the Johns Hopkins School of Advanced International Studies. A long-time observer of political transformation in African countries, her most recent works include *South Africa: The Struggle for a New Order* and *Democratization and Ethnic Nationalism: African and Eastern European Experiences.*